T0407925

Wagner

and the Creation of

The Ring

Wagner

and the Creation of

The Ring

Michael Downes

PEGASUS BOOKS
NEW YORK LONDON

Pegasus Books, Ltd.
148 West 37th Street, 13th Floor
New York, NY 10018

Copyright © 2025 by Michael Downes

First Pegasus Books cloth edition July 2025

All rights reserved. No part of this book may be reproduced in whole
or in part without written permission from the publisher, except by
reviewers who may quote brief excerpts in connection with a review in
a newspaper, magazine, or electronic publication; nor may any part of
this book be reproduced, stored in a retrieval system, or transmitted
in any form or by any means electronic, mechanical, photocopying,
recording, or other, or used to train generative artificial intelligence
(AI) technologies, without written permission from the publisher.

ISBN: 978-1-63936-915-7

10 9 8 7 6 5 4 3 2 1

Printed in the United States of America
Distributed by Simon & Schuster
www.pegasusbooks.com

For Clara, Gabriel, James, Juliet and Olivia

Contents

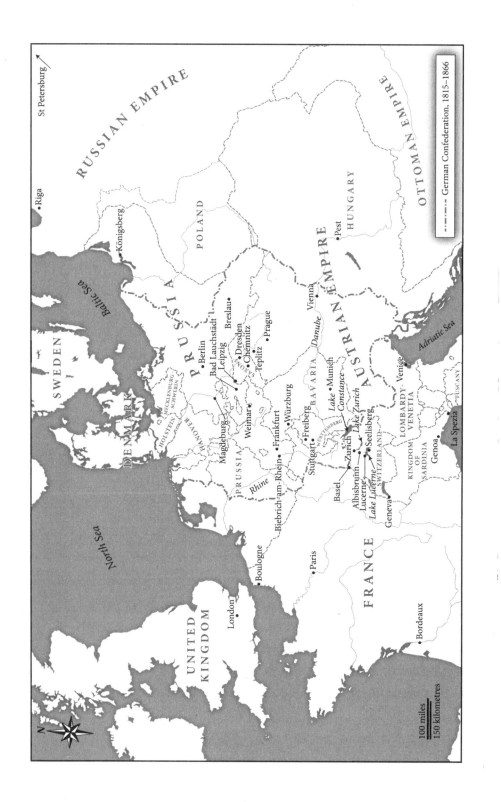

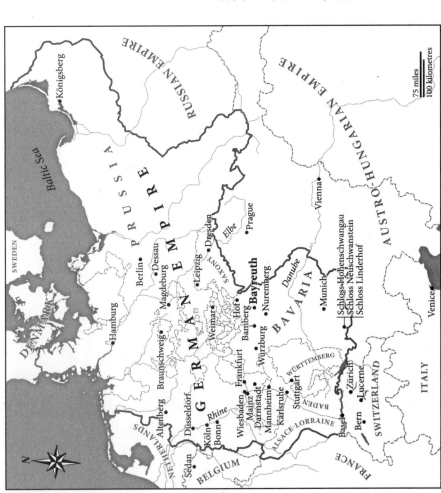

FACING PAGE Wagner's travels around Europe: boundaries shown are those of 1843, the year in which Wagner took up the post of Royal Saxon Kapellmeister in Dresden

THIS PAGE Wagner's Germany: boundaries shown are those of 1876, the year in which *The Ring* was first produced in Bayreuth

Prologue

BERLIN, JANUARY 2022. The final run of performances of Stefan Herheim's new production of *The Ring of the Nibelung* for the Deutsche Oper has coincided with the peak in cases of Omicron, the latest variant of COVID-19. The new government of Chancellor Olaf Scholz has tightened the restrictions on theatres, as on everything else. In order to gain admission to the building, audience members must produce four separate documents: proof of double vaccination, evidence of a negative test taken within the last twenty-four hours, a passport or other proof of identity, and finally the ticket. All these documents are checked with admirable efficiency and the daily routine of taking COVID tests, checking the results, gaining entry to the theatre, depositing coats and buying a programme quickly becomes familiar. The FFP2 masks mandatory throughout the evening have an angular profile that gives audience members a curiously bird-like appearance, as though we are white-beaked versions of Wotan's ravens.

Despite the obstacles placed in the way of taking a seat, barely any are empty: indeed, the difficulty of gaining admission has if anything heightened the occasion's intensity, creating a sense of pilgrimage. Quiet camaraderie develops between audience members, born of shared appreciation of the Deutsche Oper's colossal achievement in mounting a production of this complexity during a pandemic. Born, too, of the long periods of time we spend in close proximity to one another, very unusual at the moment: we are in our seats for two and a half hours for *Das Rheingold*, and in the theatre for well over six hours for *Siegfried* and *Götterdämmerung*. The orchestral players feel like old friends by the fourth night, particularly the chatty double-bass section ranged across the middle of the pit.

One spectator in the front row of the stalls has a teddy bear discreetly placed as a mascot, while another enters the auditorium in a horned helmet and brightly coloured trousers, and banters with the players in the intervals. Such exuberance, however, is the exception. Most audience members spend the intervals chatting quietly or studying programmes, libretti or musical guides, and dress in subdued colours that tone well with the dark wood and the black and beige fabrics of the Deutsche Oper's elegantly minimalist foyers. In a stunning *coup de théâtre*, the curtain opens at the start of *Götterdämmerung* to an exact replica of one of those areas, complete with the familiar paper lanterns and Wagner-inspired wall sculpture, as if to implicate the audience in the horrific events that are about to unfold.

The cast is an intriguing mix of seasoned Wagnerians and newcomers. Clay Hilley, a physically imposing *Heldentenor* from Athens, Georgia, who has not quite turned forty, is playing his first Siegfried: there are approving murmurs in the intervals that he may become the Siegfried of his generation, such is his command of the role. At the other end of the spectrum, Brünnhilde is played by Nina Stemme, a fifty-eight-year-old Swedish soprano who has performed this part all around the world for the last decade and a half. If there are occasional hints that her voice has lost some of its bloom, then such concerns pale into insignificance in the face of her evident command of every bar of the score, her superb acting and the profound humanity she brings to her interpretation. The conducting is in the safe hands of Sir Donald Runnicles, the Deutsche Oper's Scottish music director and a veteran of several *Rings* both here and in San Francisco. The orchestra sounds magnificent, the brass section resplendent.

A few critics have objected to the production's repeated reminders that we are in a theatre watching a drama, to the presence on stage of invented characters or those who are not supposed to be in the scene concerned, and in particular to the frequent appearance of a crowd of extras, with a propensity to strip to their underwear at the slightest provocation. To my mind – and it seems that I am among an overwhelming majority, judging from the rapturous reception at the curtain calls for *Götterdämmerung*, during which the hundred and more orchestral players join the cast and Runnicles on stage to accept the applause – these supposedly controversial interventions are justified interpretive decisions within an utterly compelling production. The motivations and movements of every character – not just principals, but non-singing supernumeraries too – are realised with great detail, while each drama's big moments are clearly articulated with dazzling visual effects, giving the staging a multi-layered richness comparable to that found in Wagner's score.

The production is full of incidents that draw attention to its own theatricality. Alberich paints his face at the start of *Rheingold* with a crudely drawn clown's mask; Hagen is portrayed in *Götterdämmerung* as a theatre director who adjusts the movements of the other characters – at one point he joins the audience to watch, replacing a COVID-masked Waltraute in the front row of the stalls. On the night I see *Rheingold*, the singer due to play Loge is indisposed, so an understudy sings from the wings while a female stage manager acts the part – or rather dances it, such are the energy and ebullience she brings to the fire-god's pantomimic gestures. There are welcome touches of humour, even at some of the darkest moments of the story. The hunting party who join Hagen as he prepares to kill Siegfried in the final act of *Götterdämmerung* dine on pretzels, the main form of sustenance available in this as in other German theatres; I get through quite a few myself over the course of the week, even if I can't afford the house champagne with which the hunters wash them down.

The production was conceived long before COVID, but some of its themes have particular resonance at the moment. At the centre of the stage is a grand piano, used not only as a setting for significant moments in the action (Brünnhilde is placed inside it by Wotan at the end of *Die Walküre*, and turns it into her own funeral pyre at the end of *Götterdämmerung*), but also as an instrument on which different characters mime a keyboard reduction of the music played by the orchestra. Musical objects appear frequently as props: the gold is revealed to Alberich at the start of *Das Rheingold* in the form of a Wagner tuba; the dragon in *Siegfried* speaks through the bell of a vast brass instrument; the printed scores of the dramas feature prominently on stage. To spectators who have been deprived of live performance for much of the last two years, these reminders that *The Ring* is, among other things, a musical performance feel heartening rather than gimmicky. Another prominent visual theme of the production – the battered suitcases brought on to the stage by a group of travellers at the start of *Das Rheingold* and subsequently used to represent everything from Valhalla to the huge dragon killed by Siegfried – also feels particularly relevant right now. The suitcases remind us not only of the barriers to travel that COVID has imposed, but also – this was Herheim's original intention – of the increasing numbers of people seeking refuge from political conflict and environmental catastrophe.

This feels like a peculiar time to be experiencing *The Ring* – but then, perhaps any occasion on which *The Ring* is performed is by definition peculiar, since everything the work demands is antithetical to the routine and everyday.

The Ring is many things: the practical realisation of a revolutionary theory of how musical theatre should be constructed; a compendium of brilliant orchestral sounds; a monumental physical and psychological challenge for singers; for some, a philosophical meditation or a political tract. But it is also, perhaps above all, a supreme piece of storytelling, created by a man who was, alongside Charles Dickens, Victor Hugo and Leo Tolstoy, one of the nineteenth century's greatest storytellers. Like *Bleak House*, *Les Misérables* and *War and Peace*, *The Ring* is a story not only *from* the nineteenth century, but also *about* it. Despite the non-naturalistic setting, Wagner's gods and giants, heroes and dwarves, Valkyries and Rhinemaidens play out the ambitions and insecurities of the nineteenth century – just as clearly as the soldiers and businessmen, working girls and wives of Wagner's novelist contemporaries.

But the theatrical nature of *The Ring* – the fact that it only truly exists when played out in a real theatre with live audiences – means that it is also, inescapably, a story of the time in which it is performed, absorbing and reflecting the preoccupations of its directors and audiences. In 'Gilded Age' New York, *The Ring*'s spectacular US premiere at the city's newly founded Metropolitan Opera was a story of American cultural bravado. In turn-of-the-century Vienna, Gustav Mahler and the Secessionist painter Alfred Roller conceived a startling production that told of the era's overturning of old certainties. In 1950s Bayreuth, audiences traumatised by the still-recent experience of Nazism witnessed the efforts of Wagner's grandson Wieland to purify *The Ring* of the noxious associations that had become attached to it. On each of these occasions, interpreters and audiences together created a set of meanings that made

The Ring relevant to their own preoccupations, just as they do now in COVID-stricken Berlin. After a century and a half of retellings, this nineteenth-century story has lost none of its power to speak to new audiences of contemporary concerns.

The stories that Wagner told in *The Ring* and those that others have told through it weave their way through this book, intertwined with another that is at its core: that of Wagner himself. If *The Ring* is a great nineteenth-century story, then so too is the story of how Wagner brought it into being. The ways in which he conceived and researched, moulded and shaped, wrote and composed, funded and produced his most ambitious work are the product not only of his extraordinary characteristics as an individual, but also of the social conditions and historical situation in which he found himself. The endeavour is phenomenal: the number of words that flowed from Wagner's pen, together with a similar outpouring of notes, testify to an almost superhuman capacity for hard work. Whatever one thinks of Wagner's music or personal character, his sheer industry surely arouses admiration, however grudging. Admiration, however, by no means implies ignoring Wagner's often repellent political views, particularly but not exclusively on the subjects of Jews and Jewishness, nor the appalling uses to which his work has been put, particularly but not exclusively by Hitler and the Nazis – and these aspects of *The Ring* and its reception will not be overlooked here.

Like the story of *The Ring* itself, the story of how it was created is not straightforwardly linear and cannot plausibly be reduced to an easily digestible plot summary. This book, therefore, like *The Ring* itself, includes digressions, excursions, anticipations, flashbacks, and reinterpretations of previous actions in the light of present experience. By contrast with *The Ring*, however, this story features in Wagner a protagonist whose identity remains the same throughout, even if his outlook and personal circumstances change beyond all recognition.

Of course there is no single, correct way in which to relate this complex narrative. A hundred different writers would arrange the facts of Wagner's story in a hundred different ways, and this book makes no claim to greater authority than any other telling of the story. Nor does it presume to offer a comprehensive musical analysis or philosophical interpretation, though it will touch on both those methods of approaching the work. The last word on *The Ring* will never be written, and having the last word is the last thing that this relatively short account of a long and complicated story aspires to do. I hope, however, that it will be welcomed by some readers and opera-goers as a *first* word: as a way in to this imposing work for those figuring out how – or indeed whether – to approach it.

The Ring can be one of the most overwhelming events that live theatre has to offer, particularly when its four parts are seen in quick succession, as Wagner intended. It is also a story whose meaning seems to become richer with successive generations, as it draws in the fresh and sometimes contradictory insights of new interpreters. For these and other reasons, engaging with *The Ring*, whether in the opera house or at home, is a necessarily intense experience. Although there is no shortage of secondary literature to guide the listener, the length and complexity of many of the available books can often add to rather than assuage the newcomer's sense of bewilderment. By telling the story of how *The Ring* came into being, and of why it takes the form it does, I hope to explain why it fascinates and obsesses so many of its audiences – and ultimately, why it *matters*.

* * *

A few words about the book's organisation. I do not attempt to give a blow-by-blow account of the action and music of each of *The Ring*'s dramas, both because to do so at all adequately would occupy more pages than I am able to allot, and also because this has been done very well in other books and audio sources, many of which are listed in my 'Further reading, viewing and listening' section. The stories of each drama will instead emerge gradually and non-sequentially across the course of my seven chapters. However, those readers who wish to be told or reminded of the events of each drama in the order that Wagner presents them will find synopses at the back of the book. The Chronology is similarly intended as a quick reference point as readers move through the story of *The Ring*'s creation, a story that – for reasons that I hope become clear as the book proceeds – I do not tell in strict chronological order.

I have tried to keep quotations to a minimum, for several reasons. Wagner and many of his associates were so verbose that had I quoted them to any significant extent, my word count would rapidly have disappeared without me getting a word in. And when it comes to secondary reading, so many insightful interpretations of *The Ring* have been published that to offer even a superficial account of the range of views would have required a book many times the length of this one. Those quotations I have used are mostly from Wagner's autobiography (*Mein Leben*), prose works and correspondence, and from Cosima Wagner's diaries, except in the last couple of chapters where a wider range of sources becomes indispensable. Translations of extracts from the libretti of *The Ring* are my own, though naturally informed by the several excellent versions I have read, which are also listed at the back of the book. I have supplied references for all the direct quotations I have used, for the benefit of those who wish to read the passages

I have cited in their original context. I have made no attempt, however, to give sources for all the pieces of information I present: so many of them crop up in multiple locations, often with a slightly different spin, that to attempt anything comprehensive in the way of referencing would have produced a 'Notes' section that was unwieldy without being helpful. The sheer amount of information available on Wagner can make the discovery of *The Ring* a daunting process, but it can – should – also be an exhilarating one. Wherever readers of this book begin and end their own journey with this huge and endlessly fascinating work, I hope they will enjoy it as much as I have.

1
Wagner's story

Kapellmeister and revolutionary

D RESDEN, 2 MARCH 1846. Wilhelm Richard Wagner, the
thirty-two-year-old Royal Kapellmeister of Saxony, addresses
a letter to Wolf Adolf August von Lüttichau, long-standing director of the Dresden Court Theatre. It concerns the orchestra for
which Wagner is responsible, and which plays for opera performances in the city; since 1841 these have taken place in the
magnificent new house designed by Gottfried Semper. Wagner
laments that during the three years of his tenure, he has achieved
only a limited amount. This is not through laziness – Dresden
has witnessed the premieres of three of his own operas, *Rienzi*,
The Flying Dutchman and *Tannhäuser*, during the last four years,
so he can scarcely be accused of that. However, he could achieve
much more were it not for the structural constraints that prevent
him from developing the orchestra as he wishes: its interests are
always trumped by those of the theatre, and singers swallow up a
large proportion of the available cash. In an attempt to improve
the situation, the Kapellmeister has spent three months drafting
(and redrafting) a report that he now has the privilege to enclose
for Lüttichau's consideration.

The report is long – some fifteen thousand words, plus tables
of actual and projected expenditure – and very detailed: it deals
not just with the abilities of individual players but with matters as
practical as the design of chairs and music stands and the shape

I

of the orchestral pit. Its message, however, is simple: unless the membership, schedule, working conditions and remuneration of the orchestra are thoroughly overhauled, it will fall into irreversible decline. Too much is expected of exhausted and underpaid musicians, but with only a modest increase in the salary bill (3,050 thalers added to the current annual expenditure of 28,000) standards could be transformed, if the rest of Wagner's proposals were also adopted. He concludes his letter with an offer: should his comments on the orchestra suggest his organisational advice might be helpful, he would be honoured to turn his attention to the larger and infinitely more complex organism that is the opera company.

Since the era of Carl Maria von Weber – Royal Kapellmeister from 1817 until his untimely death in 1826, and an occasional visitor to the home of Wagner's twice-widowed mother, Johanna – Dresden has been a renowned centre for opera. Wagner reveres Weber's *Der Freischütz*, not just for its exhilarating score but as a premonition of what German opera could become; Weber's widow, Caroline, helped to convince Wagner to accept the post as Kapellmeister, calling him the only worthy successor to her husband. Given his enormous debts and the hardships he had suffered over the preceding three years in Paris, why was he reluctant to accept such a prestigious position? It offered him a steady income and opportunities to have his operas performed, benefits conspicuously lacking in his career to date. Admittedly, he was not offered the top job straight away: first he was sounded out for junior posts, vacant since the deaths of Joseph Rastrelli and Francesco Morlacchi, but he declined both in quick succession, piqued perhaps by the requirement to serve a probation period, and by the posts' inferiority of status and salary to that of Carl Gottlieb Reissiger, Weber's long-standing successor, of whose abilities and work ethic Wagner holds a poor opinion. Only in February 1843, when he was offered a new position as Royal Court Kapellmeister for life, with a rank equal to Reissiger's and an improved salary of 1,500 thalers, did Wagner feel compelled to accept, though he remains unhappy at the lack of authority the post confers. On important occasions or when conducting services at the Court Chapel, he has to wear (and pay for) a silver-embroidered blue uniform with a lyre on the collar – a requirement with a whiff of servant status, of Haydn at Eszterháza, difficult for the fiercely independent Wagner to bear.

Reissiger is not the only Dresden colleague for whom Wagner has limited respect. The recipient of his letter, Lüttichau, has been in post since 1824: a former forestry administrator approaching sixty, he seems to have been appointed so that he can serve King Friedrich August II as a privy counsellor and gentleman of the bedchamber, rather than because of any enthusiasm for the theatre. Despite Lüttichau's role in securing his own appointment, Wagner treats him with contempt, missing meetings without explanation. The king himself, in his mid-forties when Wagner is appointed, has largely abandoned the liberal tendencies he displayed when he became co-regent in 1830: he now resists calls for greater civil rights and a united Germany and replaces liberal ministers with conservatives. Though he is intelligent and cultured, and aware of the exceptional qualities of his fiery new Kapellmeister, he does not concern himself closely with the theatre, and meets Wagner only four times during his six years of service.

Wagner must have hoped that the king himself would consider his report into the state of his orchestra: it includes proposals – for a new concert series, and the replacement of Dresden's old opera house with a new concert hall – that could proceed only with royal approval. Whether or not the report reaches the king's desk, it is more than a year before Wagner receives a response – and then the document is dismissed without explanation. Undeterred by this lack of support – or sufficiently bloody-minded to carry on regardless – he proceeds, uninvited, to the more ambitious proposal hinted at in the first scheme's final paragraph. On 11 May 1848, Wagner submits a 'Plan for the Organisation of a German National Theatre for the Kingdom of Saxony'. This time the covering letter is addressed to Martin Oberländer, Minister of the Interior, and includes a request for an hour-long meeting in which Wagner will present his plan to Oberländer and the Minister for Public Worship and Instruction, the Bavarian-born Baron Ludwig von der Pfordten. Oberländer has only been in office a couple of months, as part of Friedrich August's so-called 'March ministry', hastily installed in response to the uprisings that convulsed Germany after the February Revolution in Paris and the abdication of Louis-Philippe. It is unlikely that theatre reform is at the top of his agenda.

Like Wagner's earlier plan, this document delves into the composition and salary structure of the orchestra. This time, the Kapellmeister argues that better results could be achieved even while reducing the wage bill: noting that annual orchestral costs regularly exceed the 40,000 thalers allocated from the Civil List, he proposes increasing the number of salaried players but reducing the number of occasions on which they play and eliminating the use of poor-quality extras. Maintaining a stable group of players will improve the outcome – good wind intonation, for example, will be easier to achieve – but will require a number of other changes that Wagner argues will be beneficial in themselves. The use of orchestral players in church services will be phased out: the imbalance of forces between a large orchestra and a smaller choir is musically unsatisfactory, and the presence of instrumentalists distracts worshippers and encourages composers to displays of virtuosity unbecoming in a devotional context. Orchestral players will no longer be routinely required to play between the acts of spoken dramas – no one listens to them anyway – though high-quality incidental music such as Beethoven's score for Goethe's *Egmont* will naturally still be performed. Overall there will be fewer performances, which Wagner believes can be managed without reducing total box-office income: opening every night leads to the theatre being undervalued and regarded as a place merely for entertainment, rather than instruction and enlightenment.

Striking though these proposals are, this time the plan goes far beyond the orchestra. Wagner hopes to establish both a stage school offering aspiring actors a three-year training programme, thus raising the status of the profession, and a conservatoire for musicians, which will absorb the institution recently established in Leipzig by Mendelssohn. Leipzig will be compensated for the loss of its conservatoire by the establishment of a satellite branch of the national theatre – it will be the only city in Saxony other than Dresden with such an institution. Choristers will be selected and trained to work specifically in churches or theatres, depending on their abilities and the nature of their voices. A union of poets and theatre composers will be established, with opportunities for regular hearings of their work, privileged access to the theatre and representation in its governance; this union, alongside the orchestral musicians, will elect the music director. Most controversially, the budget for the theatre and its associated institutions will be transferred from the Civil List to the State, making it directly accountable to the State Assembly and marginalising the current administration. Though Wagner emphasises that the king

5

remains at the pinnacle of this imagined theatrical edifice, in this febrile political climate – only a week after Wagner's letter, the German National Assembly meets for the first time in Frankfurt – to propose such radical upheaval is fatal to his chances of success.

Wagner secures his meeting, and some apparent signs of interest from Oberländer, but once the minister shares the document more widely, contemptuous comments proliferate in the margins. Lüttichau, now approaching a quarter-century in post, can hardly be expected to be supportive, given Wagner's pointed references to courtiers responsible only to the monarch, and appointed with no knowledge of the theatre. And the hint that Reissiger should be shunted aside to concentrate on church music, giving free rein to a music director with an enhanced remit, does nothing to dispel the impression that Wagner is intent on a power grab. Although his convictions are clear – theatre has a moral purpose, and organisational change is essential if that purpose is to be realised – his political acumen is currently less developed. The Kapellmeister has overplayed his hand, and this failure marks the effective end of his attempts to give Dresden the theatre he believes Germany needs. Henceforth, according to the preface to the published version of the plan that eventually appears in 1871, Wagner chooses 'to league [himself] with Chaos, rather than with the Established'.

Reckless, self-serving, treacherous, spendthrift – these and other uncomplimentary epithets are regularly thrown at the young Wagner, both by his contemporaries and by subsequent commentators, and with good reason. But the detail and reasoned argument found in these two plans (today they would be called 'strategic') show that he can also on occasion be measured, shrewd, practical, public-minded, and even financially prudent – at least in theory, with theoretical money. He will need all these qualities decades later, to ensure that *The Ring* succeeds not just as a score and libretto but also as a practical project.

* * *

The theatrical utopia that Wagner envisages for Dresden could not have been more different from the operatic chaos he endured in Magdeburg twelve years earlier at the premiere of *Das Liebesverbot*, the first of his works to be staged. Wagner was offered the theatre's music directorship in summer 1834: it was a good position for a twenty-one-year-old, and certainly a step up from his previous job as chorus master at Würzburg, but he was reluctant to commit himself, just as he would be in Dresden. His visit to Bad Lauchstädt, where the company was presenting a summer season, confirmed his fears: he found its director, Heinrich Bethmann, in squalid circumstances, and the company manager despairing of being able to persuade the local bandsmen to put in the rehearsal time required for *Don Giovanni*. Wagner resolved to refuse the appointment and return to Leipzig, but before he could act on this decision, a friend from Würzburg took him to see some lodgings also occupied by the company's leading actress, Minna Planer, whom he described to Wagner as the prettiest and nicest girl in town. Wagner's first encounter with Minna overcame his antipathy to the company and he instantly decided to accept both position and lodgings.

Despite never having conducted an opera, or anything other than a few short pieces of his own, Wagner performed creditably in *Don Giovanni*, and grew rapidly in confidence when he returned with the company to Magdeburg for the winter season. Both his fortunes and those of the constantly impoverished troupe improved markedly the following year when Bethmann secured new funding from the King of Prussia. Previously a Prussian-controlled Duchy, Magdeburg had been the capital of the Prussian Province of

Saxony since the 1815 Congress of Vienna carved up the German lands in the wake of the Napoleonic Wars. Friedrich Wilhelm III's affection for the impresario's late wife, a celebrated actress at the Berlin Court Theatre, persuaded him to overlook Bethmann's shortcomings. Wagner was given a salary increase and licence to travel round Germany in search of singers whose reputation would justify the king's support. He secured some guest appearances from the star soprano Wilhelmine Schröder-Devrient, whose inspirational effect on the adolescent Wagner is memorably if somewhat inaccurately conveyed in his autobiography *Mein Leben*.

Meanwhile, Wagner had fallen desperately in love with Minna. She was four years older than him, and considerably more worldly: at fifteen she had been seduced and abandoned by an army officer and had subsequently given birth to his daughter, Natalie, whom she passed off as her sister. Minna was by no means unresponsive to Wagner's advances, but nor was she willing to give up her other suitors. Wagner's letters from this period reveal a jealousy that only intensified in November 1835 when Minna accepted a role in Berlin. He pleaded with her to return to Magdeburg and marry him; she reluctantly rejoined Bethmann's company, but soon left for an engagement in Königsberg, the remote Prussian 'coronation city' on the Baltic Sea. In May 1836, abandoning his hopes of a post in Berlin, Wagner followed her, and it was in Königsberg, that November, that the couple formalised their tempestuous relationship.

Minna and Richard were surely aware of each other's shortcomings as life partners by the time of their marriage, but the faultlines became increasingly obvious through the quarter of a century during which they continued, on and off, to live with each other. However, during his time in Magdeburg Wagner saw in Minna, whatever she thought of him, the possibility of an all-consuming, all-fulfilling love, physical and spiritual – an ideal he continued to nurture, both personally and artistically, for the rest of his life, and which informed his work on his second completed opera, whose title literally translates as 'the ban on love'. Wagner derived his libretto from *Measure for Measure*: he transposes Shakespeare's action from Vienna to Palermo, but gives his hypocritical governor the German name Friedrich, as if to contrast Teutonic repressiveness with unbridled Sicilian sensuality.

Though it was premiered in Magdeburg, *Das Liebesverbot* was conceived in Leipzig, the city where Wagner was born, and to which he returned as an adolescent, having moved to Dresden as a baby after the death of his father, when his mother quickly married the actor-playwright Ludwig Geyer. At seventeen, Wagner was caught up in the rioting that swept Leipzig in the wake of the July 1830 uprising in Paris, and excitedly proclaimed himself a revolutionary. The possibility of regime change was quickly averted: the newly appointed co-regent Friedrich August introduced a constitution and other liberal measures, earning the approval of Wagner, who composed a 'political overture' including a theme labelled 'Friedrich and Freedom'. This is perhaps the very first instance in Wagner's music of what later became known as a leitmotif: a short musical theme linked to an idea, character or object in the drama.

If the threat of a revolutionary uprising quickly dissipated, the new thinking that accompanied it was not so easily suppressed: Leipzig was one of the centres of the 'Young Germany' movement that argued for political and social change, and Wagner became close to several of its leading figures, including his schoolfriend Theodor Apel and the writer Heinrich Laube. Although Wagner rejected Laube's suggestion that he should set his libretto about the Polish freedom fighter Tadeusz Kósciuszko, the writer's advocacy of free love and the overthrow of bourgeois values, as expounded in the novel *Das junge Europa*, profoundly influenced the composer's own libretto for *Das Liebesverbot*.

This was in fact Wagner's third attempt at an opera, but neither of the others had reached the stage: he destroyed the unfinished score of *Die Hochzeit* after some harsh criticism from his sister Rosalie, by then a well-known actress and singer, and his efforts to get *Die Feen* performed in Leipzig had failed. He pinned all his hopes on *Das Liebesverbot*'s Magdeburg premiere, but it was dogged by misfortune.

By the time Wagner completed the score, Bethmann had once again run out of money; singers were resigning to take more secure jobs elsewhere; only ten days' rehearsal time could be spared for this long and complex work with numerous ensembles. Two performances were scheduled: at the first, for which the company would take the proceeds, many of the singers, particularly the men, forgot their parts, and because the theatre failed to produce a libretto, none of the audience knew what was supposed to be happening. The second performance, intended to benefit Wagner himself, fared even worse: a fight broke out backstage among the cast – prompted by sexual jealousy, appropriately enough – and the manager informed the small audience that the show was cancelled. These events are related in *Mein Leben* in a tone of self-deprecating humour that is – perhaps unfairly – not generally associated with Wagner. But this does not disguise the painful nature of the experience.

From the castanet solo that begins the overture to the relentless, rumbustious Rossini crescendos that conclude each act, there is scarcely a bar in *Das Liebesverbot* that sounds anything like the mature Wagner. But taken on its own terms, it is tremendous fun, and its melodic inventiveness and madcap shifts of tone prove beyond doubt that Wagner could have enjoyed a successful career as a composer of operetta – something that could hardly be further from his subsequent intentions. But if the musical impact of *Das Liebesverbot* on Wagner's later work was negligible, his subsequent career as theatrical reformer and his determination to secure the best conditions for the creation of future operas, particularly his own, owe much to its catastrophic premiere.

* * *

Once his second proposal for reform is rejected, the Kapellmeister turns away from organisational structures and salary bills and back to history and myth. He retains his belief in his vision – of a musical theatre characterised by artistic excellence and moral integrity – even if he cannot realise it in the Dresden of 1848, with its government seized by fear of revolution. Wagner revisits ideas for scenarios that he had previously set aside. Underpinning this search for a subject is the realisation that whatever the merits of his operas to date, and despite the variable success they have achieved, neither their stories nor their heroes any longer convince him. The scenarios Wagner drafts in the next few months vary widely in the nature and cultural origins of their sources and in the manner and extent to which he develops them, but they all feature a powerful hero who redeems not only himself but also the whole of mankind.

Friedrich Barbarossa (or 'Rotbart'; both sobriquets mean 'red beard') is the first hero to whom Wagner turns – or rather returns, since he had sketched out a five-act drama about the twelfth-century emperor two years earlier. Barbarossa's appeal is obvious: King of Germany for almost forty years, King of Italy and Holy Roman Emperor for thirty-five, he is famous for military success in the Crusades and his Italian campaigns, for his political acumen in drawing together a Germany of more than 1,600 states, and for his dealings with successive Popes. Such is his legendary status that stories circulate about his supernatural powers: like Britain's King Arthur, he is often represented as not dead but asleep with his knights – in the Kyffhäuser mountains, waiting to restore Germany to its former greatness. In 1846, when Wagner first conceived *Friedrich I*, his hero's first name must have seemed doubly auspicious, given that the composer served Friedrich August as Kapellmeister and hoped for the patronage of Friedrich Wilhelm IV of Prussia; by 1848, his faith in these fallible present-day monarchs has evaporated, but not his interest in their heroic medieval namesake. Barbarossa now becomes a vehicle for expressing his own political aspirations; to the historical scenarios set out in 1846, Wagner adds a speech in which Barbarossa vows to act in the interests of *all* his people – like the democratic, 'republican' monarch for whom Wagner yearns. But despite Barbarossa's promising credentials as a hero, there remains the problem of Wagner's waning interest in historical drama itself.

Wagner develops the Barbarossa scenario no further, but the emperor occupies a crucial place in another piece of writing from around this time, 'The Wibelungs: World History from Legend'. Wagner considers this sufficiently important to publish in 1850 as a pamphlet and to include many years later in his collected works. The exact chronology of its composition continues to preoccupy Wagner scholars – and a letter to Theodor Uhlig indicates that he was reworking the piece 'in a whole variety of new ways' as late as September 1849, some months after the Dresden uprising and his escape to Zurich – but the published version is headed 'Summer 1848', suggesting that it is at least begun by this point.

'The Wibelungs' is not a plan for a drama but an essay: ambitious, wide-ranging and decidedly heavy-going. It draws together royal dynasties and ruling classes from around the world and from the birth of civilisation onwards – from India to Troy, from Caesars to Popes; it considers their relationships to one another and how they used mythology to support their claims to authority. Most important for Wagner is the dynasty of Frankish kings, of whom Charlemagne is the most distinguished, and from which Barbarossa traces his lineage. Wagner argues that the myth of the Nibelung hoard – the gold that confers absolute power on whoever possesses it – is crucial to the Frankish royal family, and that the weaker the dynastic claims of the 'Kaisers' who succeeded Charlemagne became, the more insistently they asserted their ownership of the symbolic hoard. For the purposes of 'The Wibelungs' (it will be different in *The Ring*), possession of the hoard de facto confers Nibelung identity.

Even the essay's bizarre title is an attempt to drive home the connection between the Frankish dynasty and the potent myth of the Nibelungs: noting that the Hohenstaufen family to which Barbarossa belonged were also known in Italy as 'Ghibellines' and in Upper Germany as 'Wibelingen', Wagner asserts the identity of this name with that found in the myth ('if the change of the initial letter N to W could be accounted for'), ridiculing the conventional wisdom that the name stemmed from the 'wholly indifferent hamlet' of Waiblingen. Ultimately more important than this tortuous etymological sleight of hand, however, is the identity between dynasty and myth that Wagner himself creates in his essay's concluding panegyric to Barbarossa, whom he imagines sitting in a cave like that in which Siegfried slew the dragon, surrounded by Nibelung treasure. Wagner never writes his Barbarossa opera, but far from abandoning Friedrich, he subsumes him into his fast-developing idea of Siegfried, legendary conqueror of the Nibelung hoard.

Wagner's ideas develop fast. On 4 October 1848, he completes a prose treatment originally entitled 'Die Nibelungensaga', though it is known to posterity by the rather more unwieldy title under which Wagner publishes it: 'The Nibelung Myth as Sketch for a Drama'. By contrast with the sprawling 'Wibelung' essay, this treatment is focused and – at least by Wagner's standards – succinct. Here, as in *The Ring*, the Nibelungs, led by Alberich, are synonymous with the occupants of Nibelheim, a land of 'gloomy subterranean clefts and caverns'; in this telling, gaining possession of the hoard does not make Siegfried, or any other conqueror, into a Nibelung. Most of the story is told in summary, without dialogue: only from the point when Brünnhilde enters the Hall of the Gibichungs and sees her ring on Siegfried's finger does Wagner resort to direct speech. There are numerous differences from the version of the story that Wagner eventually sets down in his libretti – and some of these are important – but it is recognisably the same narrative, containing most of the major characters of *The Ring* (though not Loge, Erda or the Norns), and Wagner tells it with a conviction and brio that make its operatic potential clear.

A few weeks later, in late November, Wagner completes a libretto entitled *Siegfrieds Tod* (The Death of Siegfried). All the singing characters in *Götterdämmerung* – Gunther, Gutrune; Hagen, Alberich; Siegfried, Brünnhilde; Norns, Rhinemaidens, vassals – are present here. The libretto's bone structure, too – three acts preceded by a substantial two-part prologue, the first for the Norns and the second for Brünnhilde and Siegfried – is similar to that of the drama that eventually concludes *The Ring*, despite differences of detail. The scene for Brünnhilde that Wagner later refines into a poignant dialogue with a single Valkyrie sister, Waltraute, is represented here by a rather more matter-of-fact encounter with all eight Valkyries speaking together. A more important difference concerns the place of the gods. Even though they do not sing in *Götterdämmerung*, their importance is clear from the drama's title: they feature as silent characters and are ultimately destroyed in the conflagration that envelops Valhalla. In *Siegfrieds Tod*, by contrast, the gods are conspicuous by their absence, though Wotan's name is invoked by Siegfried, Brünnhilde and the chorus. It is not that Wagner does not realise their importance to his story: the mutual dependence of gods and heroes, Wotan and Siegfried, is clear in 'The Wibelungs' and the 'Sketch for a Drama', but he has not yet worked out how to integrate them within the same libretto, nor will he do so for some years. Although a slightly expanded version of *Siegfrieds Tod* follows in December, Wagner then abruptly abandons work on this story: he will not return to it until he has left Dresden for good.

Meanwhile, during 1849, as life in Dresden becomes increasingly complex, Wagner continues to explore other stories, auditioning two other famous figures as potential heroes. A drama about Achilles – described in 'The Wibelungs' as 'that foremost vanquisher of Troy' – appeals for a while: Wagner has a long-standing interest in Greek mythology and spends 1847 immersed in the *Oresteia*. Only fragmentary notes for the Achilles drama survive, but it is clear that Wagner regards Achilles, like Siegfried, as a man who supersedes the gods: refusing the offer of immortality made by his mother, Thetis, Achilles asserts himself as the man of the future. Wagner's plans for a drama about Jesus progress rather further: in early 1849 he produces twenty-eight pages of prose that set out ideas for a five-act drama entitled *Jesus of Nazareth*. His interest in Jesus, like his attraction to Achilles, is adumbrated in 'The Wibelungs', where he argues that Wotan can be completely identified with the Christian God and that Siegfried and

Christ are essentially the same figure.

Jesus of Nazareth – the last creative project of his time in Dresden, according to his autobiography – is a curious document. It is not published until four years after his death, and the sequence in which its three sections appear in print may not reflect the order in which they were written. In the published edition, at any rate, the first part is a detailed synopsis in five acts of a drama that begins with Barabbas and Judas Iscariot plotting against Roman rule in Judaea, and ends with Peter, inspired by the Holy Spirit, proclaiming the message of the crucified Jesus to an enthusiastic crowd. The second and longest section is a commentary on Jesus' teaching that articulates issues that resurface in *The Ring*, *Tristan und Isolde* and *Parsifal*: the conflict between mankind's natural instinct to love and laws that shackle this impulse; the immorality of loveless marriages; the relationship between sex and death; the necessity of death as a sacrifice for the well-being of the community. The final part consists of verbatim quotations from Luther's translation of the New Testament – the most heavily annotated book in the substantial private library that Wagner builds up in Dresden, and has to leave behind when he flees the city in haste. It is not clear how – or even whether – this rather disparate and unwieldy raw material will be turned into a libretto, let alone an opera, though Wagner produces eleven bars of music entitled 'Christ in the nave', and hints to Liszt in December that he is considering completing the work for a performance in Paris.

In the end, *Jesus of Nazareth*, like *Friedrich I* and *Achilles*, remains one of those tantalising phantom operas that litter Wagner's career, but the heroes who obsess him at this turning point of his life do not simply evaporate from his work. Barbarossa, Achilles and Jesus, for Wagner, are men of action who inspire revolutionary change in the real world; but they are also figures whose lives and deaths carry metaphysical significance. All of them leave their imprint on the character of Siegfried, whom Wagner ultimately chooses as the most suitable central character for the new music theatre he wants to create. Soon, once he is over the Swiss border, he will again take up the story of his chosen hero. But before that happens, the Kapellmeister himself plays the part of revolutionary activist, as Dresden is belatedly entangled in the upheavals sweeping Europe. Wagner's role may only be peripheral, and over quite quickly, but the mark it leaves on *The Ring* is indelible.

* * *

Wagner's desire to portray revolutionary leaders in his dramas is not new. It was his stirring depiction of Cola di Rienzo – the fourteenth-century Roman who dramatically seized power from the aristocratic families who controlled the city – that established his reputation in Dresden almost overnight. His second operatic premiere, which took place at Gottfried Semper's magnificent Court Theatre on 20 October 1842, could not have been more different from the Magdeburg debacle six years earlier. In Dresden the singers were well prepared and enthusiastic about their roles; rehearsals took place over months rather than days and the entire company was confident of success; the audience remained attentive despite being in their seats from six o'clock until after midnight, and applauded the composer ecstatically at the end of each act. Wagner wrote in his autobiography that this performance affected him in a way no subsequent rendition of any of his music could match, despite the dislike he came to feel for the work itself. The premiere transformed his material prospects, too: from barely having had enough money for food, he immediately became an obvious candidate for the vacancy that unexpectedly arose at the Court Theatre twenty-six days later with the death of the music director Joseph Rastrelli.

Wagner had initially imagined *Rienzi* on a very different stage: that of the Paris Opéra. From the moment in 1837 when he read a German translation of *Rienzi, the Last of the Roman Tribunes*, by the English novelist and Whig MP Edward Bulwer-Lytton, Wagner realised the story's potential to make a *grand opéra* like those currently taking Paris by storm. Works such as Daniel-François Auber's *La Muette de Portici*, Fromental Halévy's *La Juive* and Giacomo Meyerbeer's *Les Huguenots*, all premiered within the last decade, traded on spectacular scenic effects, lavish ballet scenes, elaborate choruses and thrilling arias, and the Rienzi story offered ample opportunities for all those features.

In August 1837, shortly after completing the first prose draft of *Rienzi*, Wagner moved to Riga – at that time capital of the Russian-controlled province of Livonia – to take up a post as the city's music director; two years later, when his contract was not renewed, he persuaded Minna that they should make their way to Paris in the hope of securing a production of his new opera, whose first two acts were now complete. The journey was famously tortuous – in order to dodge their creditors, the couple took a boat from East Prussia to London, with an unplanned detour along the Norwegian coast that helped to inspire some of the astonishing music in *The Flying Dutchman* – but even before they reached Paris, Wagner had shown his work on *Rienzi* to Meyerbeer, whom he encountered in Boulogne. After this auspicious introduction to France, the three years that followed were a bitter disappointment. The optimism aroused by his meeting with Meyerbeer and by the letters of recommendation the older composer provided soon dissipated, as Henri Duponchel, the Opéra's director, showed no interest in Wagner's work. He eked out a living by writing articles for German newspapers and making vocal scores and arrangements from other composers' operas; lack of income together with unwise accommodation choices left him invariably impecunious and at one point close to imprisonment for debt.

Despite these tribulations, by late 1840 the orchestral score of *Rienzi* was complete; abandoning any hope of a production at the Opéra, Wagner resolved to try his luck in his childhood home. He petitioned King Friedrich August directly – but ironically it was Meyerbeer, whom he later unfairly blamed for his failure in Paris, who intervened decisively in March 1841 when he wrote to recommend *Rienzi* and its composer to Lüttichau. A year on – by which time Wagner had largely completed a further and very different opera, *The Flying Dutchman* – he was sufficiently confident of a production of *Rienzi* to return to Germany; from late April, supported by a small loan from his family, he based himself again in Dresden and devoted himself to ensuring the opera's success.

The rehearsal process was joyful, and helped Wagner establish good working relationships with a group of talented individuals who soon became close colleagues. The idol of his youth, Wilhelmine Schröder-Devrient, took the role of Adriano, scion of the aristocratic Colonna family, who falls in love with Rienzi's sister Irene: though Schröder-Devrient was displeased to be playing a trouser role rather than the heroine, and Wagner in turn began to realise her personal and professional shortcomings, their continuing mutual regard ensured a committed performance. The theatre's principal tenor, Josef Tichatschek, was at the peak of his vocal powers and enthused by the herculean challenges of the title role: if his interpretation did not locate the ambiguities of Rienzi's character quite as Wagner would have liked, his magnificent voice and unfailing energy were ample compensation. Tichatschek was delighted, too, by the silver armour and other sumptuous costumes created for him by Ferdinand Heine, whom Wagner had known since childhood among the circle of his stepfather, Ludwig Geyer. *Rienzi* made severe demands of the chorus, so it was fortunate that the chorus master Wilhelm Fischer was another ally, who had learned the opera thoroughly before Wagner's arrival: the pair spent many hours before the premiere discussing what cuts could be made, but could never agree on which passages might be dispensed with. Wagner even found a way to get the best out of Reissiger, who was conducting, by bringing to each rehearsal fresh pages of a libretto he had offered to the older composer; Reissiger had complained that the libretti he had previously been obliged to deal with were not worthy of his talents, though he eventually became so suspicious of Wagner's motives that he declined to set his work, in case it contained a trap intended to expose his deficiencies.

Rienzi was a triumph: some smart appropriation of the tricks of Meyerbeerian grand opera and some glorious melodies, none more memorable than the theme of 'Rienzi's Prayer' that snakes through the score from the overture to its final apotheosis in Act V, ensured its popularity with audiences. And it firmly consolidated its composer's position in Dresden society: King Friedrich August attended the second performance; Wagner himself conducted the sixth to great acclaim; once he saw off an attempt to divide the opera into two parts, it became a mainstay of the Court Theatre's repertoire.

But *Rienzi* was also a dead end. By the time it reached the stage, Wagner had left behind the operatic model on which it was based. He was busy promoting the more forward-looking *Flying Dutchman*, which he described as a 'dramatic ballad' rather than a traditional 'number opera': its move towards greater continuity of sections and its daring choral and orchestral sonorities foreshadow his mature work much more clearly than does *Rienzi*. He had already drafted a scenario for *Tannhäuser*, whose source materials and themes are more closely aligned than those of *Rienzi* with his growing aspiration to create distinctively 'German' opera, even if he never brings his story of the minstrel-hero's adventures to a form with which he is quite content. He had also conceived the idea for another project that, like *Tannhäuser*, would draw on medieval German poetry: this is *Lohengrin*, the Romantic opera that more than any other establishes him as a worthy successor to Weber, even if he will no longer occupy Weber's former post as Royal Saxon Kapellmeister by the time it is produced.

Wagner's disinclination to write anything more in the vein of *Rienzi* meant that it was not the springboard for future success that it might have been for a less original, less restless composer. And although the opera contains some magnificent music, its intimidating length and its association with its most infamous admirer, Adolf Hitler – who attributed the birth of his political consciousness to experiencing *Rienzi* in 1905 in Linz, used its overture to open Nazi rallies, and accepted Wagner's manuscript as a fiftieth-birthday present – have made revivals infrequent. Recent productions, such as Philipp Stölzl's 2010 staging for the Deutsche Oper, often make severe cuts and present the title character as a proto-fascist: an approach that can be theatrically compelling and offers a chance to hear some rarely performed music, but gives only a partial understanding of the grandeur of Wagner's original conception.

Two operas performed, one about love, the other about power. Wagner's portrayal of these forces – whose opposition drives the plot of *The Ring* – will become infinitely more subtle as his career progresses, but his obsession with both is already clear.

* * *

18 June 1848. Another letter to Lüttichau. A month after presenting his ill-fated plan to reform Saxony's theatres, Wagner pleads with the esteemed director for two weeks' leave of absence, to help him deal with a digestive complaint. He follows this brief request with a much longer paragraph justifying his recent prominence in the state's increasingly heated political disputes. He concedes that he does indeed support many of the progressive faction's aims, including the 'noble concept' of a republic, but he denies that any of this is inconsistent with the continuation of the monarchy. On the contrary, the speech he gave four days ago to three thousand members of the Dresden Vaterlandsverein, 'How Do Republican Aspirations Stand in Relation to the Monarchy?', expresses his support for the king: his praise of Friedrich August's virtues prompted spontaneous applause, an unprecedented event in the society's meetings. The lecture subsequently appears in the *Dresdner Anzeiger* – anonymously, to be sure, but no one has any doubt of Wagner's authorship.

Two weeks later, Wagner writes again to Lüttichau, asking him to extend his leave, perhaps for another three or four weeks, in order that he can make a journey that will, he anticipates, refresh both body and soul. The theatre's director grants the request, seemingly on the condition that his Kapellmeister makes adequate arrangements to cover his duties, since Wagner writes Lüttichau a much longer letter the following day that combines extravagant professions of gratitude with expressions of hope that Reissiger will absorb his workload. A letter written to Reissiger that same day, 3 July, lays it on thick: Wagner pleads with his colleague to reassure Lüttichau that the theatre will manage without him; he plays on Reissiger's reputation for laziness by dangling vague promises that on his return he will renegotiate the division of responsibilities in a way that will make the older man's life easier; but for the moment, Wagner mysteriously adds, his fellow Kapellmeister should regard him as if he is terminally ill. He tells Reissiger that Lüttichau wishes to see him at 10 a.m. the following day to negotiate the terms of his leave; Reissiger's intervention must have been successful, since Wagner is allowed to go.

Both men might reasonably assume from Wagner's letters that he intends to retreat to the mountains, or perhaps a spa. Instead, he makes his way, via Breslau, to Vienna, at this point probably the most politically unstable of all German-speaking cities. It has been in turmoil since the March Revolution and the hasty departures of the long-serving Chancellor, Klemens von Metternich (for London, in March) and the Emperor Ferdinand (for Innsbruck, in May). A revolutionary coalition of workers, students and the Civil Guard now co-exists uneasily with an anxious government and an Austrian parliament elected for the first time in July. In this unstable situation, Wagner sees an opportunity to realise his plans for theatre reform, but on the grander scale that a cosmopolitan capital city will allow. On 20 July, only eleven days after his arrival, the *Wiener Abendzeitung* reports that the composer of *Rienzi* and *The Flying Dutchman* intends to put a plan to the Minister for Education to reorganise the five competing Viennese theatres into a single co-operative institution under the control of a committee of authors and musicians. Unfortunately for Wagner, his plan not only fails to gain support in Vienna, but also makes trouble for him back in Saxony when the *Abendzeitung*'s report is picked up by the Leipzig journal *Signale für die musikalische Welt*. Wagner's excuse for leaving his post and his denial of any political motivation are exposed as lies. Though he returns to his duties in late July, his Dresden employers will never trust him again.

For Saxony, by contrast with most other German-speaking countries, the bloodiest period of the mid-century revolutions is still to come. It is difficult to establish Wagner's precise actions, let alone his motivations, during the cataclysmic ten months that separate his abortive trip to Vienna from his eventual flight to Switzerland. Is he part of the plot to overthrow the government, or merely an innocent bystander caught up in events that spiral beyond his control? Is he really interested in politics, or is reform merely a means to achieve his theatrical goals? Is he sincere in his protestations of admiration for the monarchy, and for Friedrich August in particular? The surviving correspondence provides only limited assistance with these questions, since – as his dealings with Lüttichau and Reissiger show – the image of Wagner that each letter conveys depends largely on what its recipient wants to read. His autobiography, dictated to his second wife Cosima from 1865 onwards, suffers from a similar problem: the account of the Dresden uprising is compellingly written, but its value as evidence is compromised by the fact that it was written at the request of King Ludwig II of Bavaria, to whom Wagner would scarcely have wished to present himself as an anti-monarchist revolutionary.

Despite his later attempts to play down his role, Wagner is – at the very least – near to the centre of the activity that comes to a head with the May 1849 uprising, and well acquainted with many of its ringleaders. One of these could not have been closer at hand. Since 1843 Wagner's assistant has been August Röckel, a composer and conductor eighteen months his junior whom he persuaded the Court Theatre to appoint against Reissiger's wishes. Despite a distinguished musical pedigree – Röckel's father, Joseph, was a friend and collaborator of Beethoven, and August's own résumé includes assisting Rossini at the Théâtre Italien in

Paris – Wagner's assistant is increasingly known for his political activities, and for views much more unambiguously republican than those of his superior. In the summer of 1848 Röckel writes a pamphlet arguing for the establishment of national militias across Germany; he submits it to the Vaterlandsverein, the same group to which Wagner gives his controversial lecture, who distribute it among the delegates to the Frankfurt Assembly. He establishes a weekly journal, *Volksblätter*, whose first edition appears on 26 August; he publishes a provocative 'Open Letter to the Soldiers', which urges Friedrich Wilhelm's Prussian army not to intervene should there be a revolution in Saxony. All this is too much for the theatre authorities to tolerate: by the end of September Röckel is dismissed and loses what modest income he had to support his large family; in November he is briefly imprisoned before a wealthy sympathiser pays his bail. But at the end of the year, his fortunes change, as he is elected as one of the deputies who make up the new democratic majority in the Saxon parliament, usefully bringing him immunity from arrest.

Three months later, Röckel introduces Wagner to the Russian anarchist Mikhail Bakunin, one of the most influential political thinkers of the century, and later Karl Marx's most determined opponent within the international revolutionary movement. If Marx favours a democratic and peaceful route towards the ultimate victory of the proletariat, Bakunin has no hesitation in advocating political assassination and violent insurrection. The Russian has hurriedly left first Paris and then Prague, following his part in unsuccessful uprisings, and is now living in Dresden under the pseudonym of 'Dr Schwarz' – chosen as a tribute to Berthold Schwarz, the legendary fourteenth-century monk believed to have invented gunpowder. Photographs of Bakunin depict a burly, wild-eyed, scruffily dressed man with unkempt hair and an out-of-control beard – an image matching the ferocity of his writings – but he has a personal charm that belies his fearsome appearance and reputation. Only a year apart in age, he and Wagner get on famously, despite Bakunin's lack of enthusiasm for the Kapellmeister's Nibelung and Jesus projects – the Russian suggests spicing up the latter with lines such as 'Off with his head' and 'To the gallows'. He is more complimentary about *The Flying Dutchman* when he hears Wagner sing and play the opening scenes.

Wagner contributes at least three articles to Röckel's journal during its short existence – they are unsigned, but as with the article that preceded his trip to Vienna, his authorship is an open secret. 'Germany and its Princes' appears in October 1848. Whereas previous articles on this subject had taken care to distinguish Saxony's House of Wettin from more reprehensible ruling houses, here Friedrich August is represented as part of the same general problem: that despite the noble pledges made in March, nothing has changed to benefit the lives of ordinary people. The theme is developed in 'Man and Existing Society', published on 10 February 1849. Though Wagner sets out his discussion mainly in abstract terms, with only passing references to the privileged ruling houses of Prussia and Austria and none to the specific situation in Saxony, his central argument is clear: union between isolated individuals in order to overthrow a society that prevents mankind from fulfilling its destiny is both necessary and inevitable. Two months later, on 8 April, Wagner publishes a still more forthright article entitled 'The Revolution', which depicts Europe as a huge volcano, about to erupt. Wagner personifies Revolution as an 'eternal destroyer' whose paradoxical mission is to bring 'ever-youthful life'; he urges the 'upright, thrifty burgher' not to resist the approaching onslaught but to lift up his eyes and look at his fellow humans, for whom Revolution brings liberation.

This last article is written after Wagner has fallen under the spell of the charismatic Bakunin, and it is not difficult to detect the anarchist's influence beneath its expansive, bloodthirsty rhetoric. But Bakunin is not the only reason for the marked hardening of Wagner's views in what turn out to be his final months in Dresden. Until the end of 1848, he still nurtures the hope that the Court Theatre will produce his latest opera, *Lohengrin*, whose score he completes in April. This prospect is of vital importance, not just artistically, but also as a means of repaying some of his ever-increasing debts. The Act I finale is performed at a concert in September celebrating the three-hundredth anniversary of the Court Orchestra, but attracts little interest. The following month, Lüttichau informs him that the premiere has been cancelled, and adds that the Court is deeply dissatisfied with his conducting: apparently he made errors beating time in a performance of Meyerbeer's *Robert le diable*. Lüttichau's decision may reflect reluctance to allow a 'King of Germany' – the tenth-century Henry the Fowler – to appear on stage at this sensitive moment; it may, as Wagner assumes, be revenge for the composer's own insubordination and duplicity. Regardless of Lüttichau's motive, Wagner loses any hope of the premiere ever taking place – and perhaps, any lingering belief that his artistic aims can be fulfilled under the existing government. The increasingly inflammatory nature of his writings in the first few months of 1849 may reflect this artistic impasse – and a corresponding desire both to bring about a new regime and to ingratiate himself with whatever new administration results from the revolution he anticipates – as well as the influence of his revolutionary associates.

The fragile calm that has so far been preserved in Saxony is about to be shattered. In February, the king dismisses Martin Oberländer and the rest of the cabinet who have been in office since the previous March, and who have achieved very little of the reform they intended to enact. He summons Count Friedrich Ferdinand von Beust – a reactionary career diplomat from a noble family, currently acting as Saxony's envoy to Prussia – back from Berlin to become minister of state and effective head of the government. The following month, the Frankfurt Assembly approves a draft constitution providing for a German national parliament elected by universal suffrage, albeit under a hereditary emperor. Friedrich Wilhelm of Prussia is elected to this position, but shortly afterwards announces that he will not accept it if it is offered by a parliament. Meanwhile, Beust persuades Friedrich August that Saxony should reject the draft constitution, setting himself in conflict with those pressing for change. Until now, Wagner's sympathy with these agitators has been demonstrated largely through speeches and writings, conversations and meetings, but as events gather pace he becomes more active.

During April, Wagner holds meetings in his summerhouse with colleagues including Röckel, Bakunin and Gottfried Semper, to discuss how to arm the people in preparation for the violence that everyone believes is coming. Wagner himself probably takes direct steps to achieve this goal: Karl Wilhelm Oehme, a brass founder, later testifies that Wagner and Röckel asked him to produce large numbers of hand grenades in early April, and that on 4 May Wagner tells him to fill them with explosives. Needless to say, this episode does not find its way into *Mein Leben*, but the presence of the word 'shrapnels' in Wagner's diary for 3 May seems to corroborate Oehme's account.

The long-anticipated conflict is eventually triggered on 30 April, when Friedrich August dissolves the Saxon parliament and dismisses most of his cabinet, three days after a similar move by Friedrich Wilhelm in Prussia. As Wagner speculates on 2 May in a letter to Röckel – who has fled for Prague, having lost his parliamentary immunity – there is now a danger that the revolution may come too soon; indeed, it may be Beust's intention to provoke an outbreak of hostilities before the insurgents can establish a strong position across the state. The day after writing this letter, Wagner hears the sound of the tocsin from the tower of St Anne's Church, or perhaps rings it himself; whichever is true, it is interpreted as the start of the uprising. Wagner calls at the house of Tichatschek, who is away, and asks the tenor's wife whether he can borrow the singer's collection of rifles – though he will claim in his autobiography that he makes this request only to ensure that the firearms do not fall into the hands of a dangerous mob.

On 4 May, Friedrich August and his ministers flee the city; the army, confronted by crowded barricades, agrees to a truce. The printer of *Volksblätter*, for which Wagner is now responsible in Röckel's absence, later testifies that Wagner asked him to make a large number of flyers reading 'Are you with us against foreign troops?'; he was seen distributing them around the barricades and handing them to members of the Saxon army. A provisional government is formed at the city hall and requests citizens to take up arms in its support; Beust returns to Dresden and issues an ultimatum calling for the provisional government's unconditional surrender. Wagner is a conspicuous presence, appealing for information, offering advice and – according to some witnesses – addressing the crowds from the city hall's balcony.

The following day, the Kapellmeister climbs the three-hundred-foot tower of the Kreuzkirche, the city's highest vantage point. He watches troop movements and reports back to the city hall by wrapping notes around stones and dropping them to the street; he remains throughout the night and is heard discoursing on philosophy and music. In the morning, he witnesses rebel forces entering Dresden to support the provisional government, and also Prussian troops, summoned by Beust, who intend to suppress the uprising. That same morning, the city's old opera house goes up in flames; the fire also destroys the sets and costumes used in Semper's new opera house, forcing the cancellation of all forthcoming performances – to Reissiger's distress and Wagner's grim satisfaction. No conclusion is reached on the responsibility for this act of vandalism, but Bakunin and Röckel are both suspects, though the latter claims not to have returned from Prague until the following morning.

While he is in the tower, Wagner receives a message from Minna begging him to return home. He devises a plan to remove her from the firing line of the Prussian troops entering the city: the following day, 7 May, they meet in the countryside and travel to Chemnitz, where Minna will stay with Wagner's sister Clara, and her husband Heinrich Wolfram. On their way there, Wagner is arrested by leaders of the Chemnitz Communal Guard under suspicion that he is deserting the revolutionary cause; he is released only when he promises to return to Dresden as soon as he has deposited Minna. He arrives back on the 8th and heads for the city hall, where he finds the insurgency on the point of collapse; the next day, he is sent to Freiberg to rally reinforcements and bring them to Dresden. Travelling back by coach, the exhausted Wagner falls asleep but is woken by shouting from a large group of insurgents marching away from the city. It is pointless to return: the uprising has been crushed.

* * *

The old opera house that was destroyed in the uprising – disingenuously described in *Mein Leben* as an 'eyesore' and a 'temporary structure' that everyone always feared would burn down

– was in fact a beautiful baroque building with excellent acoustics. Three years earlier, it was the scene of one of Wagner's greatest triumphs as a conductor: his first performance of Beethoven's Ninth Symphony. The concert took place on Palm Sunday, the one occasion of the year on which the Court Orchestra was allowed to perform on its own, rather than in a church service or opera. The proceeds from these annual events went towards a pension fund for the widows and orphans of orchestra members, and Wagner alternated their direction with Reissiger, who had led a couple of apparently disastrous renditions of the Ninth in 1838. Scarred by this experience and fearful for the consequences for their fund, some players went to Lüttichau to object to Wagner's choice of repertoire. But the Kapellmeister was insistent: when the orchestral committee refused to release the funds to purchase the players' parts, he borrowed a set from Leipzig and devoted his energies to ensuring the success of the performance.

Wagner's obsession with Beethoven's final symphony went back to his schooldays in Leipzig. After hearing some unsatisfactory rehearsals at the Gewandhaus in 1830, only six years after the premiere, he copied out the full score, then made a piano arrangement of the first movement. With characteristic chutzpah, he sent this to the work's publisher, Schott of Mainz, with the proposal that he should arrange the whole piece should they accept it for publication. Wagner's offer was rejected, but his fascination with Beethoven continued: he studied the other symphonies, the string quartets and the piano sonatas; he composed a Beethoven-saturated symphony of his own in C major; he conducted six of Beethoven's symphonies in Riga. In 1840, soon after arriving in Paris, he heard François Habeneck conduct the Ninth Symphony with the Conservatoire orchestra, an experience he later described as revelatory, due to the care and precision with which the performance had been prepared. It made him hear the symphony's continuous melodic line for the first time, and prompted a decisive shift in his taste (or so he claimed): he saw now that the French and Italian operas on which he had spent so much of his time as a conductor were essentially trivial (though he maintained an admiration for the melodies of Bellini), and began planning a massive symphony of his own based on Goethe's *Faust*.

This symphony only ever materialised in the form of an overture, but the connection Wagner had established between Goethe's and Beethoven's crowning achievements resurfaced six years later as he prepared to conduct the Ninth. In an attempt to build his audience's understanding of a work that even professional musicians dismissed as incomprehensible (Reissiger was heard at the dress rehearsal lamenting how far Beethoven had gone astray), Wagner prepared elaborate programme notes that used quotations from *Faust* to explain his interpretation of each movement. In accordance with his Paris insight about the symphony's fundamentally melodic nature, and in anticipation of the theory of music drama he would develop after leaving Dresden, Wagner imagined a voice 'singing' throughout the symphony, using Goethe's words to suggest the ideas the voice might be seeking to articulate. It is tempting to imagine Wagner discussing this programme note with another Dresden resident interested in the links between literature and music, Robert Schumann. *Mein Leben* records Schumann mentioning on a walk that he was looking forward to Wagner's performance, though Wagner dismisses him as unstimulating company. He seems to have deliberately disguised the extent of their acquaintance, since Schumann's diaries record at least twenty-four such meetings between late 1845 and the start of 1849, usually instigated by Wagner and involving lengthy discussions of various operatic issues.

The care Wagner took with the programme notes was matched by the attention he lavished on every other aspect of the performance, despite the initial resistance of the Dresden authorities to his choice of repertoire. He annotated each part with dynamics and expression markings that he felt brought out Beethoven's intentions, carefully considering when the wind parts should be doubled; he supplemented the usual theatre chorus with the boys of the Kreuzschule and the singers of the Dresden Seminary to produce a choir of more than three hundred; he devoted numerous rehearsals to the tricky cello and double bass 'recitative' passages in the final movement; he secured funding to rebuild the theatre's stage, so that the chorus surrounded the orchestra in sharply raked seats arranged in the fashion of an amphitheatre. The performance was an artistic triumph and raised more for the pension fund than any previous Palm Sunday concert had achieved.

Biographers have tended to focus on Wagner's frustrations in Dresden, but this concert was just one of a number of significant achievements that demonstrated the Royal Saxon Kapellmeister's unique combination of talents. In 1844, for example, Wagner persuaded the king and Lüttichau that the remains of Carl Maria von Weber, who had died in London, should be returned from Moorfields Chapel to Dresden: to accompany the torchlit procession from Dresden's train station to Weber's final resting place, he composed a *Trauersinfonie* (symphony of mourning), based on themes from *Euryanthe* and scored for seventy-five wind instruments and six muted snare drums; he gave a moving oration from memory by the side of Weber's new grave; afterwards he conducted an elegy for men's voices, *An Webers Grabe*, for which he supplied both text and music. The previous year, Wagner had marshalled a hundred musicians and no fewer than twelve hundred male singers from across Saxony into the vertiginous galleries of the Frauenkirche to perform a work for Pentecost entitled *The Love Feast of the Apostles* – a formidable feat of logistics, even if the musical outcome disappointed him. Like the Beethoven performance – and like *The Ring* – these events required not just musicianship but also impressive organisational, political, diplomatic, literary and rhetorical skills.

Wagner conducted the Ninth Symphony twice more in Dresden – and then on only two further occasions, in London in 1855 and in Bayreuth in 1872, at a concert to mark the laying of the foundation stone of the Festspielhaus. The final Dresden performance took place in a very different political context from the first. By Palm Sunday in 1849, 1 April, preparations for the uprising were well under way. Many of those present interpreted the performance as a tribute to Robert Blum, who represented Saxony at the National Assembly and had been executed in Vienna the previous October, causing outrage across Germany: Blum was known also for co-founding the first 'Schiller Society', linking the text that Beethoven set with the republican cause. An unexpected attendee at the final rehearsal was Bakunin, not renowned for his interest in music: at the end, he told Wagner that even if all other music was destroyed in the global conflagration that was surely about to begin, this symphony must be saved. Beethoven, Blum, Bakunin – these coincidences reinforced the connection already present in Wagner's mind between the Ninth Symphony and the idea of revolution, whether political or artistic.

* * *

Wagner is extremely fortunate to escape arrest and a long spell in prison for his part in the Dresden uprising. On 9 May, as he aborts his return to the city, he realises that the retreating revolutionaries are accompanied by Bakunin and the writer Otto Leonhard Heubner, now the effective leader of the rebellion. He joins them on their journey to Freiberg and the three men agree to continue to Chemnitz where they will try to re-establish the provisional government. In the confusion, Wagner loses his comrades and travels to Chemnitz separately; at five in the morning on 10 May, he walks to his sister Clara's house, where Minna is staying. It is only later that day that he learns that Heubner and Bakunin arrived before him in Chemnitz, where they were arrested and taken to prison under armed guard. Had Wagner travelled with them from Freiberg, he would have stayed at their inn and shared their fate.

Heinrich Wolfram realises the danger his brother-in-law is in and arranges a discreet nocturnal journey to Weimar, where Wagner will stay with Franz Liszt, the Court Kapellmeister. Liszt has mounted a production of *Tannhäuser* and is expecting his colleague's visit, but not in these circumstances: he wisely dissuades Wagner from attending a performance, though he allows him to listen to a rehearsal from a hiding place in a box. Wagner clearly has no conception of how much trouble he is in. In a letter to a Dresden friend, the theatre producer Eduard Devrient, he distances himself from the uprising, admitting to sympathy but not to any active involvement; he intends to return to his Court duties after a six-month leave of absence. He tells Minna he is safe from prosecution, but she already knows this is not true: the police have visited her in Dresden and warned her that her husband faces a charge of treason. They have plenty of evidence, including the testimony of Oehme the brass founder, and a letter found on Röckel when he was arrested, which makes clear the Kapellmeister's complicity. The warrant for Wagner's arrest is published on 19 May: in Saxony, treason carries a death sentence, though if he is treated similarly to Röckel and Heubner, this will be commuted to a decade or more of imprisonment. Liszt can no longer safely harbour the fugitive, so he suggests that Wagner should make his way to Paris on a route that minimises the chances of detection, perhaps via Bavaria and Switzerland, and provides him with an out-of-date passport from a Swabian friend.

Wagner is fortunate again: the passport is not questioned and he makes his way without mishap via Lake Constance to Zurich. He stays with an old friend, Alexander Müller, who arranges a passport that allows him to reach Paris on 2 June. Wagner soon regrets this: Paris is stiflingly hot and enduring a cholera epidemic, and he has no real prospects of a commission from the Opéra, despite Liszt's optimistic predictions. He certainly cannot expect any help now from Meyerbeer, as a chance encounter during one of his rival's frequent visits to Paris makes clear: the General Music Director of the Prussian Court, a position Meyerbeer has held since 1842, would hardly compromise his position by associating with a notorious political refugee. During Wagner's short stay in Paris, he drafts a fiery essay entitled *Art and Revolution* which makes clear that his hopes for drastic social change have not disappeared with the failure of the Dresden uprising.

Six days after his arrival, Wagner leaves Paris; two weeks later he returns to Zurich and the hospitable Müller. For Wagner, Zurich increasingly seems the best place to settle for as long as he is unable to return to Germany: it is beautiful, tranquil and wealthy, and offers the prospect of congenial intellectual companionship. But Minna, who is in poor health, is unenthusiastic about leaving her friends and family in Saxony for what she perceives as a backwater: in July she suggests that she and Wagner should break off all contact. Wagner writes to his stepdaughter Natalie and pleads with her to win her mother over, telling her that the Müllers have space to accommodate all three of them. In late July,

Minna reluctantly agrees, though not without making clear to Wagner how much she has suffered from his reckless behaviour; in August, she sells most of the couple's belongings in Dresden and, with the help of a hundred thalers provided by Liszt, travels to Zurich – together with Natalie, Peps the dog and Papo the parrot.

As this unusual family embarks on a new life in Switzerland, Wagner's immediate prospects could scarcely be more uncertain: he has no job, no income, and owes his creditors at least 20,000 thalers – more than ten times his annual salary as Royal Court Kapellmeister. But he could not be better equipped to embark on the monumental project that will define the next three decades of his life. He knows he will plan a musical drama on the grandest possible scale, and he understands the infrastructure and range of expertise that will be required if it is to be successfully produced. He has thought about what it means to change the world; and for a brief but unforgettable period, he has tried to do so himself. Neither the Kapellmeister nor the revolutionary alone could have conceived *The Ring*, let alone realised it, but the unique combination of experiences that Wagner has undergone in the first thirty-six years of his life makes it possible for him to do so.

2
Sourcing the story

Song and saga

ZURICH, AUGUST 1849. Wagner reads *Siegfrieds Tod* to a group of male friends. The small audience is entranced by the poem, whose manuscript the fleeing revolutionary has brought from Dresden: in *Mein Leben*, Wagner will boast that he has 'never had more attentive listeners than on that evening'. Neither the precise date of the reading nor the exact composition of the audience is recorded, but Alexander Müller, Wagner's first Zurich host, and his pupil Wilhelm Baumgartner are certainly there; so too are the Cantonal Secretaries Jakob Sulzer and Franz Hagenbuch. Only weeks after his arrival in Zurich, Wagner is already well known both in musical and political circles. It helps that his music has travelled here first: concert performances of *Rienzi* and *The Flying Dutchman* have been given, and a production of *Tannhäuser* has been mooted.

It will later suit Wagner to depict mid-century Zurich as provincial, uninteresting and uncultured – his trajectory towards international celebrity will seem more impressively meteoric if its starting point is represented as unpropitious – but the truth is rather different. Zurich has had a democratic constitution since 1830, and despite a brief period of reaction (it is Zurich's 'Putsch' of September 1839 that gives this *Schweizdeutsch* word to the world), by the time Wagner arrives liberal values are once again ascendant. The University of Zurich, founded in 1833, is a refuge for radical young Germans – notably Georg Büchner, author of *Woyzeck*, who was a lecturer in anatomy there for the last few months of his short life – and the city's politicians play a leading role in the Swiss Confederation established in 1848. The new state's first President is Jonas Furrer, previously Zurich's mayor; he has been replaced in that role by Alfred Escher, brother of Clementine Stockar-Escher who paints a famous portrait of Wagner and is his first landlady in the city; Escher is replaced as Cantonal Secretary, meanwhile, by Sulzer, who becomes one of Wagner's closest friends and on his first full day in the city secures him the Swiss passport that allows him to visit France.

Wagner's easy familiarity with Zurich's politicians and administrators contrasts with the strained, servile relationships he endured with Lüttichau and Dresden's other royal functionaries. He finds stimulating company, too, among Zurich's writers and academics, many of them fellow exiles: Hermann Köchly, who also flees Dresden after an unwisely prominent role in the uprising, appointed Zurich's Professor of Classical Philology in 1851; Georg Herwegh, Stuttgart-born poet, activist in Germany's *Vormärz* movement, associate of Marx and Bakunin; the German-born Willes (former newspaper editor François and novelist Eliza) at whose house outside Zurich Wagner will give his first readings of *The Ring*; Bernard Spyri, who edits the *Eidgenössische Zeitung* to which Wagner will soon contribute, and whose future wife Johanna will later write *Heidi*; Ludwig Ettmüller, another Saxon, and an authority on old German sagas on whose expertise Wagner will draw heavily. When he claims that Zurich offers little intellectual stimulation, Wagner is even more disingenuous than usual.

The city's musical life, though far less developed than Dresden's, is by no means primitive. Huldrych Zwingli – leader of Zurich's Reformation in the early sixteenth century, who believed that music had no place in the church – still exerts a baleful influence, ensuring that, unlike most other German-speaking territories, the city has not developed a tradition of ecclesiastical music. It is only in the nineteenth century that anything resembling a professional orchestra and opera company appears. But the Allgemeine Musik-Gesellschaft Zurich (General Music Society of Zurich) has promoted concerts since 1812, though the mixture of professional, amateur and visiting players it still employs is not conducive to musical excellence. The Zurich Theatre opened its doors in 1834 with *The Magic Flute*, and enjoyed considerable success between 1837 and 1843 under the leadership of Charlotte Birch-Pfeiffer, actor, author and entrepreneur: among the singers she attracted to Zurich was Wilhelmine Schröder-Devrient.

The failure of the theatre and the Music Society to cooperate is perhaps the city's biggest musical weakness, one to which Wagner devotes much thought. He quickly gets to know Zurich's prominent musicians: apart from his old friend and Würzburg colleague Alexander Müller, a well-respected choral conductor, these include Franz Abt, a protégé of Birch-Pfeiffer who now conducts the Music Society's orchestral concerts; Baumgartner, a talented composer who introduces Wagner to the writings of Ludwig Feuerbach; Ignaz Heim, a choral conductor who becomes a generous supporter of Wagner; and Heim's singer wife, Emilie. He quickly assesses the capabilities of these and other Zurich musicians in an effort to discern what he can offer the city's music, and perhaps more pertinently, what it can offer him.

While he waits for musical opportunities to materialise, he begins the series of polemical 'Zurich writings' with which his time in the city will become associated. Through the intercession of Liszt, *Art and Revolution* is accepted by the radical Leipzig publisher Wigand, who pays Wagner a substantial fee. That essay's vision of the ethical, unified and freely available art that will become possible after a revolution is elaborated in *The Artwork of the Future*, completed in November 1849, and published by Wigand the following year with a dedication to Feuerbach. This essay imagines the bringing together of artists in all media – architecture, painting, sculpture; music, dance, poetry – in a communal art-form which Wagner describes as a *Gesamtkunstwerk* (a 'total work of art'). This is one of the few occasions on which Wagner himself uses this term – so frequently attached to his name, although he was not the first to use it and disavowed it in later life.

It does not take long for the Music Society to become aware of the box-office potential of Zurich's newest and most notorious resident, and it has no compunction in moving Abt aside. Wagner makes his debut with the semi-professional orchestra on 15 January 1850, and is well paid: for conducting a single work, he receives thirty-seven Swiss francs – a rather better hourly rate than Abt, who receives 107 francs in total for a season of seven complete programmes. He chooses to conduct Beethoven's Seventh Symphony, praised in *The Artwork of the Future* for its 'bacchanalian power . . . [it] is the Apotheosis of the Dance . . . the loftiest deed of bodily motion'. His performance lives up to his words, and from this point on, he conducts in Zurich almost whenever he pleases, commanding ever higher fees and the freedom to choose players from across Switzerland and beyond.

Intellectual companionship, political freedom, admiring colleagues, well-paid conducting engagements, not to mention beautiful scenery – all in all, and despite the city's musical shortcomings and the frustrations of not hearing his own music performed, Zurich seems to offer Wagner most of what he needs to develop his ideas for the drama he intends to produce when circumstances allow. But Minna is an unhappy exile: increasingly troubled by a heart condition and missing her family in Saxony, she cannot understand why her husband has abandoned his prestigious post in Dresden for a quixotic dream of revolution. She would like them to return – but if that is not possible (and nothing the couple hears from Saxony suggests that it is) then the next best place for Wagner, as far as she is concerned, is Paris. Why can't he do what any other ambitious opera composer would do and cash in on his talents there, she urges, heedless of the miserable failure of Wagner's two previous Parisian escapades. She has a powerful ally in Liszt: unable to keep meeting his friend's requests for financial support, he has tried to help him to provide for himself in Paris, publishing an encomium to *Tannhäuser* in the *Journal des débats* and suggesting possible projects and collaborators. Neither Minna nor Liszt realises, however, how far Wagner's thinking has moved from what is likely to find favour in the French capital – perhaps even Wagner himself does not quite realise this yet, since he will soon make yet another attempt to succeed there.

His latest idea for an opera is *Wieland der Schmied*, based on the legend of a master blacksmith who takes revenge on the king who has crippled and enslaved him by killing his sons, before using the winged cloak he has crafted to make his escape back to his wife, Schwanhilde. In Wagner's libretto, Wieland is enslaved not by a king but by a mortal princess who wants to win him away from Schwanhilde, and who steals the magic ring he has acquired from his wife; he is also an allegorical representation of *das Volk*, the people of Germany who seek liberation from tyranny. In the final pages of *The Artwork of the Future*, Wagner invokes the 'glorious saga' of Wieland to exemplify the *Gesamtkunstwerk* to be staged in the ideal theatre of which he dreams; but as he reluctantly leaves Zurich, a fortnight after his triumphant conducting debut, he contemplates refashioning it for the far-from-ideal stage of the Paris Opéra. He hopes to enlist the help of Gaetano Belloni, Liszt's secretary, whom he knows from his brief stay in Paris the previous year, but Belloni is out of town throughout Wagner's six-week visit. It is as fruitless as his previous Parisian ventures: even the modest plans to perform his overtures come to nothing. The Opéra audiences are obsessed with Meyerbeer's *Le Prophète*, to Wagner's disgust: he will claim in *Mein Leben* that he walked out in protest, though a letter to his Dresden friend Theodor Uhlig makes clear that he witnessed the applause at the end. His rival's spectacular success with a work he regards as empty and vulgar makes him abandon any attempt to refashion *Wieland* to suit Parisian taste: as he tells Uhlig, his own work must be 'German! German!'

It is from Dresden rather than Paris, ironically enough, that the financial support Wagner is seeking ultimately comes. Julie Ritter is a widow who has met Wagner only once, when he attended a musical soirée organised for the benefit of her son, Karl – a former pupil of Robert Schumann and an aspiring composer, now aged nineteen. Such was the impression the Kapellmeister made on Karl that Julie intimates that she would like to support his activities now he is in exile. Furthermore, she will be joined by other unexpected benefactors, the Laussots: together, the two families offer Wagner a yearly payment of 3,000 francs, a sum equivalent to about three times the annual rent on a Zurich apartment. Jessie Laussot, English by birth, has been fascinated by Wagner's music since attending the premiere of *Tannhäuser* in Dresden with the Ritters; a few years later, she met Wagner in person when Karl took her to the Kapellmeister's apartment during a brief visit she made from Bordeaux, where she has lived since marrying a wine merchant at eighteen. The Laussots – Jessie and Eugène, along with Jessie's widowed mother Ann Taylor – now invite Wagner to visit, even offering to pay his travel expenses. Desperate to escape Paris, he happily accepts, despite Minna's anticipated misgivings; he arrives in Bordeaux on 16 March 1850.

Events move fast. Wagner quickly realises that the Laussot marriage is unhappy; Eugène had previously been the lover of Ann, who used her inheritance from her husband to salvage his wine business and instigated the match with her daughter. Jessie is young, beautiful, fluent in German, an accomplished pianist and obsessed with Wagner's music; Wagner is frustrated by Minna's lack of understanding of his aspirations and her angry refusal to celebrate the generosity of his new benefactors; Eugène is often away on business and often cruel to his wife when he is not. An affair quickly begins and before Wagner returns to Paris he and Jessie have made wild plans to flee to Asia Minor (the Asian portion of present-day Turkey) via Marseilles, Malta and Greece. He writes a farewell letter to Minna; horrified, she enlists Sulzer and Baumgartner, loyal friends since Wagner's earliest days in Zurich and the *Siegfrieds Tod* reading, to persuade him to change his mind. Minna makes her way to Paris in search of Wagner; he escapes her by fleeing to Geneva, though he pretends he is already on his way to Greece. Jessie foolishly confides the couple's plans to her mother, who immediately tells Eugène; he removes Jessie and Ann to the country amid threats of shooting Wagner in the head, and ensures that if the composer were to reappear in Bordeaux the police would investigate his dubious passport and eject him from the city. Jessie is persuaded to break off all contact with Wagner and he has little option but to return to Zurich and attempt a reconciliation with Minna.

She acquiesces, mindful of how much she has already invested in the family's new life in Zurich, and also perhaps remembering Wagner's willingness to take her back after her own infidelity a few years earlier. On 3 July Wagner arrives for the first time at the upper-floor apartment Minna has rented on his instructions in the suburb of Enge, a short distance from the shore of Lake Zurich. Sulzer and Baumgartner jokingly christen it 'Villa Rienzi', an appellation that belies its modest proportions – and causes some annoyance among Wagner's many creditors in Dresden, who imagine the fugitive Kapellmeister living in luxury. This is far from the case: although he still receives Julie Ritter's modest share of the proposed joint annuity, he can scarcely expect any money from the Laussots, and he has returned the down payments that Ann Taylor advanced to Minna over the summer. But Enge's seclusion from the city suits Wagner well, and he credits his still-extant dog and parrot, Peps and Papo, with 'an extraordinarily effective contribution to our domestic ease'. The episode with Jessie, like Minna's own previous infidelity, is not mentioned between the couple. Wagner resumes work.

* * *

Perhaps the greatest deprivation Wagner experiences in Zurich is the absence of the extensive personal library he had assembled in Dresden. Heinrich Brockhaus – the guiding force of one of the most important German publishing houses, and brother to two of Wagner's brothers-in-law – seized the Kapellmeister's prized collection shortly after his hasty departure from Dresden, as security for a loan of 500 thalers advanced three years earlier. The loan was never repaid, and the library never returned: the Brockhaus family kept it until 1974, when they passed it to the Wagner Foundation in Bayreuth. The 169 books that remained at this point – a list compiled by Minna mentions another couple of dozen whose whereabouts are unknown – can now be seen at Wahnfried, Wagner's Bayreuth home, which opened to the public in 1976, a hundred years after the premiere of *The Ring*.

Wagner bought most of these books in 1843, directly after taking up his post in Dresden, and arranged for them to be expensively rebound. The purchase was at once a demonstration of his new-found status as Royal Kapellmeister and a declaration of his intentions as musical dramatist. The library included poetry and plays by Shakespeare and various French and Italian authors, translations from classical literature and a number of historical works – all useful to a composer in search of inspiration – but Wagner's primary aim was to lay his hands on as much material as possible relating to German mythology. Renditions, faithful and otherwise, of medieval stories, some very hard to track down; commentaries, learned and fanciful, on the stories' significance and relationship to each other; theories on what the stories revealed about Germany, ancient and contemporary – Wagner worked his way systematically through all this, supplementing what he owned with what he could borrow from Dresden's libraries or from friends. His years of patient reading found their outlet in his months of frenetic writing in 1848, most fruitfully in the version of *Siegfrieds Tod* with which he left Saxony and which he read to his new friends in Zurich on his arrival.

According to Wagner's autobiography, it was turning the twelve hundred pages of Jacob Grimm's *Deutsche Mythologie* that opened his mind to the possibilities of German mythology as a source for musical drama. The chronology – not for the only time in *Mein Leben* – is somewhat suspect, since Wagner places his first revelatory encounter with this magnum opus in 1843, while the edition he owned was published only in 1844, but this is no reason to doubt the importance of Grimm to his thinking. Both the Grimm brothers – now remembered primarily for their retellings of fairy stories – were formidable scholars: *Deutsche Mythologie*, whose first

edition appeared in 1835, is an encyclopedic account of every possible strand of German myth, much of which survives only in very
fragmentary form. Grimm's book accompanied Wagner through
a hot summer vacation in Teplitz: it led him through a world of
gods and heroes of whom he had been dimly aware since childhood but had never before seen clearly. 'Nothing in it was complete, nor was there anything resembling an architectural line,'
he noted; he 'often felt tempted to abandon the seemingly hope-
less effort to make something systematic out of it'. The numerous
lacunae and discontinuities in Grimm's narrative may have been
an inspiration in themselves: if Wagner was going to make a story
from this material, he would need to forge the links himself. But
a still greater spark to his imagination was Grimm's argument –
academically disreputable, though eloquently expressed – that
the mythology of Scandinavia was not only deeply connected to
that of Germany, but derived from it: Norse legends, for Grimm,
always originated from an authentically German urtext, even if
no actual evidence of that source remained. Wagner's decision
to believe in this dubious proposition licensed him to populate
his burgeoning drama with figures who appeared only in Nordic
sources – gods and giants, Valkyries and Norns – while still repre-
senting it as impeccably German.

The most obvious primary source of mythology at hand, however, was the ostentatiously German *Nibelungenlied*, represented
in Wagner's library in no fewer than three editions of the Middle
High German original as well as Karl Simrock's 1827 translation. This epic poem was first written down around 1200 by a
now unknown author (or authors), but versions of it had been
declaimed – or quite possibly sung, perhaps even with instrumental accompaniment – to audiences at least from the fifth century
onwards. Further manuscripts of varying versions of the 'Lay of

the Nibelungs' were produced at regular intervals until the early sixteenth century, but it was the rediscovery in 1755 of a crucial *Nibelungenlied* manuscript at Hohenems Castle in the Vorarlberg region of Austria that kickstarted the modern appreciation of the poem. Two years later, the Swiss scholar Johann Jakob Bodmer published an edition of the final section, and in 1782 his pupil Christoph Heinrich Myller published the first edition of the complete text, which he dedicated to Frederick the Great.

In the early nineteenth century, as translations into modern German started to appear, and figures such as the Grimms and Goethe (in an introduction to Karl Simrock's 1827 translation) argued its importance, the *Nibelungenlied* began to attract mass interest for the first time. For advocates of German unification, the lay met a need for a national epic that the fractured country had previously lacked: favourable comparisons with the *Iliad* became commonplace, and special editions were produced for soldiers going into battle. The poem achieved almost cult status in the 1840s as new editions poured from the presses. In 1844 F. T. Vischer proposed that the *Nibelungenlied* would make an ideal source for a new form of heroic German opera: Mendelssohn, Schumann, Gade and Liszt all considered turning the poem into an opera, and in 1854 the now-forgotten Heinrich Dorn actually did so.

The poem's apparently straightforward title, 'Song of the Nibelungs', is liable to confuse a contemporary reader, certainly one who is already familiar with Wagner's *Ring*. The subjugated, subterranean-dwelling race of dwarves who go by the name of 'Nibelungs' in *The Ring* make only a shadowy appearance here, as characters in a story that is already over before the poem's plot begins. By the time we first see him, Siegfried has already conquered the Nibelungs and acquired their priceless hoard of gold, which he brings to the kingdom of Burgundy when he arrives to woo a beautiful princess, and which the Burgundians appropriate after his murder. For much of the epic, the name 'Nibelungs' is used to describe the Burgundians themselves.

Several of the characters in the *Nibelungenlied* are derived from real-life historical figures. The Burgundian king whose court Siegfried visits, Gunther, is based on Gundaharius, who died in AD 437 alongside twenty thousand of his troops in a battle against the Huns. In the *Nibelungenlied* Gunther rules Burgundy alongside two of his brothers, Gernot and Giselher, who are also kings; they share guardianship of their sister, the princess Kriemhild (Wagner uses her Norse name, Gutrune). The legendary dragon-slaying hero Siegfried, son of King Siegmund of the Netherlands and his wife Sieglinde (who are still alive at the start of the poem, unlike in Wagner's versions), visits Burgundy in the hope of marrying Kriemhild, whose beauty is legendary. Gunther agrees to this only on the condition that Siegfried uses his supernatural powers to help him win the Icelandic princess Brunhild, who may be based on a Visigothic princess, Brunhilda, who ruled Burgundy during several periods in the late sixth and early seventh centuries. Siegfried uses his cloak of invisibility to assist Gunther, but the consequences of the deception are severe: Brunhild and Kriemhild quarrel over the respective status of their husbands; Kriemhild hints at the questionable role the disguised Siegfried may have played on Brunhild's wedding night, forcing her into submission so that Gunther could exercise his conjugal rights; Kriemhild is tricked by Hagen (here a kinsman of Gunther, but not a half-brother as in Wagner) into revealing the one part of Siegfried's body where the hero is vulnerable to attack; Hagen stabs him in the back on a hunting trip and kills him. This happens about halfway through the poem; the rest of the epic (with which Wagner does not directly engage) is a slow, dreadful playing-out of Kriemhild's revenge, culminating many years later in the slaughter of the Burgundians at the hands of the Huns, whose king, Etzel (based on Attila but of a very different character), Kriemhild has married.

Wagner will later try to play down the contribution of the *Nibelungenlied* to *The Ring* as much as he can. In 1851, in *A Communication to My Friends*, he will tell anyone who will listen that it was only when he saw Siegfried in 'purest human shape, set free from every later wrappage' that he believed he could make him the hero of a drama, 'a possibility that had not occurred to me when I only knew him from the medieval *Nibelungenlied*'. Yet the number of narrative threads from the lay that Wagner incorporated into *Siegfrieds Tod* and which survive even in the final version of *Götterdämmerung* – the hero's uninvited but assertive appearance at Gunther's court; the deceitful claiming of Brünnhilde as Gunther's bride; the double marriage; and above all, the sequence of events that leads to Siegfried's death, from the revelation of his single point of weakness to his dying moments – suggest that its importance to him remained greater than he was willing to acknowledge. Some of Wagner's characterisation owes more to the *Nibelungenlied* than to any other possible source, particularly that of the weak and ineffectual Gunther and the demonic, avaricious Hagen. So too does Hagen's positioning within Wagner's story as Gunther's principal counsellor and Siegfried's prime antagonist. The lay may even have given Wagner the idea for the three Rhinemaidens who greet Siegfried and encourage him to return his ring to them in order to escape the effects of its curse: although Siegfried in the *Nibelungenlied* does not encounter any mermaids in the Rhine, Hagen meets some in the Danube. It is perhaps revealing that as late as 1856, when Wagner has completed all the *Ring* poems and is asked by Franz Müller to catalogue the sources he has used in preparing them, he contradicts his earlier dismissal of the *Nibelungenlied*'s importance by placing it at the top of the list. Yet for all their similarities, it would be misleading to regard *Siegfrieds Tod* (and even more so *Götterdämmerung*) as an adaptation of the *Nibelungenlied* – and the rough-edged Siegfried whom Wagner brings to life in *The Ring* is certainly not the courtly figure found in the poem. Even in Dresden, the Nordic sources that Wagner was able to borrow from public libraries and procure for his own occupied at least as important a place in his thinking, as is amply demonstrated by that other great *Ring* prototype of 1848, 'The Nibelung Myth as Sketch for a Drama'. Over the next few years in Zurich, the importance of these Nordic sources would only increase, and that of the *Nibelungenlied* recede, as Wagner refined his conception of *The Ring* and extended its narrative scope further and further back into the pre-history of the hero.

* * *

Lucerne, 28 August 1850. Wagner and Minna are taking a short holiday at the Hotel Schwanen, overlooking the lake. Some four hundred miles away, at the Weimar Court Theatre, Liszt conducts the first performance of *Lohengrin*. Wagner experiences the premiere only in his imagination, using a pocket watch to tell him when each act should be starting and finishing. He is distressed to discover, some days later, that the performance lasted more than an hour longer than it should have done – this is probably the fault of the singers, not of Liszt, as Wagner first assumes. Had he been present in Weimar he would probably have been more distressed still: the orchestra is small – only half a dozen first violins play in this premiere – and not particularly expert; scenery and costumes fail to match Liszt's expectations; the twenty-three-year-old tenor, Karl Beck, is unequal to the title role's formidable demands. Nonetheless, for Wagner, forbidden from entering German territory and denied any other opportunity to hear his own music, this imagined performance in Weimar is as good as it currently gets. The advocacy of Liszt and the support of the Grand Duke of Weimar – whose anonymous gift of a hundred thalers pays for Wagner's stay in Lucerne – represent his best hope of bringing *Siegfrieds Tod* to the stage.

Encouraged by Liszt's interest in the project, Wagner had begun sixteen days earlier to sketch some music to accompany his libretto. He completes about twelve minutes of music for the drama's Prologue, encompassing the Norns' scene and the beginning of the scene showing Siegfried and Brünnhilde in domestic bliss before the hero's departure for the Rhineland. Hindsight allows us to detect faint pre-echoes of the finished *Ring*: the sketch starts in E flat minor, anticipating the key in which Wagner will ultimately begin *Götterdämmerung* as well as the E flat major with which he will launch *Das Rheingold*. The following year he notes down a melody in B minor to be sung to Brünnhilde by the Valkyries, which he will ultimately use for their famous 'Ride': it strikingly recalls a theme in the same key from *Das Paradies und die Peri*, Schumann's 'secular oratorio' of 1843, which Wagner knows and admires, whatever he later says about its composer. But he has not yet found an approach or a musical style appropriate for a drama that he already knows will be very different from *Lohengrin*. He quickly abandons his efforts and does not even bother to hold on to the manuscripts: he gives the 'Valkyrie' sketch to Robert Radecke, a young violinist who visits him from Leipzig, and whose son will publish a facsimile almost seventy years later.

A few days after Wagner returns from Lucerne, the *Neue Zeitschrift für Musik* publishes an essay entitled *Jewishness in Music* under the byline 'K. Freigedank' – a pseudonym chosen by Wagner presumably in order to suggest that he is 'free-thinking'. Though there are antisemitic remarks in Wagner's earlier writings, he has not been regarded until now as actively hostile to Jewishness, perhaps because of his friendly relationships with a number of Jewish individuals. The immediate prompts for this diatribe are his outrage at *Le Prophète*'s popularity and frustration at his own lack of performances. But its roots perhaps lie in his increasing preoccupation with German mythology: the 'German hero' of his new drama will be defined in part by his opposition to everything that is 'not German' – which for Wagner means above all Jews, though he will also subject the French to virulent attacks. *Jewishness in Music* does not mention Meyerbeer by name, but it does not need to: Wagner believes that his readers will identify his rival as the archetype (as he perceives it) of the Jewish composer who succeeds with music that is fluent but superficial and emotionally empty. Not only does he believe that Jews produce worthless art, he also draws offensive parallels between their creative work and their 'unpleasantly foreign' appearance and 'repulsive' manner of speaking – and hopes that his readers will do the same. This appalling piece of writing – and Wagner's bizarre decision to republish it in 1869 under his own name, with a sinister preface calling for the 'forceful ejection of this destructive foreign element' in German culture – permanently stains the composer's posthumous reputation.

Soon after *Jewishness in Music* is published, Wagner embarks on *Opera and Drama*, the longest and most ambitious of his 'Zurich writings'. He works with such intensity that he completes a first draft by early January, and manages to publish the entire tract by November. This is Wagner's most comprehensive theoretical account of what he hopes to achieve in what will become *The Ring*. He first turns his attention to his operatic predecessors: with a few honourable partial exceptions – Gluck, Mozart, Beethoven, Weber – he condemns them for writing melody that is excessively concerned with the interests of the singer, and insufficiently attentive to the necessary primacy of language. Music, for Wagner, is like a woman who requires the 'fertilising seed' of a male partner (poetry) in order to be truly expressive.

Spoken drama is similarly despatched in the second section of the treatise, before Wagner turns in the third and most interesting part to the 'drama of the future' and sets out how it will differ from the opera of the past. The alliterative verse – *Stabreim* – that he has used for the libretto of *Siegfrieds Tod* creates the possibility of a new form of 'musical prose' that will be more flexible and expressive than the regularly structured melodies found in most operas. Modulation away from the home key will be much more extensive and ambitious than before, expanding the music's expressive range, though it will always be initiated and strictly justified by the meaning of the text. Finally, the new drama will endow the orchestra with the capacity to 'speak', to convey information and ideas aurally in a way analogous to what is done visually by actors on a stage: the technique that will later be called 'leitmotif' will play a key role in enabling Wagner to achieve this aspiration. None of these concepts is as yet fully formed, but Wagner will continue to explore their practical application for the next quarter-century as he refines the poetry and music of *The Ring*.

Completing *Opera and Drama* seems to liberate Wagner: his thoughts on *Siegfrieds Tod*, which has not fundamentally changed since he drafted it three years ago in Dresden, now develop rapidly. On 9 March 1851 he presses Liszt to turn his vague promises of support for the project into a concrete plan, whether that involves sending money himself or securing a commission from Weimar. Liszt does both, and in early May Wagner receives an offer of

500 thalers for *Siegfrieds Tod*, on the condition that the score is delivered by the following July. The offer focuses Wagner's mind, though not with the result that Liszt expects. On 10 May, Wagner tells Uhlig that he intends to set aside *Siegfrieds Tod* in favour of a drama dealing with the hero's earlier life which he will call *Der junge Siegfried*. This, Liszt is led to believe, will be a lighter piece that will be easier for the Weimar company to mount, and which will prepare the way for the eventual acceptance of *Siegfrieds Tod*. Wagner completes a prose sketch of the new drama by the start of June, and a libretto three weeks later, though he does not yet send it to Weimar, requesting instead that Liszt should come to Zurich to hear him read it.

Over the summer, Wagner becomes increasingly doubtful that Weimar will be able to stage a satisfactory performance even of this more straightforward work, let alone anything more elaborate. Uhlig, who attended the *Lohengrin* premiere, is staying with him and no doubt now gives him a fuller account of the production's shortcomings. Despite his frustrations with Zurich – he tells Liszt he is 'bound to go mad here', and Minna is more dissatisfied still – Wagner flirts with the idea of making the city the site for the new theatre he believes his new form of drama will require. Letters written the previous autumn to his Dresden friends Uhlig and Gustav Kietz float the possibility of building a wooden theatre just outside Zurich, where the best German singers and instrumentalists would gather for a festival of his music; once it was over the theatre would be demolished. And in April he writes 'A Theatre in Zurich', a plan to improve the standard of the city's dramatic performances by training local singers and instrumentalists – it meets with no more enthusiasm from those in charge than his similar plans for reform in Dresden. For the moment, Wagner has no evidence that Zurich's performers or theatrical infrastructure could rise to what he needs – and he remains contracted to Weimar.

He is increasingly troubled by various health problems: neurasthenia, constipation, abdominal pains, insomnia, shingles, and above all erysipelas, a painful bacterial skin infection which produces inflammation, often on the face, and seems to be linked – in Wagner's case at least – to episodes of nervous exhaustion. He has suffered from this condition since his early twenties, and has often sought relief in hydrotherapy, placing an almost mystical faith in the power of the waters in spas such as Teplitz and Marienbad to effect both physical and spiritual cleansing. In mid-September, at the prompting of Uhlig, he leaves Zurich to begin a course of treatment at a sanatorium in Albisbrunn, a tiny settlement a dozen miles south of the city.

The regime is miserable for him – woken up at five every morning, icy-cold baths, a diet of dry bread, cold soup and water, total abstinence from alcohol, tea and coffee – and it seems to make him worse rather than better. However, his mood greatly improves when he hears from Julie Ritter in Dresden that an inheritance from a wealthy family member means that she can now pay him an annual stipend of 800 thalers. He decides to abandon the increasingly unappealing plan to mount one or more of the Siegfried dramas in Weimar, and to return the 200 thalers he has already been paid for the commission.

Wagner's new-found state of relative financial freedom enables him to think about his Siegfried project on a grander scale than could ever have been realised in Weimar. A letter written to Uhlig in October hints at 'great plans' for new dramas. By 3 November he is more specific, telling Uhlig of his intention to create 'three dramas (the second and third of which are the two *Siegfrieds*) and a big *Vorspiel [Prelude]*' – his first reference to what will become *The Ring* as a one-plus-three structure – and

57

to produce them 'in my own way'. Nine days later, he is more explicit about what his 'own way' means, telling Uhlig of his plans to 'erect a theatre on the banks of the Rhine and issue invitations to a great dramatic festival': after a year's preparation he will mount all four dramas across the course of three or four days. He has already finished the first prose draft for a drama currently entitled *Der Raub des Rheingoldes* (The Theft of the Rhinegold); by 23 November, when he returns to Zurich, the first prose draft for the cycle's 'first evening' is also complete, though its title, too, has not yet reached its definitive form – Wagner is weighing up the merits of *Die Walküre* against those of the rather more cumbersome *Siegmund und Sieglind* [sic]*: der Walküre Bestrafung* (The Valkyrie's Punishment). It only remains for him to inform Liszt (which he does in late November; his friend is characteristically generous in response, and perhaps rather relieved not to have to shoulder responsibility for the production), and to tell the world (which happens in the closing paragraphs of *A Communication to My Friends*, published in December). From this point onwards, although almost everything is uncertain about how what will become *The Ring* will actually be produced, his conception of the work as an intricately integrated four-part structure does not change.

* * *

Wagner's library in Dresden contained, alongside the four versions of the *Nibelungenlied*, as much Nordic mythology as he could lay his hands on. Impatient with the courtly game-playing and anachronistic detail of the Middle High German epic, which depicted figures from the ancient past as though they were medieval aristocrats, the Kapellmeister regarded the Scandinavian sources as purer, more authentic and older versions of the stories they told. He believed this even though the earliest surviving written versions of all of them date from rather later than 1200, when the *Nibelungenlied* itself was composed. Perhaps they seemed to him less marked by the historical circumstances of their composition, less coloured by the Christianity that reached Iceland only in the mid-tenth century, more than half a millennium after the conversion of Germany. Icelandic mythology, in particular, was indispensable to Wagner even in 1848: that year's 'Nibelung Myth as Sketch for a Drama' would not have been possible without the route it offered for joining the story of the gods to that of Siegfried. By 1851, now the imaginative leap to expand that essay into four evenings of drama has been taken, the importance of the Icelandic sources to Wagner has only increased.

Among the Norse literature that he purchased in Dresden were two German translations (both from the 1810s) of the *Prose Edda* – also known as the *Snorri Edda* after its probable author Snorri Sturluson, the son of an Icelandic chieftain, who became the country's richest and most powerful leader. This text was composed in the 1220s, but the title 'Edda' was attached to it only much later. Possibly derived from the Latin 'edo', meaning 'I compose', the word and its derivations came to be associated with the principles of poetics, and part of the *Prose Edda* is essentially a treatise on the ancient Norse genre of skaldic poetry. But the text's most substantial section, 'Gylfaginning', constitutes the most complete account that survives of the Norse belief system, conducted through a dialogue between the disguised King Gylfi of Sweden and three manifestations of Odin. The gods who appear in *Das Rheingold* have their stories told here, although their names are slightly different from those Wagner gives them: as well as Odin (Wagner's Wotan), we encounter Frigg (Fricka), Freyja (Freia), Frey (Froh), Thor (Donner) and the ambivalent, elusive Loki (Loge). A preliminary section traces Odin's descent from a daughter of King Priam, as if to endow the Norse gods with glory reflected from Troy; this genealogy may have influenced Wagner's similar attempt to connect the Norse and Trojan worlds in 'Die Wibelungen', though no trace of this suggestion survives in *The Ring*. Many of the stories in the *Prose Edda* also feature in other Nordic sources consulted by Wagner, making it difficult to retrace lines of derivation, but one clear borrowing from 'Gylfaginning' is the story of how Loki unwisely persuades the gods to promise Freyja to 'a master builder from Giant Land' if he completes the construction of a fortress over a single winter.

Many of the stories told by Snorri are also found in a collection of heroic and mythological poems generally known as the *Poetic Edda*. By contrast with the *Prose Edda*, there is no single narrative thread: the poems were originally written by different authors at different times and places for different reasons and in different modes (monologue, dialogue, third-person narrative). The exact age and geographical origin (Norway or Iceland?) of these texts is unknown – most of the mythological poems and some of the heroic ones probably predate the conversion of Scandinavia to Christianity – but all of them clearly circulated in oral tradition long before they were copied down by an anonymous Icelandic writer in the 1270s. This book – known as 'Codex Regius' because it was presented to the King of Denmark in 1662, before finally being repatriated to Reykjavik in 1971 – is the *Poetic Edda*'s principal source, though poems found elsewhere were also added to the collection.

German translations of parts of the *Poetic Edda* were published at various points from 1814 onwards. Wagner's Dresden library contained a translation of some Eddic *Heldenlieder* (heroic songs) published by the Grimm brothers in Berlin in 1815, as well as an edition in Old Norse by Friedrich von der Hagen. He also owned a volume entitled *Mythologische Dichtungen und Lieder der Skandinavier*, translated by Friedrich Majer and published in Leipzig in 1818. This included several Eddic *Götterlieder* (songs of the gods), including 'Völuspá' (The Seeress's Prophecy), which especially influenced Wagner throughout his work on *The Ring*: it contains references to the World Ash Tree (named here, though not by Wagner, as Yggdrasil), to three women who shape the fate of mankind (Wagner's Norns), and to Odin's loss of his eye, and to his summoning of a dead giantess (probably a model for Wagner's Erda) who foretells the downfall of the gods. The poem's word for this is 'Ragnarök', translated by many of the scholars of Wagner's day as 'twilight of the gods' and therefore giving him the title he will ultimately adopt for the final drama of *The Ring*.

Though Wagner was familiar with many of the Eddic poems throughout his time in Dresden, it is not until February 1851 that a translation of the complete *Poetic Edda* into German (by Karl Simrock) is published. This is three months before Wagner completes *Der junge Siegfried*, which reveals a knowledge of poems that had not appeared in German until that year: some scholars conclude that Wagner must have read Simrock's translation as soon as it appeared; others believe that the timing is too tight and that Wagner's expanded knowledge of the *Poetic Edda* must come from his friendship with the noted Eddic translator Dr Ludwig Ettmüller of the University of Zurich, whom he has known since he first arrived in the city. Whatever the exact means by which Wagner has come by his information – no correspondence survives that can settle the issue either way – the debt of *Der junge Siegfried* to the *Poetic Edda* is clear. The sequence of poems that relate the story of the slaying of the dragon Fafnir by Sigurd (Wagner's Siegfried) and the hero's difficult dealings with the dwarf Regin (Wagner's Mime), who has brought him up, contain numerous details used by Wagner to bring his drama to life.

Another Nordic source that is of prime importance to *The Ring* – the *Volsung Saga* – reached Wagner by a still more indirect route, initially at least. This is an extended prose version of the tragic tale of three great heroic families, preserved in a single vellum manuscript, now in the Copenhagen Royal Library, written down around 1400 by an anonymous author. The saga draws on earlier cycles of heroic poetry – the text includes stanzas of poetry taken from items in the *Poetic Edda* – but the story also fills in some of the gaps in what has survived of the poetic sources. The saga is structured chronologically, following five generations of the Volsung family from the grandfather of King Volsung to Sigurd the Dragon Slayer. The tale of Sigurd is the longest episode, and includes many features also found in Wagner's telling, including stories of a great pile of treasure containing a cursed ring; of the slaying of the dragon Fafnir; and of an encounter with Brynhild (Wagner's Brünnhilde), whom Sigurd wakens from magic sleep, vows to marry, and then betrays because he has been given a potion that has caused him to forget her. The motif of an incestuous relationship between brother and sister that produces a son, so crucial (and controversial) in *Die Walküre*, is found here too, though the offspring of that union is not Sigurd but his half-brother, Sinfjotli. The *Volsung Saga* also features a direct blood relationship between god and hero, though in the saga Odin is Sigurd's great-great-great-grandfather, whereas in *The Ring* Wotan is Siegfried's grandfather. By tightening up these familial relationships – and adding the dimension that Wotan is Brünnhilde's father (no such relationship exists between Odin and Brynhild in the saga) – Wagner both simplifies and intensifies his story, but its debt to the saga remains clear.

So close is the connection with the *Volsung Saga*, in fact, that it comes as something of a surprise to realise that Wagner did not have direct access to this source until the very end of his time in Dresden. It was not until 21 October 1848 – after completing the 'Nibelung Myth as Sketch for a Drama', and shortly before writing *Siegfrieds Tod* – that he borrowed the saga (published as the fourth volume of Friedrich von der Hagen's *Nordische Heldenromane*) from the Dresden Royal Library. Though von der Hagen's translation had been published in 1815 in Breslau, it 'no longer existed in the booktrade', as Wagner would later complain to Uhlig. But even before reading it for himself, Wagner had learned about the saga from at least two secondary sources. He was very struck by the analysis of it, and in particular of the incest story, in Wilhelm Grimm's *Die deutsche Heldensage* – first published in 1829, and one of the items in his Dresden library. Perhaps more importantly still, the saga was the principal source for Friedrich de la Motte Fouqué's 1808 play *Sigurd der Schlangentödter* (Siegfried the Serpent-Slayer), the opening drama in a trilogy entitled *Der Held des Nordens* that constituted the first modern attempt to put the Nibelung legends on stage. Although Fouqué's work was not in Wagner's library, nor are there any records of him borrowing it from elsewhere, the parallels with his own poems are so extensive that he must have known it well; Wagner's Leipzig uncle Adolf Wagner was a friend and frequent correspondent of Fouqué, so may well have introduced his nephew to his work.

One final Nordic source which there is no direct evidence of Wagner having owned or borrowed, but which he almost certainly knew, is *Thidrek's Saga*, also known as the *Saga of Dietrich of Bern*. Although the saga was written down in Norway around the middle of the thirteenth century, the stories it tells seem to come from the Germanic rather than the Scandinavian tradition. The saga was translated by Friedrich von der Hagen as volumes 1 to 3 of the *Nordische Heldenromane* (the same set of which the *Volsung Saga* made up volume 4), and these volumes, too, were in the Dresden Royal Library, but Wagner does not seem to have borrowed them from there. However, the saga is included on the list of sources for *The Ring* that he sent to Franz Müller in 1856, and he may well have read it before leaving Dresden, judging by the number of parallels it exhibits with the 'Nibelung Myth as Sketch for a Drama'. The saga may have been the source of Wagner's notion that there were mermaids who bathed in the Rhine; of the characterisation of Alberich as devious and avaricious (Alpris in *Thidrek's Saga* is a notorious thief and the most cunning of all the dwarves in any saga); and of the idea that Hagen is Alberich's son (in *Thidrek's Saga* he is sired by a dwarf). But in addition to these specific similarities, the tone of the depiction of Sigurd in *Thidrek's Saga*, and of his relationship with the smith Mymmer (Wagner's Mime), matches more closely than any other version the knockabout comedy for which Wagner seems to have been striving in *Der junge Siegfried*.

The shopping list of books that Wagner devised when he first moved to Dresden, and the reading he undertook throughout his time there, furnished him with a deep understanding of mythology from both the Germanic and, more importantly, Norse traditions. And despite being deprived of his library, he continued to engage with myth as best he could even once he was in Zurich. Whether or not Ludwig Ettmüller was the source of his final *Edda* translations, he was surely a helpful source of advice as Wagner put the finishing touches to his poems; and Wagner's request to Uhlig (still in Dresden) in November 1851 that he should smuggle the *Volsung Saga* out of the Royal Library so that he could check a few details shows his continuing determination to absorb as much as he could from mythological sources. Without this deep engagement with myth over so many years, the set of poems that Wagner produced for *The Ring* would never have become so rich and resonant. And yet for all the depth of their engagement with myth, they are ultimately pieces of creative writing rather than mere adaptations. While incorporating features and motifs from all the sources discussed above and more, Wagner also makes connections that do not exist in any of the sources. In particular, the extent of Wotan's involvement in the affairs of the world – and his desire to ensure that Siegfried carries out the actions that he himself cannot – is Wagner's invention, and as a result his Wotan is a richer and more complex character than the Odin found in any of the sources.

* * *

Zurich, 25 April 1852. Wagner conducts the first of four performances of *The Flying Dutchman* at the city's theatre. It is the first time for more than a year that he has conducted there, and the orchestra is more than a third larger than its usual size, with players brought in from Bern and elsewhere. Wagner takes the opportunity to make some changes to the overture and final scene and to refine the orchestration. His influence over the production is not confined to the music: he closely supervises the work of the set designer, Ludwig Caësmann, and advises Liszt to purchase his sets for the production he is planning for Weimar later that year.

Wagner declines to take a fee for this production, in a display of largesse that helps cement his prominent position in Zurich society. He is once again living in the city: since his return from Albisbrunn, he and Minna have rented a handsome ground-floor apartment in Zeltweg, a leafy street not far from the university, and they have used the funds provided by Julie Ritter to furnish it luxuriously. Wagner's appearances with the Music Society's orchestra, which has recently recruited several star players from Germany, are the highlights of the city's musical life: last month's concert featured Beethoven's 'Pastoral' Symphony alongside the overture from *Tannhäuser*.

That opera is at the centre of what Wagner describes as a 'hail-storm' of interest in his work from theatres across Germany. It is taken up by theatres in several smaller cities, including Wiesbaden, Würzburg and Breslau; there is a revival in Dresden, despite its composer's continuing status there as a wanted man; the following year there will be twenty performances in Wagner's native city of Leipzig. This sudden interest in his music causes Wagner as much frustration as satisfaction – he is annoyed at the paltry income these provincial performances generate, and concerned that his work will not be performed according to his wishes, given that he cannot attend in person. He writes a pamphlet, 'On the Performing of *Tannhäuser*', and has it printed and distributed to theatres across Germany at his own expense – but he suspects that no one reads it.

The prospect of producing *The Ring* is as distant as ever – after Napoleon III's coup in Paris, disillusioned with Europe, Wagner tells Kietz that it will have to be taken to the banks of the Mississippi – but he nonetheless continues to work on the poems. By the start of July 1852, the poem of *Die Walküre* is complete; *Das Rheingold* (now given this shorter name) is written by November; by 17 December Wagner has made the changes needed to *Der junge Siegfried* and *Siegfrieds Tod* (still known by those titles) as a result of the drafting of the earlier two works; and over the next few days he reads the poems in sequence to a small gathering of friends at the country house of François and Eliza Wille.

By the New Year he is ready to share the poems more widely. In

January he arranges a private printing of fifty sumptuously bound copies and distributes them to friends. And on 16 February 1853, a large audience gathers for the first of four successive evenings on which Wagner will read the poems. The venue is the Baur au Lac, then as now perhaps Zurich's most luxurious and best-situated hotel: long-term guests at the time of Wagner's readings include Otto Wesendonck, a wealthy silk merchant who has been based in Zurich since returning from the USA in 1850, and his wife Mathilde. Wagner declaims all the roles and his performances are, by all accounts, compelling; the audience grows each night and includes many of Zurich's most prominent politicians and academics. Perhaps for the first time in his life, Wagner feels understood and respected by a discerning and knowledgeable public.

During his three and a half years in Zurich to date, at a time of life when most composers would be approaching a creative peak, Wagner has – remarkably – written virtually no music, though his published output as a writer over the same period stretches to hundreds of thousands of words. He arrived in Switzerland with one Siegfried drama to read to his new associates; now he has sent no fewer than four dramas into the world in what – for the moment at least – he regards as their final versions. Before long, he will regret putting his Nibelung cycle into the public domain so soon: he comes to realise that his intentions will not be properly understood until the music that will reveal his characters' inner life is composed. He understands the monumental nature of the work that is still to be done, though he cannot possibly have imagined how many years it will take.

3
Shaping the story

Stabreim and Schopenhauer

Z URICH, 22 MAY 1853: Wagner's fortieth birthday. He marks
the occasion by conducting a concert consisting entirely of
his own music, the third time within the last five days that he has
presented this programme. The programme consists of substantial extracts from *The Flying Dutchman*, *Tannhäuser* and *Lohengrin*,
preceded by the 'Friedensmarsch' from Act IV of *Rienzi*: the sim-
ilarity of this structure to that which Wagner had recently devised
for *The Ring* (three main parts with a shorter introduction) is probably not a coincidence. He has carefully prepared his audiences'
understanding of the programme by giving public readings of the
libretti of *Dutchman*, *Tannhäuser* and *Lohengrin* in the Casino concert hall. The birthday festival itself, however, takes place in the
much larger Aktien Theatre, specially equipped with an acoustic shell constructed to Wagner's own specifications that projects
the performers' sounds from the stage into the auditorium. The
Music Society's forces expand for these concerts to a chorus of
over a hundred and an orchestra of more than seventy; Wagner
personally writes to instrumentalists across Switzerland and from
several German cities to invite them to play. Visitors flood into
the city specially for the concerts, and audiences respond raptur-
ously: Wagner is urged to repeat the programmes immediately,
both in Zurich and elsewhere, requests that he politely declines in
order to preserve the festival's uniqueness. At the birthday concert
itself he is presented with a laurel wreath and an anonymous poem

of praise – in fact written by Johanna Spyri; the previous night he was lavished with extravagant compliments at a banquet held in his honour. Wagner probably derives even greater satisfaction, however, from the chance the concerts offer him to hear his ethereal Prelude to *Lohengrin* for the very first time, more than five years after he completed the opera.

The costs of this festival, at around 9,000 francs, are far beyond what the Music Society itself can secure. A month before it begins, subscriptions have reached only 3,600 francs. Wagner himself is in no position to cover the shortfall: he has just moved up two floors within his Zeltweg apartment block into a larger and airier flat which he is now furnishing lavishly – he and Minna will remain there for the next four years. Ever entrepreneurial, he devises a scheme of 'patronage certificates' to encourage individuals and organisations to sponsor the project; he will use a similar system two decades later to help finance the first Bayreuth Festival. Despite the success of the scheme and the large box-office income, however, a deficit of around 1,200 francs remains after the festival is over. This is paid off by a consortium of eight benefactors, including Jakob Sulzer, Konrad Ott-Imhof (the Music Society's clarinettist, who leads the tributes to Wagner at the banquet) and Otto Wesendonck. The businessman and his wife Mathilde, a talented amateur pianist, have become increasingly friendly with Wagner and Minna since meeting them in early 1852. Wagner quickly identifies Otto as a promising source of financial support: three months later, he will subsidise the trip to Italy which the composer credits with providing the first inspiration for the music of *Das Rheingold*. Inconveniently, Wagner begins to fall in love with Mathilde: a week after his birthday, he presents her with a piano miniature in the style of a polka, the first piece he has composed for more than five years.

On 1 July Liszt arrives in town for a week's stay at the Baur au Lac. It is the first time that he and Wagner have seen each other since he offered the Kapellmeister sanctuary in Weimar on his flight from Dresden: the reunion is emotional for them both. Liszt is reassured to find his friend looking well and living in a state of surprising luxury: throughout his time in Zurich the Wagners' apartment welcomes a constant flow of guests, cooked for by the patient Minna, refreshed from the couple's well-stocked wine cellar, waited on by Liszt's own servant. The two composers talk constantly, listen to each other's work (Liszt playing the piano, Wagner reading from the poems of *The Ring*), sing duets from *Lohengrin*; together with Georg Herwegh they make an excursion to Lake Lucerne and swear an oath of eternal brotherhood. Wagner feels a deep affinity with his fellow composer, with whom the outside world increasingly associates him as co-leader of the 'new German school', even if it is still six years before the *Neue Zeitschrift für Musik* will coin that phrase. He is bereft when Liszt leaves Zurich: in the autumn he will follow him to Basel, and later to Paris, where he will make his first acquaintance with the three children of Liszt's relationship with Marie d'Agoult, including the sixteen-year-old Cosima – all Wagner will recall of this first meeting is Cosima's shyness. He tries to persuade his friend to move to Zurich, telling him of his plans for a temporary theatre near the city specially designed for *The Ring*: he is confident that he can raise the hundred thousand francs that he believes it will cost. François Wille overhears the conversation and interjects that the project will surely require over a million francs; Liszt grandly responds that the million will be found.

Despite the limitations of its musical infrastructure, Zurich remains for the moment Wagner's only realistic prospect for staging the dramas whose music he is now, at long last, beginning to compose. The Saxon government's arrest warrant still stands and makes it too risky for him to enter any of the states in the German Confederation, and nothing emanating from Dresden suggests any likelihood of this situation changing. Liszt lobbied energetically on his friend's behalf in June 1853 when the King and Queen of Saxony visited his employer, the Hereditary Grand Duke, in Weimar; the Duke is sympathetic, and the King may even be so too, but the reactionary government led by Count von Beust that was installed after the uprising remains in control, and reports that reach Saxony from Switzerland of Wagner's extravagant lifestyle and his continuing association with known radicals such as Herwegh scarcely endear him to the authorities. A bulletin issued by the Dresden police on 11 June 1853 noted Wagner's apparent intention to return to Germany, reiterated that he was a wanted man, and attached his portrait to facilitate his arrest. And even if the composer were able to enter Germany to hear it, his work no longer seems to be satisfactorily promoted there: despite his friends' efforts, it will be many years before *Lohengrin* is staged in Berlin, and a long-awaited Leipzig production that eventually takes place in January 1854 is a fiasco. Wagner reluctantly resigns himself to creating the music of *The Ring* without having heard more than a few extracts from his previous opera.

The choirs and orchestras of Zurich appreciate the lustre that the city's most distinguished musician brings them: Wagner is particularly touched by the torchlit procession from the Zurich Choral Society who, shortly after Liszt's visit, sing their way up to his apartment to present him with a beautifully inscribed honorary diploma. He once again lavishes his attention on the city's musical institutions, in the hope of transforming them into something capable of realising his artistic ideals, but he moves faster than they are willing to go: the Music Society rejects his proposal to perform Beethoven's Ninth Symphony in the theatre, fearful of the likely overspend. Wagner's motivations for involving himself in the musical life of Zurich are not purely artistic: in the absence of significant income from the performance of his operas in Germany, he needs conducting fees to maintain the lifestyle he has started to enjoy. Nonetheless, when the theatre's entire workforce is sacked in January 1854 following the death of the previous director and a period of chaotic management from his widow, Wagner magnanimously declines a fee for a concert he conducts for their benefit; for a short while he even considers taking on the job of director himself. He submits a third proposal to the Music Society to reorganise its orchestra in close alignment with the needs of the theatre, complete with detailed costings, but in June this plan, like its predecessors, is rejected. Wagner once again faces an impasse: although he is proceeding at pace with *The Ring*'s music – he completes the draft orchestral score of *Das Rheingold* in May and begins work on *Die Walküre* in June – the prospect of the cycle's staging seems as remote as ever.

* * *

As Wagner finally began to compose again, his *Ring* poems were making their own way in the world – printed without the encumbrance of their author's name in the hope that they, unlike that author, could pass freely across the Swiss border into Germany. Wagner sent ten of the fifty copies that he produced in January 1853 to Liszt for distribution to royal personages as distinguished as the Grand Duchess of Weimar and the Princess of Prussia, and to friends including his imprisoned former assistant August Röckel, and Hans von Bülow, a brilliant twenty-three-year-old conductor and pianist whom Wagner has known since he was sixteen. Liszt quickly requested a further three copies, and acted as the conduit for some of the responses to what Wagner had boasted to Uhlig would be 'the greatest poem I have ever written'. Wagner was dismayed by the misunderstandings of admirers and detractors alike: the former, such as Louis Köhler, who published a book entitled *The Melody of Speech* in 1853, misguidedly attempted to second-guess how Wagner would turn his new form of poetry into music; the latter, such as Adolf Stahr, an admirer of *Lohengrin* who believed that the *Ring* poems were a 'total mistake', failed altogether to consider their ultimate dramatic purpose and mistakenly judged them purely as literature. By August 1853, Wagner had come to regard the publication of the poems as a matter of 'immense regret', as he wrote to Louis Schindelmesser:

I now feel that even my friends ought not to have had sight of the poem until it had been set to music . . . I wish I could recall all the copies I gave away. Come and visit me here soon, and I shall *read* it aloud to you, *sing* what is already finished, and *talk* to you about it; only *then* shall you take away a copy, if you wish to have one.

The failure even of Wagner's sympathisers to recognise in the poems of *The Ring* the masterpiece he felt he had already created was the result, however, not just of the poems' incompleteness – the absence of the music to which they would be set and the intentions that Wagner could currently convey only in person – but also of their novelty. These are poems unlike any opera libretto that had ever previously existed – even those by Wagner himself – in almost every respect. Indeed, Wagner himself felt that the term 'libretto' was no longer adequate to describe what he had produced. *A Communication to My Friends*, the autobiographical essay that Wagner published in December 1851 as a preface to the libretti of *The Flying Dutchman*, *Tannhäuser* and *Lohengrin*, describes the creation of *Dutchman* as the moment at which his career as a 'poet', rather than as a 'mere concoctor of opera-texts', properly began. Until then the shapes and styles of his libretti had been determined by his impulse to imitate the qualities he found attractive in various different genres, whether German Romantic opera (in *Die Feen*), Italian opera (in *Das Liebesverbot*) or French *grand opéra* (in *Rienzi*): when writing the libretto for the last of these, duets, trios and so forth 'found their own way in, here and there, because I looked upon my subject exclusively through the medium of "Opera"'. From *The Flying Dutchman* onwards, he becomes less interested in satisfying the tastes of a generalised 'public', more concerned with the judgements of specific individuals whom he respects. He credits himself from this point with paying much more attention to the specific poetic (and musical) requirements of each of his subjects, which unlike his previous choices did not necessarily lend themselves to being transformed into conventionally constructed operas. And yet, as he rightly acknowledges, there was no 'sudden leap'. A 'mechanical reflex' ensured that many of the 'traditional forms' of opera – arias, ensembles and choruses – persisted in the poem of *Dutchman*. Though he gradually liberates himself in *Tannhäuser* and *Lohengrin* from his reliance on these conventional structures, it is only when he begins work on *Siegfrieds Tod* that he genuinely breaks with the old model of the opera libretto. The differences – in *Siegfrieds Tod* and the three other *Ring* poems he goes on to write – are apparent at every level of the text, in units of every size from the smallest to the largest: word, line, scene, act.

Wagner's word choices in the *Ring* poems are governed most obviously by his decision to adopt as their guiding principle a form of alliteration closely related to the medieval technique of

Stabreim. The technique is ubiquitous in the Eddas and many of the other Germanic and Norse sources he consulted in his research, but until his efforts *Stabreim* had scarcely been used since the ninth century. The surviving medieval sources in which he discovered *Stabreim* were sophisticated works of literature, but he romantically represented the technique as though it were once an everyday means of communication: 'alliterative verse, bending itself in natural and lively rhythm to the actual accents of our speech . . . *Stabreim*, which the Folk itself once sang, when *it* was still both Poet and Myth-Maker'. Unlikely to the point of absurdity as Wagner's description is, his belief that *The Ring* was harnessing a form of language deeply rooted in German folk memory was a vital component of the myth of authenticity he constructed around his entire project. The only significant recent precedent for Wagner's adoption of *Stabreim* was *Der Held des Nordens*, the trilogy of plays by Friedrich de la Motte Fouqué, friend of his Leipzig uncle. Fouqué's example was probably a decisive influence on Wagner, alongside Ludwig Ettmüller's renderings of *Stabreim* into modern German in his book of translations of Eddic poetry. Wagner borrowed Ettmüller's collection, which contained a detailed introductory explanation of the technique, from the Dresden Royal Library in October 1848, a year before he first met Ettmüller in Zurich.

The prevalence of alliteration is obvious from the very first lines of *Das Rheingold*. The repeated Ws with which so many of the first actual words sung by the Rhinemaiden Woglinde begin – 'Woge, du Welle, walle zur Wiege' (Rise, waves, circle our cradle) – establish a continuity with the expressive but literally meaningless sounds that she, like her sisters, periodically emits throughout the scene: 'Wagalaweia! Wallala weiala weia!' Here, at the outset of the cycle, sound rather than sense seems to govern Wagner's word choice. But such extravagant alliteration, memorable though it is, is relatively unusual. More typical is the sort of alliteration found in the first speech made by the Nibelung Alberich as he emerges from the abyss, where a single consonant – 'n' in this case – dominates, but not to the exclusion of all others:

Hehe! Ihr Nicker	Hey! You nymphs!
Wie seid ihr niedlich	How gorgeous you look,
neidliches Volk!	you garrulous folk!
Aus Nibelheims Nacht	From Nibelheim's night,
Naht' ich mich gern,	I'd gladly emerge,
neigtet ihr euch zu mir!	if you'd come closer to me!

The repeated use of the 'n' sound in Alberich's speeches helps to establish his character: his use of his 'own' consonant to address the Rhinemaidens ('Nicker') and to express what he would like them to do ('neigtet') hints at his solipsistic nature. It also reinforces his relationship with his place of origin (Nibelheim), and that place's association with the darkness of night ('Nacht').

But alliteration in *The Ring* – and indeed in the Germanic and Norse sources that inspired Wagner – is not simply a matter of piling up repeated uses of the same consonant for maximum effect. *Stabreim* is often translated into English simply as 'alliteration', but the more literal rendering – 'stave-rhyme' – gives a better idea of its function. Alliteration within *Stabreim*, unlike in other poetic traditions, is not just a decorative effect or a device to draw attention to connections between words. Here it is also the poetry's principal source of order and structure – of *rhyme*. Connections and consonances between words in the middle of lines serve the same purpose here that those between words at the end of lines do within the much more familiar tradition of end-rhyme. Units of *Stabreim* are typically made up of two short lines, each containing stresses that fall within or (more usually) at the start of important words – the *Staben* or 'staves' that give the technique its name. The strongest stress falls on the first stave of the second line of the unit: in 'Aus Nibelheims Nacht / Naht' ich mich gern', for example, the main stress is on 'Naht'. And unlike in the end-rhymed iambic pentameters Wagner crafted for his previous libretti, in *Stabreim* the total number of syllables in each line is not a defining feature.

It is not only in their individual lines and speeches, however, that the *Ring* poems break with Wagner's previous practice, but also in the way they structure each scene and act. *Lohengrin* anticipated the through-composed music drama of Wagner's maturity more than any of his previous works, but its libretto nonetheless provides for arias and ensembles redolent of traditional number opera, and contains public and ceremonial scenes – such as the famous bridal march in Act III – that recall the French *grand opéra* that Wagner by this point affected to despise. The *Ring* poems, by contrast, break more completely and radically with established operatic structures. For Wagner – as he attempted to show in *Opera and Drama* – the structure of the poetry contained within itself the harmonic framework that the musical setting would ultimately work through, with movements away from and back to the local tonic key for each passage. And although it was difficult for him to demonstrate this in *Opera and Drama*, since no musical settings of any of his new-style poems had yet been completed, he envisaged that excursions away from the home key would sometimes be lengthy. The poetic-musical period – to adopt a phrase that Wagner coined in *Opera and Drama* and over whose precise meaning critics have quarrelled ever since – might be short or long, depending on the specific dramatic context. But the crucial point was that the poetry (if properly understood) contained within itself the basis of the musical form. What Wagner regarded as the conventional and arbitrary parcelling up of operatic scenes and acts into self-contained and harmonically rounded-off numbers would have no place in *The Ring*.

But however interesting and important Wagner's new method of constructing the speeches and scenes of his dramatic poem might be, this is poetry – as some of his early critics forgot or failed to see – that was always intended to be set to music, not read on its own. The true value of Wagner's adoption of *Stabreim* and the structural innovations to which it led him became apparent as he started to compose. He had an early intimation of this in September 1851 as he began some initial sketches, now lost, of what eventually became *Siegfried*; he wrote to Uhlig of his delight at how easy his new style of poetry made the task of composition: 'The musical phrases make themselves for these stanzas and periods, without my even having to take pains with them; it all grows out of the ground as if it were wild.' This particular boast would turn out to be well-founded, notwithstanding the length of time the cycle's composition actually took. To adopt Wagner's own somewhat extravagant metaphor, his new form of poetry was indeed the seed from which his revolutionary new drama grew.

* * *

Zurich, 14 September 1854. Wagner informs Jakob Sulzer that his current debts total ten thousand francs – a figure similar to the entire cost of the previous year's festival of his music. Some of this debt is to Karl Ritter and can be defrayed gradually by reducing the allowance that Karl's mother continues to pay him, but the majority requires immediate settlement. No significant source of income is on the horizon: Wagner concedes that he has been living beyond his means ever since he moved into his new apartment. Otto Wesendonck, frustrated by Wagner's constant requests for support, has been urging him to provide such a total for most of the year, but Wagner prefers to use the less forbidding Sulzer as an intermediary. It is Otto, however, who comes to his rescue, agreeing to advance him seven thousand francs to liquidate his debts and an annual allowance of two thousand to cover his living expenses, payable in quarterly instalments; in return, Otto will receive Wagner's fees from the future opera productions that he confidently anticipates. Two days later, a sheepish Wagner admits to Sulzer that he has miscalculated and needs a few hundred francs more if he is to pay his rent. Otto once again bails him out, but he insists that Sulzer tell Wagner that this is the very last time he will do so, and that Sulzer himself should henceforth take control of the composer's financial affairs.

Minna, meanwhile, seeks to advance her husband's interests in Germany; the Saxon government's arrest warrant does not apply to her. She secures a meeting with Botho von Hülsen, intendant of the Court Theatre in Berlin, in the hope that he will finally agree to mount *Tannhäuser*, but this would be much easier to achieve if the composer himself were allowed to enter Prussia to supervise the production. Wagner hopes that an amnesty may be forthcoming now there is a new King of Saxony: his former employer, Friedrich August, died in August 1854 after falling in front of a horse during a journey to the Tyrol, and was succeeded by his brother Johann, a noted scholar who has pseudonymously published a highly praised translation of Dante. The composer floats the possibility that the couple might be permitted to live in Weimar, as long as he promises to give up politics and they do not leave the Grand Duke's territory without permission; Minna visits Weimar for discussions with Liszt and to obtain a letter of support from the Grand Duke; on her arrival in Dresden, she presents a petition in person on behalf of her husband, whom she represents as an 'erring artist' motivated only by the desire to hear singers and orchestras perform his music. The Saxon Minister of Justice's reply does not reach Minna until December, by which time she is back in Zurich: it once again rules out the possibility of any pardon until 'the fugitive has returned and submitted himself to examination'. *Tannhäuser* will not be staged in Berlin until January 1856, and then without Wagner's involvement: his autobiography laments the 'miserable presentation' it receives, but rejoices in the 'continuing flow of income' it generates.

While Minna is away, Wagner once again becomes embroiled in the musical politics of Zurich. Frustrated by the Music Society's rejection of his plan for reform, he refuses its invitations to conduct until they agree to co-operate with the theatre, but by December 1854 a compromise is reached and Wagner deigns to appear with the Music Society orchestra. As always, his arrival on the podium has a galvanic effect on box-office receipts. His programmes in early 1855 include the first performances of a revised version of his *Faust Overture*, which he began in 1839 as the first movement of a projected *Faust Symphony*; it may be Liszt's recent completion of a work with this very title that prompts him to resuscitate his own more modestly proportioned piece. The score of this new rendering is marked with a dedication to 'S.l.F.': 'S.l.' stands for 'Seiner lieben', though whether the 'F' refers to his 'Frau', Minna, or 'Freundin', Mathilde Wesendonck, is open to question. Certainly Wagner's feelings for Mathilde are deepening at this point, even if her reticence and his financial dependence on her husband prevent him from acting on them too openly. Meanwhile, the new director of the theatre has programmed what will be the Swiss premiere of *Tannhäuser* as part of his first season,

and as a gesture of support Wagner has agreed to assist the conductor, Louis Müller. He is pleasantly surprised by the quality
of the musicians' work, and on 23 February – apparently at the
particular request of Mathilde – he takes the baton for the third
performance. The theatre is filled beyond capacity for what turns
out to be Wagner's final appearance as a conductor in Zurich.

Nine days later, Wagner is in London: he has accepted an offer
to conduct the Philharmonic Society orchestra's spring season.
No doubt he is flattered by the personal visit to Zurich that the
Society's treasurer, George Frederick Anderson, makes in order
to negotiate with him; but he is in fact the fourth choice, behind
Sir Michael Costa (who refuses to withdraw the resignation he
submitted in the wake of a quarrel with the Society), Louis Spohr
(who declines, perhaps feeling that at seventy he is too old to make
the journey from Kassel), and Hector Berlioz (who is already committed to conducting the rival New Philharmonic). Wagner's time
in London is unhappy. He dislikes the dank weather, the stodgy
food and the London orchestras' predilection for overlong and
incoherent concert programmes. His inability to speak English is
an obstacle to acceptance; so too is his refusal to ingratiate himself with the London critics in the way that they have come to
expect; this inevitably leads to poor reviews, despite some enthusiastic responses from his audiences. The high point of his visit
comes when Queen Victoria and Prince Albert attend his penul-
timate concert and ask to hear the *Tannhäuser* overture; Victoria
suggests that the large number of German singers in London's
theatres might help him mount his operas there in the future.
Wagner is alert to the irony that the Queen of England should
so warmly greet a figure whom her German cousins regard as a
traitor. He returns to Zurich on 30 June 1855 with a mere forty
pounds (around a thousand Swiss francs) remaining from his fee

of two hundred – this is scant reward for the arduous work he has done, but perhaps just enough to suggest to Otto Wesendonck and his other Zurich benefactors that he might be able to earn his own living in the future, rather than depending on their largesse.

He and Minna leave Zurich again after less than a fortnight, on 13 July. Wagner is beginning to suffer frequent and painful recurrences of his erysipelas, and Minna too is unwell, so the couple decide to visit the tiny spa of Seelisberg on Lake Lucerne – taking with them Jacquot the parrot (purchased four years previously as a replacement for Papo), but not their beloved spaniel Peps, who died the previous day. Seelisberg enjoys spectacular views across the lake to the town of Brunnen: Wagner identifies a pretty spot by the lake where he believes he will be able to work in peace, and begins discussions with a local hotelier he knows about the prospect of building a house there. And he starts to contemplate the idea that *The Ring* might be staged on a floating stage formed of barges in the lake, with the Alpine scenery forming a magnificent natural backdrop. Nothing will come of either of these schemes, but the fact that Wagner even considers them suggests that he has given up on Zurich itself as somewhere worthy of the investment of his musical energies.

When he returns to the city, he is true to his word – rather to the Music Society's surprise – in refusing all further invitations to conduct. Instead, he settles down diligently – whenever his erysipelas does not prevent him, which it quite often does – to the orchestration of *Die Walküre*, on which he made little progress in London. His social circle in the city has been enriched by the arrival of Gottfried Semper, architect of the Dresden opera house, a fellow political exile for whom Wagner has helped line up a professorship at Zurich's newly created technical university; and his mood is lifted by reports of the enthusiastic response to productions of *Tannhäuser* in Munich and Berlin, even if he is sceptical about the musical quality of what these audiences will have heard. His financial worries remain, however: he cannot conceive of how he will pay a copyist for the mammoth task of transcribing his scores for *The Ring*, and in January 1856 he asks Liszt for yet another loan.

Despite his financial and medical difficulties, Wagner completes the monumental task of orchestrating *Die Walküre* in March, and on 26 April 1856 he presents the first act to a small group of friends for the first time. Wagner himself takes the roles of both Siegmund and Hunding; Emilie Heim sings Sieglinde; Theodor Kirchner from Winterthur – himself a talented composer though even more financially reckless than Wagner – plays the piano. This cannot have been how Wagner imagined bringing his greatest music to date into the world, but the makeshift performance brings him one concrete benefit. Otto Wesendonck is so impressed that he immediately offers to match Julie Ritter's annual allowance by paying Wagner a stipend of 250 francs per month, so that he can concentrate on completing *The Ring* without having to worry about the vagaries of royalties from his other operas. The pathway to completing the music seems clear at last; but before composing any more, Wagner will make some small but vital changes to the words he plans to set.

* * *

Siegfrieds Tod was drafted at a time when Wagner firmly believed in the potential of political change to enhance the well-being of individual people and society as a whole. Siegfried, as Wagner conceived him in October 1848, embodies this optimistic view of the world; Brünnhilde, in the final speech she gives at Siegfried's funeral pyre in this first version of the libretto, celebrates the

84

liberation of the Nibelungs, before she takes the 'freest of heroes' to Valhalla. In this version of the story, the rule of the gods is shored up rather than ended by the death of the hero – Wagner was still a servant of the King of Saxony, not yet a committed revolutionary nor ready to depict the violent overthrow of an old order – but the positive mood of the ending is clear. Wagner's optimism about what the future might hold is evident, too, in the much more ambivalent ending he drafted probably in December 1848, in which Brünnhilde suggests that the gods will 'fade away in bliss before man's deed'. This is a remarkable change of emphasis in a short period of time, one that reflects the febrile nature of the political situation and of Wagner's state of mind. But the two endings, however different in what they foretell of the fate of the old order, share an entirely positive interpretation of Siegfried as the representative of the new.

Wagner's growing involvement in revolutionary activity undoubtedly entrenched his belief in the potential of politics to effect positive change, but the philosophical underpinnings of this attitude went back much further. His involvement with the 'Young Germany' movement as a young man in Leipzig developed his belief that society would be improved if it were not restricted by bourgeois values, particularly those relating to sexual morality: he gave voice to this view, which coincided conveniently with his personal inclinations, in the final section of *Das Liebesverbot*. After he settled in Dresden he began to study Hegel, whose *Philosophy of History* was the only recent philosophical work in his personal library. It encouraged Wagner, like so many of his contemporaries, to think of reality – including the structures that governed society – as something that was not immutable but always in the process of change: indeed, every situation contained within it the forces that would ultimately cause its transformation.

Bakunin, Wagner's anarchist comrade in Dresden, had translated Hegel into Russian as a philosophy student in Moscow, and joined the left-leaning 'Young Hegelian' movement when he moved to Berlin in his twenties. Wagner's own interest in Hegel prepared the ground for his intense intellectual friendship with Bakunin, and predisposed him to be sympathetic to the Russian's view that existing social structures should be swept away, violently if needed. Whatever the composer later tried to claim, his revolutionary activities were the product of deep philosophical conviction, not just opportunism or a temporary whim.

The 'Young Hegelian' who exerted the greatest influence on Wagner was Ludwig Feuerbach, an anthropologist and philosopher nine years his senior, whose perceived hostility to organised religion effectively denied him an academic career. As with Hegel, Wagner was probably well aware of Feuerbach's importance and familiar with his ideas long before he read him. His autobiography gives the credit for his discovery of Feuerbach to a preacher in Dresden, but it was not until he had settled in Zurich that he immersed himself in Feuerbach's writing – in particular, *The Essence of Christianity*, published in 1841 and known in the English-speaking world through George Eliot's 1854 translation. This book helped Wagner to understand the nature of his own fascination with the gods whose fundamental importance to his Nibelung project he was starting to realise. For Feuerbach, it is human beings who have created the gods – or God – they worship, not the other way around, so the truths that religion has to tell us are not metaphysical but concern human motivations and behaviour. The qualities that humans have attributed to the separate gods of Greek or Norse mythology – bravery, wisdom, kindness, eternal youth – are those to which they themselves aspire; and the supreme quality that Christians attribute to their

God – that of love – is for Feuerbach the most important quality that humans themselves can display. Love, for Feuerbach, was the force that would bring about mankind's liberation from its state of subjugation.

Feuerbach's ideas both of religion and of love imprinted themselves on Wagner's poems for *The Ring* as he worked on them in Zurich – and especially on the first two poems that he decided to add to the scheme in 1851, during his stay in Albisbrunn. Wagner's depiction of the highly flawed and all-too-human gods who populate *Das Rheingold* draws on Feuerbach's insight that human beings invent divine ones to epitomise aspects of their own behaviour; *Die Walküre*'s celebration of the overwhelming but socially proscribed love between the Volsung siblings, Siegmund and Sieglinde, echoes Feuerbach's characterisation of love as a force for social change. And the words that Wagner added to the ending of *Siegfrieds Tod* before he read it to his friends at the end of 1852 underline his conversion to Feuerbach's world-view. Brünnhilde now proclaims, much more clearly than in 1848, the destruction of Valhalla and the downfall of the gods. The world to which she bids farewell no longer has any figures of authority; the wisdom she offers as her parting gift stems not from wealth, social status, legal rights or ancient customs, but from love. It is love – as embodied by Brünnhilde and Siegfried – that has equipped mankind to free itself at last from the oppressive rule of the gods.

At some point between writing those words and completing the final version of *Götterdämmerung*, Wagner lost his belief that mankind could come together to create a better world, a belief that had endured through the turbulent years of revolution and exile. Probably no one single factor caused this change. Many writers – including Wagner himself in his autobiography – have pointed to Louis-Napoleon's dissolution of France's National Assembly in December 1851 and his assumption of dictatorial powers as Emperor as the episode that destroyed the composer's faith that political action would or could produce a juster society. Certainly Wagner retrospectively attached great symbolic importance to this betrayal – *Mein Leben* tells of his suggestion to Uhlig that they should henceforth date all their letters 'December 1851', as if to pretend that this historic rupture had not happened – but the fact that the optimistic 'Feuerbach ending' to *Siegfrieds Tod* was written a year after the coup indicates that his turn to pessimism was neither as sudden nor as absolute as he later implied.

If Louis-Napoleon contributed to the shattering of the beliefs that had shaped Wagner's outlook since early adulthood, then it was another philosopher who enabled him to construct a world-view that made sense of his disappointment. Wagner's first encounter with Arthur Schopenhauer's *The World as Will and Representation* came in autumn 1854, by which time he had already composed the music of *Das Rheingold* and Act I of *Die Walküre*. Wagner himself was in no doubt of the significance for his future development of Schopenhauer's magnum opus, much of which had been published in 1819 (an expanded version appeared in 1844) but which had only recently begun to attract attention. Once Wagner had been introduced to the book by Georg Herwegh, he read its thousand-plus pages four times before summer 1855, and returned to them at numerous points thereafter, particularly when immersed in new creative projects. The diaries that his second wife Cosima kept from 1869 reveal just how much Wagner reread, referenced and revered Schopenhauer: though he was not generally given to acknowledging the influence of others, he expressed his gratitude to the philosopher regularly and until the very end of his life.

Unlike most of the thinkers who had previously influenced Wagner, Schopenhauer was no Hegelian: he famously described

88

the Berlin professor, at the peak of his celebrity as Schopenhauer was publishing his first works, as 'a commonplace, inane, loathsome, repulsive and ignorant charlatan', who disguised the shortcomings of his system with the deliberate obscurity of his writing. Kant, on the other hand, was a precursor for whom Schopenhauer maintained the utmost respect, even as he sought to distance himself from his thinking. The distinction between 'representation' and 'will' that Schopenhauer evolves in his book builds on Kant's opposition between the 'world of appearance' and the 'thing in itself'. Schopenhauer's 'representations', like Kant's 'appearances', are impressions of the world whose specificity and distinctness depend on the existence of a subject who experiences them: such 'appearances' or 'representations', however, do not constitute reality itself, but only a sort of dream, even if they are the only phenomena we can precisely grasp. Schopenhauer's 'will', on the other hand, resembles Kant's 'thing in itself' in that it exists independently of human perception, but Schopenhauer goes on to develop the concept in a surprising and complex way. 'Will' – the 'will to life' – is the world's inner essence: it includes those actions that human beings undertake in response to instinctive, perhaps unconscious urges – including, importantly, sexual urges – and also the behaviour of animals and plants.

According to Schopenhauer, the 'will to life' constantly strives for a satisfaction that can never truly be achieved. Competition between human and human, animal and animal – for food, scarce resources, sexual partners – makes suffering inevitable. Even when desires are met, fulfilment is only temporary, since satisfaction is quickly replaced by fresh desires, or by boredom. This philosophy is profoundly pessimistic – hence its appeal to Wagner at a time when his own mid-century optimism had already been shaken – but it does not entirely exclude the possibility of escaping the cycle of suffering. Schopenhauer noted that several religions – Hinduism, whose sacred texts he had studied, and Buddhism, as well as Christianity – encouraged a life of asceticism, in which believers might at times deny themselves food, physical comforts, sexual satisfaction. Despite being an atheist, Schopenhauer proposed in the fourth and last book of *The World as Will and Representation* that 'salvation' could be achieved by those who similarly denied the 'will to life', who abandoned the pursuit of egotistical ends and selfish pleasure. For those able to recognise in this way the lack of importance of an individual human life, death is something not to be feared but to be welcomed.

Though Wagner in his personal behaviour was for the most part anything but ascetic, he finds Schopenhauer's idea of the denial of the will profoundly appealing. He writes to Liszt that he has 'found a sedative which has finally helped me to sleep at night; it is the sincere and heartfelt yearning for death: total unconsciousness, complete annihilation, the end of all dreams – the only ultimate redemption'. He includes some lines that ascribe very similar sentiments to Brünnhilde in a new section of verse for the end of *Siegfrieds Tod* drafted in 1856:

> I depart from the home of desire,
> I flee forever the home of delusion
> the open gates
> of eternal becoming
> I close behind me now:
> to the holiest chosen land,
> free from desire and delusion,
> the goal of the world's migration,
> redeemed from reincarnation,
> the enlightened woman now goes.

Wagner ultimately decides not to set these words to music, though he considers them sufficiently important to include, alongside the discarded 'Feuerbach ending', as a footnote in the 1872 publication of the *Ring* text. However, the lack of music for the 'Schopenhauer ending' by no means implies that *The Ring*'s ending is not Schopenhauerian.

The other aspect of *The World as Will and Representation* that particularly influences Wagner is Schopenhauer's characterisation of music. The philosopher believes that any type of aesthetic contemplation is valuable, since it requires the temporary setting aside of the demands of the will: 'pure cognition, liberated from and rid of all willing, is highly gratifying and already as such has a great share in aesthetic enjoyment.' However, music occupies the supreme place in Schopenhauer's hierarchy of the arts, since whereas other art-forms can give some insight into the workings of the will, music – as Schopenhauer explains with detailed reference to its internal processes – is 'a copy of the will itself', and thus allows the will's longings and strivings to be comprehended in a way that no other art-form can achieve. It is music's very freedom from association with specific words and concepts that allows it to perform this role.

This is almost the opposite argument to the one that Wagner himself has recently propounded, above all in *Opera and Drama*: that music is worthwhile only when 'fertilised' by the 'seed' of a poet's words. Schopenhauer's argument challenges him, and ultimately changes the balance between words and music in his dramas in favour of the latter. The ending Wagner eventually composes for *Götterdämmerung*, with the burden of expression finally entrusted to the orchestra alone, is one of the most telling revelations of this change of heart.

* * *

Zurich, 15 May 1856. Following Minna's unsuccessful petition two years previously, Wagner himself now writes a long letter to King Johann of Saxony. His revolutionary activities in Dresden, he submits, were motivated not by political commitment but by the opportunity he felt the upheaval offered – misguidedly, as he now realises – to advance his long-held views on art and its role in society. He realises that the fervid treatises he has published in Zurich can 'only aggravate the verdict of my judges', but defends them as a form of self-therapy: 'they benefited me by gradually cooling my agitation and setting me little by little, after the manner of a morbid substance pathologically excreted, on the road to recovery.' Thus cleansed, he is able to devote himself once again to purely artistic matters. He would happily accept the punishment of exile were it not that his art itself 'directs me back to the German Fatherland to which it indissolubly binds me': only by supervising productions in Germany can he continue to produce the work he is compelled to write. To this end, he asks the king, in the most obsequious and self-abasing terms, to remove the obstacles that prevent him from taking up the opportunity of sanctuary in Weimar that the Grand Duke and his distinguished friend have kindly offered. Johann passes Wagner's request on to the Ministry of Justice; after a detailed re-examination of the depositions of those involved in the uprising, the Ministry recommends its rejection, news that Wagner hears in August.

The day after he writes to the King, 16 May, Wagner sets down a rather different document: a short prose sketch for a drama to be entitled *Die Sieger* (The Victors). The story is drawn from Buddhist legend, and concerns the passionate love of a young girl, Prakriti, for the devout Ananda. She is distraught to hear that she can only be united with him if she shares his vow of chastity, but the Buddha himself enables her to understand the cycle of death and rebirth that has led her to her current existence, and she joyfully joins Buddha's followers as Ananda's sister. Together with the new ending to *Siegfrieds Tod* that Wagner drafts in the same month, *Die Sieger* demonstrates the composer's new-found preoccupation with the idea that enlightenment can be achieved only by renouncing life's illusory temptations – including sexual desire. Wagner draws this idea from the Buddhist texts to which he has been led by his obsession with Schopenhauer; but it is also a way of negotiating the overwhelming attraction he has started to feel for the unattainable Mathilde Wesendonck. For a while, *Die Sieger* competes for Wagner's attention with *The Ring* and with the story of Tristan and Isolde: the last is an idea for an opera even more intimately connected with his feelings for Mathilde, one that he has been considering at least since December 1854, when he wrote to Liszt of his plan to make it 'a monument' to love ('this most beautiful of dreams'). Unlike *Tristan*, *Die Sieger* will progress no further than this brief sketch, though aspects of Wagner's thinking about the story find their way into several of his other works, particularly *Parsifal*.

Wagner's new philosophical priorities are confirmed in the summer of 1856, when he finally settles on the titles that he will give the later parts of *The Ring*. The drama previously known as *Der junge Siegfried* he now calls simply *Siegfried*, while *Siegfrieds Tod* becomes *Götterdämmerung*: the German equivalent of the Old Norse word 'Ragnarök', which means 'twilight of the gods' and is found in both the *Prose Edda* and the *Poetic Edda*. Together with the changes he has recently made to the closing lines of the last drama, the new titles underline Wagner's shaping of the story as a drama now focused primarily on the gods and the ultimate necessity of their destruction, rather than on Siegfried and the possibility of positive change in society that he originally represented.

In June 1856 Wagner opens negotiations with the Leipzig firm of Breitkopf and Härtel for the publication of the scores of *The Ring*. With characteristic over-confidence, he tells Breitkopf that the scores will all be complete by summer 1858, that he will then mount the cycle in the 'festival' manner that he has always envisaged for the first performances, and that there is bound to be interest from all the major German theatres in taking up the works thereafter. Because he has no heirs who will benefit from long-standing royalties on the works, he offers Breitkopf instead the opportunity to buy the works outright for a total of 10,000 thalers – half payable now in return for the two scores he has completed, the remaining amount to be paid on delivery of the final two dramas. This arrangement will buy him the time – and space, in the form of a property where he can concentrate on composition in peace – that he needs to complete his work. Negotiations continue over the summer: the publishers try to persuade Wagner to allow them to issue each opera separately, and to publish versions for solo piano, in order that they can recoup some of their investment without waiting for the entire work to be complete. It seems for a while that a deal will be possible, but on 30 August Breitkopf and Härtel informs Wagner of its withdrawal from the negotiations, citing the impracticability of producing the works as the main reason for the decision.

This is a severe blow to Wagner's prospects – and his financial problems are compounded a couple of months later when he feels obliged to relinquish his allowance from Julie Ritter, which has been his most reliable source of income for the last five years. Liszt is in Zurich again, and in the course of the first evening of his stay he quarrels with Julie's son (and Wagner's acolyte) Karl on a number of topics, including Emperor Napoleon III (whom Liszt admires and Karl does not) and Bakunin (whom Liszt believes is a Russian spy). Wagner uncharacteristically casts himself in the role of peacemaker but his efforts are misinterpreted by Karl, who relays his version of events to his mother, who takes her son's side in a letter to Wagner. Though the rift with Julie is short-lived – Wagner's allowance resumes six months later – he does not speak to Karl for another two years.

Meanwhile, robbed of any hope of either political rehabilitation or lucrative publication, and deprived – temporarily at least – of half his regular income, Wagner is once again in a state of near-desperation. In January 1857 he pleads with Liszt to ask the Grand Duke in Weimar whether he can provide him with an allowance, at least for the time it will take him to finish *The Ring*. Or if that is not forthcoming, perhaps Liszt can use his influence with Breitkopf and Härtel to persuade the firm to reopen negotiations for the scores? Once again, however, it is Otto Wesendonck rather than Liszt who proves Wagner's most reliable source of assistance. The Wesendoncks are about to move from the Baur au Lac to a magnificent newly built mansion on a hill overlooking the quiet Zurich suburb of Enge, not far from where Wagner and Minna lived after his Bordeaux escapade. There is a small piece of land with a cottage on it adjoining the Wesendoncks' estate, which Otto learns has been purchased by a doctor intending to build a mental hospital. Alarmed by this possibility, he forestalls it by repurchasing the land for himself, and offers the cottage to Wagner at a peppercorn rent which he will take from money that has already been advanced to him as administrator of Wagner's financial interests; this means that the composer will owe him nothing, at least for the next two years. Wagner accepts, grateful not only for the generous deal Otto proposes but also for the opportunity to live in close proximity to Mathilde.

Wagner and Minna move on 28 April 1857 to the cottage they

now call the 'Asyl'. This name is nothing to do with the previous owner's plans for the site: Wagner coins it in response to a comment from Mathilde that the house will be a 'refuge' for him, away from the bustle of the city and the particular annoyance of his noisy Zeltweg neighbours. The Wagners' time in the 'Asyl' will ultimately turn out to be anything but peaceful, the expense of refurbishing it makes Wagner's short-term financial situation worse rather than better, and contrary to his expectations, he will make virtually no progress with *The Ring* after his first three months there. But for the moment, at least, it feels like a fresh beginning.

4
Sounding the story

Text into music

Das Rheingold

L A SPEZIA, LIGURIA, 5 SEPTEMBER 1853. Wagner has taken
the steamship from the nearby city of Genoa in the hope
of recovering from an attack of dysentery which he attributes to
too much ice cream, but succeeds merely in adding seasickness
and insomnia to his list of ailments. Exhausted after a long walk,
he reclines on a couch, and is soon overcome not by sleep but by
what he describes in his autobiography as a 'kind of somnambulistic state, in which I suddenly had the feeling of being immersed
in rapidly flowing water'. The sound of the water soon turns itself
into a chord of E flat major, which relentlessly persists even as
he imagines himself submerged by waves. As he returns to full
consciousness, he realises that what he has heard is the music that
will begin *The Ring*, and that it has been there inside him all along.

Or so the story – Wagner's story – goes. Many have questioned
its veracity. *Mein Leben* describes the Prelude to *Das Rheingold* as
we now know it – 136 bars based on a single chord – with almost
suspicious accuracy, but the first version he writes down is shorter
and rather different. Moreover, it is most uncharacteristic of him
not to mention such an important experience for more than a year
in any of his voluminous correspondence: Emilie Ritter is the first
to hear about it, in December 1854. By this time Wagner has discovered Schopenhauer and read his arguments about the importance of dreams in artistic creation, which quite possibly influence
how he tells his own story. The account he dictates in 1869 for
inclusion in *Mein Leben* is perhaps best regarded not as a precise
description of what happened sixteen years earlier, but as a new

myth of his own devising, fashioned to explain the genesis of a mythological drama still some years from reaching the stage in its entirety. *The Ring* will be unlike anything anyone has ever seen before: Wagner wants his audiences to believe that it came into being in a unique way – and perhaps he even believes this himself.

After experiencing whatever he experiences in La Spezia, Wagner determines to cut short the Italian holiday he has planned and return to Zurich to begin work on the score. After five years during which he has barely composed a bar, his excitement at returning to the task is palpable. For various mundane reasons, however – including the trip he makes to Paris with Liszt in October – it will not be until 1 November that he actually does so. Once he is back in his Zeltweg apartment, he quickly realises that he will need a system of working different from that he has used for any of his previous operas. Previously he has begun with a sketch on three staves, the top one for the vocal lines and the lower two for a compressed version of the orchestral accompaniment, before moving on to a first sketch of the orchestration and then a first draft of the full score. But for *Das Rheingold* he needs to begin sketching individual orchestral lines from the outset, enabling him to cut out a stage of the process. Between 1 November 1853 and 14 January 1854 – only eleven weeks, of which he is too ill to work for almost two – he writes a continuous draft. This is still on three staves, like the sketches for his earlier works; but here the ideas for individual instrumental parts, though skeletal and roughly worked out, are almost ready to be turned into a draft full score.

Wagner starts work on this right away, and it is at this stage, in February, that he shapes the Prelude into its final form. Whether it is the product of a mystical vision or conscious calculation, fashioning a piece of this duration from a single chord is unprecedented, and it achieves a number of things. By stretching out the first chord to such lengths, Wagner intimates the huge scale of what is to follow, and tells us that we are embarking on a story of epic proportions. The sounds are magical: eight horns, twice as many as are usually found in an orchestra, successively introduce the same pattern of notes from the E flat major triad, entering at gradually decreasing intervals of time to form an intricate canon. By avoiding any dissonance or modulation, and emphasising the notes of the harmonic series, Wagner suggests that we are hearing the sounds of nature, of a physical phenomenon that has been present since the world began; and by decorating the chord with rapid figures that rush up and down with the regularity of waves, he identifies that phenomenon as the specific element of water. By his careful pacing of the build-up of orchestral sound and of the speed with which notes move, meanwhile, he creates a growing recognition of the inevitability of change. Paradoxically, this music at once suggests a state that has always been the same, and one that cannot remain the same any longer – stasis and momentum coexist.

With the appearance of a voice, the chord changes for the first time. The Rhinemaiden Woglinde sings a melody that Wagner drafted as far back as March 1852, one of only a very few scraps of music from before the La Spezia breakthrough that survive into the finished work. Woglinde's first speech conjures up the fast-moving river she inhabits – 'Wagalaweia! Wallala weiala weia!' – and the intimate, onomatopoeic relationship that she and her sisters enjoy with the Rhine is underlined by the continuation of the orchestral sounds from the Prelude and the frequent returns to the home key. The Rhinemaidens continually emerge from and submerge each other in the river, while their sinuous, vowel-rich vocal lines intertwine with the melodies that bob up through the orchestra.

Alberich, the Nibelung, poses the first challenge to the ecstatic state that the Rhinemaidens celebrate. As he sings the consonant-heavy speech quoted on page 77, rougher, more abrasive sounds appear in the orchestra. One by one the Rhinemaidens flirt with then deny him. The priapic dwarf's threefold humiliation is enough to drive him to renounce the possibility of love, once the Rhinemaidens have carelessly let slip that doing so will allow him to take possession of the gold they have been guarding and thus become master of the world. This is the rupture with Nature for which the Prelude's inexorable momentum has prepared us: for the Rhinemaidens, and for Wagner, to renounce love is an incomprehensibly unnatural act. Alberich's declaration is accompanied by harsh, jagged, minor-key music, the antithesis of the flowing phrases of the Prelude, as the Rhinemaidens pursue him in a vain attempt to retrieve the gold.

Wagner has largely invented the actions and motivations of his characters in this opening scene: by contrast with almost everything else in *The Ring*, the story he tells has little basis in either German or Norse mythology. His priority is to depict the two opposing forces – an urge to love; a longing for power – whose conflict will propel the entire drama, and his music conveys them with exceptional clarity and economy. Nothing else in *The Ring* will be quite so straightforward.

* * *

Paris, October 1853. Wagner and Liszt visit the workshop of Adolphe Sax in the Rue Saint-Georges. The Belgian instrument-maker shows his distinguished guests his full range of eponymous novelties: saxophones, saxhorns and saxtubas. Wagner is particularly taken with the saxhorns: instruments of various different pitches that look like small tubas. Since Sax patented them in

1845, they have already become popular in military bands and for on-stage music at the Opéra. Meyerbeer uses eighteen of them in *Le Prophète*, which Wagner heard in Paris in 1850, and Berlioz will soon deploy them in *Les Troyens*.

A few weeks later, Wagner begins the interlude that transports the audience of *Das Rheingold* from the mists of the Rhine to its first glimpse of the fortress that Wotan has recently commissioned as a home for the gods. Valhalla – Wotan gives it this name at the end of this 'preliminary evening' – has been built on a mountain summit near the Rhine; Wagner associates the scene in his mind's eye with the spectacular Julier Pass near St Moritz, which he has recently visited in the company of Georg Herwegh. The fortress's magnificence is unlike anything previously seen, and so to depict it Wagner needs to find a combination of sounds never previously heard.

His thoughts turn back to the instruments he heard in Paris – he tells King Ludwig in 1865 that he was thinking of *Sax'schen Instrumenten* when he composed this scene – but they are not quite right. He indicates in the score that the 'Valhalla' theme will be played by 'tubas', two tenor and two bass, but the instruments he has in mind do not yet exist, and do not exist even when *Das Rheingold* is premiered against Wagner's wishes in Munich in 1869. It is not until 1875, with the help of Hans Richter – who will conduct the first Bayreuth production of *The Ring* the following year, and who trained as a horn player – that a set of 'Wagner tubas' is produced to the composer's specifications. The instruments look like elongated French horns, and will be played by the extra four horn players that Wagner has introduced into the orchestra, using their own mouthpieces. However, they produce a sound that is mellower and less biting than that of the horn, due to the greater width of the channel through which the player blows. Together with the bass trumpet, the contrabass trombone and the contrabass tuba, themselves also very recent inventions for which Wagner helps develop the technology, they conjure up the unearthly vision of Valhalla to unforgettable effect.

Wagner's willingness to conceive a crucial passage of his score for an instrument that would not be manufactured for more than twenty years reveals the precision of his sonic imagination and his refusal to compromise. It also shows how timbre has now become an integral part of his initial musical idea – alongside pitch, rhythm and harmony – rather than something to be thought about once the music has been drafted, as for many earlier composers and perhaps also the younger Wagner. On a purely logistical level, too, his decision is interesting. The inclusion of the Wagner tubas means that the composer will need to engage a further quartet of horn players to play them, on top of the four normally found in an opera orchestra; he makes good use of these auxiliary players on the French horn as well, not least in the Prelude.

By comparison with *Lohengrin* – his most recently completed score, itself requiring a larger orchestra than most operas – *Das Rheingold* demands, in addition to the extra horns, an extra flautist, oboist, clarinettist and trumpeter, larger numbers of string players than normal to balance the extra wind, not to mention additional percussionists and seven harpists whose roles become clear later in the piece. Of course, Wagner is not alone among his contemporaries in writing for a greatly expanded orchestra – Berlioz is another obvious example – but his willingness to conceive *The Ring* for such a large ensemble at a time when there is no prospect of its performance is evidence of his confidence, if this were needed.

The vision of Valhalla that Wagner's orchestra conjures up is one of purity (in its careful blend of brass timbres), dignity (in its stately tempo), eternity (in the seemingly endless way that the theme ripples on): these are qualities that Wotan dreams that the fortress will symbolise, as it embodies the gods' untroubled domination of the world. As Wotan is first revealed at dawn – after an initial scene whose opening seems to stretch back to the beginning of time, the remainder of *Das Rheingold*'s action takes place between dawn and dusk on a single day – the dream seems a reality. Half-awake, he rejoices in his fortress and his own wisdom in building it, his voice sounding like an addition to the brass choir: musically as well as in his words, Wotan is at one with his surroundings.

Before long, however, the mismatch between Wotan's vision for his fortress and the shortcomings of the gods who will occupy it becomes apparent. Influenced by Feuerbach's critique of mankind's religious instincts and mindful of the downfall of the gods to which *The Ring* – as he has decided by 1853 – will lead, Wagner seeks through his music not to celebrate their divinity but to expose their shortcomings and reveal them as fallibly human. The music he assigns them exposes their individual foibles, even if they have only a few lines to sing.

Wagner casts Fricka as Wotan's principal antagonist, outraged by his actions whether as head of the family or as husband. Why is he perpetually unfaithful to her? Why does he continually wander the world rather than attending to duties at home? Why has he sacrificed his family's well-being by offering Freia to the giants in return for Valhalla? Given the strains on Wagner's marriage by this point, it is easy to interpret his portrayal of Wotan and Fricka's troubled union as autobiographical. Much of Fricka's music is lightly accompanied recitative, emphasising the interrogative tone of her discourse: only when she sings of ideals of home and fidelity is there a brief melodic flowering.

The entry of Freia (represented here as Fricka's sister; in the Eddas they are unrelated) is announced by the most emotionally charged orchestral writing so far. She is the only character in *Das Rheingold* for whom anyone expresses affection: Wagner's portrayal of her was influenced by the fifteen-year-old Marie zu Sayn-Wittgenstein, who captivated him when she and her mother Princess Carolyne, Liszt's long-term partner, unexpectedly decided to join the two composers on their trip to Paris. Donner and Froh are also represented here as siblings of Freia and Fricka, heightening the sense that these are really human beings in mythical form, rather than divinities we are intended to admire or worship. The brash Froh, a *Heldentenor* role in miniature, is accompanied by impressive but vapid brass fanfares; Donner's singing is punctuated by accented orchestral interjections that reveal his violent intentions.

The objects of Donner's aggression are the giants, Fasolt and Fafner, whom he wishes to kill to prevent them from taking away his sister. The giants' signature motif is perhaps the crudest music Wagner ever wrote, lumberingly constructed from the simplest elements, but he carefully distinguishes their vocal lines, keeping Fafner's gruff and unadorned while allotting Fasolt music of surprising, almost Puccinian lyricism. Donner is prevented from killing the giants by Wotan, who acknowledges the contract he has made with them. This is inscribed on the spear that Wagner represents with a distinctive descending figure in the orchestra. Given how important a role the spear plays in the rest of the cycle, it is a surprisingly late invention, one that does not feature even in the lengthy prose draft of *Das Rheingold* that Wagner made in March 1852.

The only figure who seems able to resolve the impasse is Loge, whose timely first appearance is accompanied by extraordinary music which flickers around numerous different keys without ever settling, as if to dissolve the harmonic stability of both Valhalla and the giants. Even Wotan mistrusts Loge, and the other gods despise him, but his proposal to free Freia by giving the giants the gold that Alberich has stolen from the Rhinemaidens offers the only solution to their dilemma. The weakness of the gods' position is soon made musically palpable in the passage that follows the giants' temporary removal of Freia. Harmonic changes are stretched out, melodies appear to retreat into the distance, the pulse of the music seems to drop almost to a standstill: Wagner vividly depicts the rapid descent into old age that is the inevitable consequence for the gods of the withdrawal of the golden apples that only Freia knows how to tend. This sudden stretching of our perception of time is all the more striking in the context of a drama that generally moves so fast. Only Loge, as a mere demigod, remains unaffected, and it is his characteristically whirling music that leads Wotan on to Nibelheim, the realm ruled by Alberich with the help of his newly acquired gold.

* * *

Geographically and musically, Nibelheim is the antithesis of Valhalla. If Wagner mentally locates Valhalla in Switzerland, he will find his real-life equivalent of Nibelheim in 1877 when he visits London for the third time: 'This is Alberich's dream come true,' he tells Cosima. 'Nibelheim, world dominion, activity, work, everywhere the oppressive feeling of steam and fog.' He finds a sound for Nibelheim no less original than his depictions of the Rhine and Valhalla. As Wotan and Loge descend through a crevice, sulphurous mists rising around them, a persistent dotted rhythm in triple time gradually emerges to pervade the entire orchestra. At the climax of the interlude, Wagner calls for eighteen anvils – nine smaller, six big, and three bigger still – to play behind the stage and literally hammer out the rhythm. Their sound is unlike anything that has ever been heard before: these lumps of metal do not produce the consistent series of overtones that a normal musical instrument generates, so the effect is cacophonous and overwhelming. With a single musical gesture, Wagner conveys the monotony of the Nibelungs' existence, their enforced activity in extracting treasure from the earth, and the violence to which they are subjected.

Both the rhythm and the timbres of the interlude seep into the ensuing scene, and the impression of darkness is heightened by the exclusive use of male voices: two tenors and two bass-baritones. From the restricted palette of orchestral colours that Wagner uses for this scene – quite distinct from those with which he paints the fast-flowing river of scene 1 and the heady mountain peaks of scene 2 – he achieves some spectacular effects. Every reference to the magical Tarnhelm, the helmet that enables its wearer to become invisible (a property found in the composer's literary sources) or to assume the appearance of another person or creature (a property invented by Wagner for purposes that become clear in *Götterdämmerung*), is accompanied by a sequence of otherworldly chords played by four muted French horns that create the sensation of time being stopped in its tracks. The knockabout comedy of Alberich's boastful deployment of the Tarnhelm, too, is vividly represented in the orchestra, with the fearsome serpent and the tiny toad into which he transforms himself represented by trios of snarling tubas and whimpering clarinets respectively. Whether by supervising the invention of new instruments or by combining familiar instruments in new ways, Wagner determines to make every moment of his new drama sound like nothing that has ever been heard before.

* * *

Wagner becomes Royal Saxon Kapellmeister in Dresden in 1843, soon after E. B. Kietz draws this portrait, one of the earliest surviving images of him. Dresden has been a renowned centre for opera since Carl Maria von Weber's time as Kapellmeister (1816–26); the opening in 1841 of Gottfried Semper's magnificent Court Theatre, the first of two Semper opera houses on this site, brings fresh lustre to the city's musical life.

Wagner's involvement in the unsuccessful 1849 Dresden uprising forces him to flee Germany and relinquish his position. As an exile in Zurich, he is financially dependent on patrons such as Otto Wesendonck – with whose wife, Mathilde, Wagner falls in love. The ensuing scandal causes him to abandon Zurich in 1858; six years later the newly crowned King Ludwig II of Bavaria starts to support him in lavish style.

Josef Hoffmann's *Ring* designs, such as this oil sketch for the end of *Das Rheingold*, are beautifully painted, but impractical as a blueprint for scenery. Carl Emil Doepler's costumes – including these for Wotan and Waltraute – draw on meticulous research and influence producers for generations to come, but fail to satisfy Wagner.

The Bayreuth Festspielhaus opens in 1876, four years after Wagner lays the foundation stone. Both its brick exterior and the austere auditorium contrast sharply with the ornate opera houses of the day; the pit is revolutionary, its wide curved cover and steeply descending rows of seats ensuring that the orchestra never overpowers the singers.

Cosima Wagner, the composer's second wife, gives birth to the couple's only son, Siegfried, on 6 June 1869. After Wagner's death in 1883, Cosima and Siegfried assume joint responsibility for the Bayreuth Festival, but their determination to replicate every detail of Wagner's original productions ultimately proves stultifying. In New York, meanwhile, *The Ring*'s US premiere in 1889 cements the fast-growing reputation of the city's newly built Metropolitan Opera House.

After the deaths of Cosima and Siegfried in 1930, Siegfried's widow, Winifred – pictured in 1938 with Adolf Hitler and Josef Goebbels – directs the festival until 1944; when it reopens in 1951, her Nazi links debar her from active involvement. Her son Wieland seeks to rehabilitate Bayreuth with a *Ring* that eliminates any hint of German nationalism: with uncluttered sets, simple costumes and (from 1953) a sloping disc that hosts most of the action, he underlines instead the cycle's affinity to Greek tragedy.

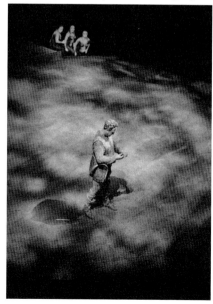

In 1976, an all-French team led by director Patrice Chéreau and conductor Pierre Boulez produces a new Bayreuth *Ring* marking the centenary of the first production. Chéreau interprets the cycle as a story about nineteenth-century industrialisation; designer Richard Peduzzi develops this theme by filling the sets with machinery, such as the hydroelectric dam from which the Rhinemaidens emerge in *Das Rheingold* and the mechanical anvil that forges Nothung's fragments back into a sword in *Siegfried*.

A grand piano features centre-stage throughout Stefan Herheim's 2021/22 production for the Deutsche Oper Berlin: often characters sit at it – or on it, as Loge does during scene 4 of *Das Rheingold* – when they try to take control of the story. Other recurring design motifs include sheets, suitcases and scores: at the end of *Siegfried*, Brünnhilde consults a score for guidance before joyfully casting it aside.

Despite the massive scale on which he is working and the numerous innovations he introduces, Wagner in one sense keeps things relatively simple during the first three scenes of *Das Rheingold*. Their sound-worlds could scarcely be more different, but they follow a similar dramatic trajectory. Wagner sets each of them in a different and strongly characterised realm (the Rhine, the mountaintops beneath Valhalla, Nibelheim), dominated by a different element (water, air, earth). Each of these realms receives an unwelcome intrusion (from Alberich, from the giants, from Wotan and Loge), and each of the intruders removes things or people that are highly prized in the realm concerned (gold, Freia, Alberich).

In the final scene – the drama's longest – Wagner sets himself new challenges. Although its physical location at the foot of Valhalla is the same as that of scene 2, its dramatic and musical landscapes are more complex and ambiguous. There are several different strands of action bringing together almost all the characters we have seen so far and introducing an important new one in Erda. Like Alberich, the gods, the giants and the Rhinemaidens, all of whose voices and distinctive musical identities are heard in this final scene, Erda offers her views on what should happen to the gold that gives the drama its title – or more specifically, to the ring that Alberich has forged from it. The motivations of at least some of these characters are ambiguous and questionable, and the resolution of the power struggle between them is less clear-cut than any of them might wish. Wagner's self-appointed task in this final scene is to convey the ambivalence that exists both within his characters and in the uneasy relationships between them, while also giving his drama a musically satisfying ending.

He begins the scene by staging a confrontation between Wotan and Alberich, the leaders of their respective realms. Though the power balance between them at this point is ostensibly all in Wotan's favour, the similarities between their positions and characters are revealed by their voice-types (both are described in the score as bass-baritones) and highlighted by the contrasting tenor interjections of Loge. Alberich's guilt is clear – he admits that he stole the gold – but Wotan is no less morally compromised: he argues that the gold belongs to the Rhinemaidens while concealing that he has no intention of returning it to them, and even as he seizes the ring by force he asserts his status as ruler of the gods (an orchestral rendition of the 'spear' motif at this point is an ironic reminder of his role as guarantor of the law). Wagner's new-found flexibility in his setting of text mirrors this moral ambivalence: he does not close off characters' speeches with decisive musical cadences as in traditional 'number' opera, but allows each character's remarks to meld harmonically into the responses of his alter ego, revealing their interdependence and the shaky basis on which their assertions are founded. At points in this episode Wagner sets the dialogue with a speed and plainness that brings it close to recitative, but he adjusts the pace of the setting and the weight of orchestral accompaniment at the approach of each key moment – Wotan's theft of the ring, the curse of destruction that Alberich places on anyone who owns it – to ensure that its significance is made clear. 'Endless melody' – the memorable if somewhat confusing phrase Wagner coins in *Music of the Future* (1860) to describe his new approach – is more diverse and more capable of articulating musical contrasts than the composer's detractors like to imply.

Wotan is not allowed to gloat over his acquisition of the ring for long: the giants demand it as the final tranche of their payment for the release of Freia, while Loge also reminds Wotan of his own promise to return it to the Rhinemaidens. Wotan refuses to surrender the ring, and the story is at an impasse. Wagner breaks it with the introduction of unison trombones and tremolo double basses – characteristically, and contrary to his reputation for orchestral extravagance, achieving maximum dramatic effect with minimal instrumental resources. The Wagner tubas play a subdued, minor-key version of the principal melody from the drama's Prelude. This version may in fact have occurred to Wagner first – the evidence from his sketchbooks is a little ambiguous – but regardless of the order in which they were conceived, by presenting the melody in these two distinct but obviously connected versions, Wagner makes clear the deep kinship between the Rhine, the Rhinemaidens, Erda – who is about to appear – and her three daughters, the Norns of whom she sings.

Like the Rhinemaidens, Erda is a figure largely of Wagner's own invention, an all-knowing earth goddess whose characterisation owes as much to the Greek goddess Gaia as to her Nordic equivalents. By introducing her at this point, Wagner darkens the atmosphere and recalibrates the pace not only of *Das Rheingold* but also of *The Ring* as a whole: hers is the first of the slow, reflective monologues that will henceforth play such an important part in the cycle. Wotan's unthinking determination to hold on to the ring cannot survive Erda's warning that he should give it up, and his attitude to what must happen next changes permanently as a result.

Following Erda's recommendation, and urged on by the other gods, he adds the ring to the pile of gold with which he pays the giants. Freia returns to the embrace of her family while the giants squabble over the gold, and then over the ring. Fafner clubs his brother to death; Wotan is horrified at this immediate demonstration of the power of Alberich's curse. He realises that Valhalla is compromised by the nature of the payment he has made for it: his instinct is to find Erda and ask for more advice, but Fricka persuades him to stay and enjoy the fortress he has caused to be built. *Das Rheingold* is approaching its close – Freia and her golden apples have returned, Alberich has been dispatched to Nibelheim, the giants have been paid, Erda has returned to sleep, the Rhinemaidens' claims have been ignored, and the gods, Loge's caustic comments notwithstanding, are free to enjoy their new home. But *The Ring* is only just beginning, and both Wotan and Loge are well aware of the instability of their position, even if they respond to it in different ways: Loge by vanishing and Wotan by taking up residence in Valhalla.

Wagner's challenge in setting this ending is to convey these contradictory states – the closure of the gods' entry into Valhalla and the open-ended nature of the story that will continue; the magnificence of the gods' home and the instability created by the compromises that have enabled it to be built – in music that matches the scale and grandeur of everything he has composed so far.

He achieves this by enabling two musical narratives to unfold at the same time. In the foreground, each of the male gods in succession embarks on his grandest peroration of the evening. Donner summons into being a thunderstorm from which emerges a rainbow bridge that leads to Valhalla. Donner and Froh vanish then reappear in the clouds – Wagner draws here on a memory of his first ascent of Mount Rigi in August 1850, during which he experienced the 'Rigi ghost', a meteorological phenomenon that allows observers to see an image of their own movements in the sky. In a final touch of orchestral profligacy, Wagner summons six harps to add their glittering sound to the musical vision: in 1875, shortly before the Bayreuth premiere, he will ask the Budapest-based virtuoso harpist Peter Dubez to help him ensure that their parts are effectively arranged. Froh invites the other gods to follow him across the bridge, then Wotan sings an encomium to his fortress, naming it as Valhalla and asking Fricka to take up her rightful position there as his consort. Through each of these speeches, the harmony and instrumentation hardly change, creating an impression of stability that is partly illusory: for all its resplendence, the orchestral sound is almost literally without foundations, so sparing is Wagner's use of the double basses and the cellos' lower register.

Alongside this narrative of harmonic and political stability, Wagner tells a second and more troubling story. Loge's rejoinder to Wotan's boasting, in which he expresses his disgust with the gods and foretells their downfall, is accompanied by the disconcerting flickering music that embodies his subversive role in the story; each of the Rhinemaidens' off-stage laments is introduced by a sudden lurch into a new key. The second and final ensemble eventually resolves in the 'Valhalla' key of D flat major, dissolving into the closing orchestral peroration. But by placing the disruptive music of Loge and the Rhinemaidens so close to the end of the drama, Wagner manages to make the ending feel musically stable and unstable at the same time, perfectly mirroring the gods' ambivalent position as they enter their new stronghold.

He perhaps surprises even himself by the success of his return to composition after the five-year lay-off. On 15 February 1854, only three and a half months after beginning the first outline draft, he begins to make his fair copy in ink of the full score, though he does not complete it until 26 September. (Unfortunately it no longer survives: it was presented to Adolf Hitler in 1939 as a fiftieth-birthday present by the German Chamber of Industry and Commerce but was lost in the aftermath of the Führer's death.) Wagner's relatively slow progress – in comparison to the lightning pace of the previous stages of work – is explained partly by his rather unrealistic hopes that someone else might be commissioned to transcribe the final version for him, but more pertinently by the fact that he is at this stage well under way with drafting *Die Walküre*. *Das Rheingold* has essentially been completed at a speed astonishing for any opera, but barely believable for one as complex and original as this. Wagner must be satisfied with his rate of progress, but he is probably even more pleased by the way in which words and music are fusing in his new work to form an indissoluble unity in his mind – just the outcome he fervently anticipated during the long years of drafting libretti and publishing theoretical treatises. As he tells August Röckel in a letter from 25/6 January 1854, 'the work's meaning . . . is only made clear by the music: I can now no longer bear to look at the poem without the music.'

Die Walküre

Z URICH, 8 JUNE 1854. Wagner writes to Liszt to explain why he has not yet sent him the full score of *Das Rheingold*. 'At present I have no time for it. I must begin the composition of the *Valkyrie*, which I feel joyfully in every limb.' His work will be aided, he tells his friend, by a recent gift from Mathilde Wesendonck: an American-manufactured gold pen 'of indestructible power', which he will use for decades to come.

As he begins his sketches for *Die Walküre* – the earliest is dated 28 June – the donor of the pen with which he writes them is constantly in his mind. Four years later – writing from Geneva, after a crisis that has precipitated both his departure from Zurich and the effective end of his marriage – he will confide to his sister Clara Wolfram that the only thing that enabled him to remain with Minna so long was 'the love of that young woman whose initial response to me was one of diffidence, doubt, hesitation and shyness, but who later approached me with increasing certainty and self-confidence'. Mathilde, fifteen years younger than Wagner (and nineteen years younger than Minna), is not only beautiful, but also musically sensitive and highly intelligent: in later life she will become a prolific poet and playwright. She seems – after Wagner's death Cosima orders the destruction of most of her letters to him, so it is impossible to be certain – to be as enraptured by Wagner as he is by her. But as Wagner tells his sister, 'since there could never be any question of union between us, our deep and mutual affection assumed that sadly melancholic character that banishes all vulgarity and baseness, and recognizes the source of all joy in the other's well-being.'

Later in 1854, Wagner starts to plan a new drama, *Tristan und Isolde*, whose story more precisely plays out his interpretation of his relationship with Mathilde – two souls whose perfect union is doomed to remain unconsummated – while also embodying his new-found interest in Schopenhauer's philosophy of renunciation. But for now, he is committed to setting the story of another love triangle that he cannot fail to identify with his own situation. Although he drafted the prose sketch of *Die Walküre* in late 1851, just a few weeks before meeting the Wesendoncks, its first act, at least, uncannily reflects the dilemma in which he now finds himself, drawn irresistibly towards a woman on whose husband he is dependent, temporarily at least: Siegmund's position as a guest in Hunding's hut parallels Wagner's reliance on the financial support of Otto Wesendonck. However, Act I of *Die Walküre* will have a very different ending from Wagner's own domestic drama, with Siegmund and Sieglinde ecstatically coupling as the curtain rapidly falls. The composition draft of Act I that Wagner presents to Mathilde contains numerous coded allusions to his own feelings: for example, 'I.l.d.g.!!' (perhaps meaning 'Ich liebe dich grenzenlos'; 'I love you boundlessly'), and 'W.d.n.w., G.!!!' ('Wenn du nicht wärst, Geliebte'; '[What would I do] if you were not [here], beloved?'). These annotations surely suggest Wagner's unusually heightened emotional state as he sketches his latest music with Mathilde's golden pen.

As he embarks on his work, Wagner remarks to Liszt – as if surprised by the phenomenon himself – on 'how curious these contrasts are – I mean, between the first love scene of the *Valkyrie* and . . . the *Rhinegold*'. Some of the contrasts are inherent in the subject-matter he has already chosen: from his expansive story of gods, dwarves and giants, unfolding in widely contrasting and vividly imagined settings, Wagner moves to a tale of three apparently mortal beings – admittedly, two of them soon turn out to be Wotan's own children – claustrophobically confined to a single room. He initially considers allowing Wotan to make an appearance in person in Hunding's hut, making the connection between the two stories more obvious, but rejects this idea in favour of an exclusive focus on the three human characters, albeit with evidence of Wotan's prior visit to the hut soon made apparent.

Other contrasts are less predictable, and are perhaps partly explained by Wagner's state of mind when composing. After a Prelude that vividly conjures up the storm that drives Siegmund to seek refuge – and parallels the equivalent section of *Das Rheingold* by sounding a single pitch, this time D, through much of its duration – Wagner proceeds to depict the tentative first exchanges between the separated siblings with music more tender and delicate than any he has previously composed. Quiet dynamics and string sonorities dominate, creating the sense of chamber music. A telling example occurs very early on: as Siegmund drinks from the horn Sieglinde offers him, he is accompanied only by a solo cello, but as his glance falls upon his hostess, Wagner divides the cello section into five separate parts, with the two principal double bassists adding a sixth. This sudden proliferation of a single sonority into multiple lines creates an effect that is both expressive and intimate, as though offering access to characters' innermost thoughts. This is one of many instances in this first act where Wagner either divides a single string line into several parts, or else instructs only a limited number of members of the section to play. Always meticulous in his scoring, here he uses the palette of instrumental sounds at his disposal with more sensitivity and precision than ever before. His frequent use in the act's first minutes of 'grace-notes' – miniature flourishes that precede the main note of the melody – further enhances this impression.

As the act proceeds, Wagner's music traces in minute detail not only the limited number of external events but also the gradual development of the Volsung twins' inward understanding of each other, and their mutual progression from diffidence to boldness. If the seams between sections are occasionally obvious in *Das Rheingold*, here the music grows in almost organic fashion. Wagner had written to Röckel a few months previously of his pleasure that the earlier drama had 'become a close-knit unity: there is scarcely a bar in the orchestra which does not develop out of preceding motifs' – but the comment is even more applicable to *Die Walküre*. Even the one section of the first act that could be described as (and is often extracted in recitals as if it were) an 'aria' – 'Winterstürme', Siegmund's encomium to the magical effects of spring's arrival – does not emerge from nowhere: Wagner prepares the ground for this melodic flowering through the passages that precede it and in the music that accompanies the unexplained opening of the door to the hut. And he writes much less music in *Die Walküre* than in *Das Rheingold* that could be described as 'recitative': here his setting of lengthy passages of narration – such as Sieglinde's account of Wotan's appearance at her wedding to Hunding – invariably lives up to his own ideal of 'speech melody', with every implication of the text matched with an appropriate inflection in the music.

Wagner tells much of the first act's story, though, without using any words at all. The arrival of the exhausted Siegmund at Hunding's hut; his acceptance of a drink from Sieglinde; Hunding's displeasure at seeing the stranger at his hearth; the positioning of the three characters at the table for the discussion that will confirm Hunding's identification of Siegmund as an enemy – Wagner conveys such moments with music written for the orchestra alone, but with detailed stage directions accompanying almost every bar of the score. The singers' silence at these and other crucial junctures speaks eloquently of the affinities and antagonisms that lie between them; meanwhile the music Wagner gives to the orchestra registers every nuance of the situation while also suggesting the pace and quality of the characters' movements. The longest and most elaborate of these 'pantomimes' – in the original meaning of that word: telling a story solely through gesture, accompanied by music – is the passage at the end of scene 2 in which Sieglinde adds ingredients to her husband's customary bedtime drink that will ensure he sleeps heavily, and indicates to Siegmund using only her eyes the location of the sword that Wotan placed in the tree for his benefit. By scoring these three crucial minutes for orchestra alone, Wagner expresses confidence not only in the acting skills of his future singers, but also in his own ability to convey precise meaning through the gradual evolution of musical motifs, without the help of words.

Rather like Mathilde Wesendonck – if Wagner's account to his sister is to be believed – Siegmund and Sieglinde initially behave with 'diffidence, doubt, hesitation and shyness', then 'with increasing certainty and self-confidence', as they recognise themselves both as lovers and as siblings. Wagner's setting of his libretto charts this trajectory with such unerring pacing that the extraordinarily erotic climax to the first act seems as inevitable as it is exhilarating. The way in which Wagner handles the metamorphosis of his themes is crucial to this effect. Just as the Volsung hero discovers his true name only during the course of the act – he refers to himself earlier on as 'Wehwalt' and 'Wölfing' while regretting that he cannot call himself 'Friedmund' or 'Frohwalt', before joyfully accepting the name 'Siegmund' from his sister – so musical motifs

develop from amorphous beginnings into a triumphantly definitive form. For example, when Sieglinde sings 'Du bist der Lenz'
(You are the spring), and Siegmund a few moments later sings 'Du
bist das Bild' (You are the image [that I keep inside me]), they do
so to a theme that Wagner has used in various ways since the start
of the act (it derives from the melody with which Freia pours out
her feelings in *Das Rheingold*), but whose full significance is only
now revealed. By the time it rings out twice in the orchestra in the
act's brief postlude, following Siegmund's exultant panegyric to
'Volsung blood', no words are necessary.

* * *

Of course, there are many moments in *Die Walküre*, as in the rest
of *The Ring*, at which Wagner's intention to use a musical theme
to convey a non-musical meaning – to represent an object, person
or idea of recurring importance to the story – seems obvious from
the outset, even if the audience's understanding of that meaning
changes during the course of the cycle. Wagner is much less keen
on the term 'leitmotif' – literally, a 'leading motif' – than his acolytes will turn out to be: he uses it only once in his own writings,
and then only to complain that 'one of my younger friends [. . .]
has viewed the characteristics of what he calls my "leitmotive"
rather in the light of their dramatic significance, than in that of
their bearing on musical construction.'

This 'younger friend' is probably Hans von Wolzogen, the first
and most egregious of the leitmotif-hunters to pore over the score
of *The Ring*. Wolzogen's *Thematic Guide to the Music of Richard
Wagner's 'The Ring of the Nibelungen'* is first published in 1876,
the year of the cycle's Bayreuth premiere. Though he is not the
first to use the term 'leitmotif', he popularises it by identifying no
fewer than ninety such themes used by Wagner over the course

of the cycle. Though Wagner scarcely disowns Wolzogen – he invites him to move to Bayreuth the year after his book is published, to begin editing *Bayreuther Blätter*, a new journal that will be devoted to his own work – nor does he endorse his analysis of *The Ring*. He probably realises that Wolzogen's dogged efforts to attach names to each of the leitmotifs will offer ammunition to those who seek to reduce his new methods to an elaborate system of musical labels; and to critics such as Debussy, who wittily but unfairly accuses Wagner of giving each of his characters a musical 'visiting card': 'they never appear unless accompanied by their damnable leitmotif, and there are even those who sing it!'

Wagner is right to distance himself from the names that Wolzogen attaches to his themes – they are generally reductive at best, misleading at worst – but despite the overuse of the word 'leitmotif' by Wagner's advocates and detractors alike, the concept it embodies is inescapable in any discussion of *The Ring*. Whatever the composer's subsequent protestations, there are numerous occasions on which he *does* use leitmotifs – or whatever we choose to call them: Wagner at different points referred to 'melodic moments' and 'basic motifs' – for 'dramatic import and effect', not only as 'elements of the musical structure'.

The most obvious way in which Wagner uses leitmotifs is to convey information which he wishes the audience to know, but which cannot be sung by the characters because they themselves are not consciously aware of it. An apparently straightforward example of this occurs in Act I, scene 2 of *Die Walküre*, when Siegmund tells Sieglinde and Hunding that he has not seen his father, whom he knew as Wolfe, since they were separated in a fierce battle. All he could retrieve from his search was a wolf-skin left at their home in the woods: 'my father found I not'. Over the word 'nicht' (not), a quartet of trombones very quietly plays the first two bars of the stately theme associated in *Das Rheingold* with Valhalla, Wotan's fortress. Wagner does not use it again in *Die Walküre* for another twenty minutes, when he instructs horns, bassoons and trombones to play a rather more extended version of it, rather less quietly, as Sieglinde tells Siegmund about the 'old man dressed in grey' who appeared at her wedding. A couple of minutes later, her story moves on to the sword that the mysterious visitor placed in the tree, which the other guests tried in vain to dislodge. 'Dort haftet schweigend das Schwert' (There the sword stays silently): over the word 'Schwert' (sword), Wagner sets yet another version of the 'Valhalla' theme. Though he now significantly changes both the melodic outline and the instrumentation (strings predominate in this latest rendition), he relies on the theme's familiarity both from its very recent appearance and from its extensive use in the previous evening's drama to equip listeners to identify it. While it is played, Sieglinde sings that she now knows who her visitor was, and for whom he left the sword.

Through his careful placement of this sequence of thematic reprises, Wagner suggests to his audiences two ideas that are not overtly contained in the text: Wolfe, Siegmund's father, is actually Wotan; Wotan is also the visitor who placed the sword in the tree at Sieglinde's wedding. By combining the theme with the words Sieglinde sings, Wagner also hints that Wotan is Sieglinde's father (would she know who he was if he were anyone else?), that Sieglinde and Siegmund are therefore siblings, and that Siegmund is the intended recipient of the sword. Just as importantly, and again without making it overt in the text, he shows the connection between the two dramas he has thus far presented – something that might reasonably have eluded an audience member surprised to find the previous evening's assembly of gods displaced on the stage by three mortals in a hut. Of course, all these connections can only be made by a listener prepared to associate the 'Valhalla' theme with Wotan himself, rather than the fortress with which it was invariably connected in *Das Rheingold*. This is a theoretical problem for those who, following Wolzogen, insist on each motif having a single, precise label, but it is not a problem in practice. Wotan's self-identification with his creation makes it an easy imaginative leap to link the motif with the god himself.

At other points in *Die Walküre*, Wagner reprises themes from *Das Rheingold* in ways that are harder to explain. The most extensively discussed case occurs at the end of Act I, where Siegmund grasps the sword his father has left for him while singing the tune to which Alberich renounced love in the opening drama's first scene. On the face of it, the juxtaposition is absurd: Alberich denied love, Siegmund runs headlong towards it, as both his actions and his words ('Holiest love . . . yearning desire') make clear. Ingenious theories are frequently advanced to explain Wagner's apparently surprising choice of theme at this point. But as with the Valhalla/Wotan theme, the problem is solved by embracing a more liberal understanding of what the motif might 'mean', one less pedantically tied to what it seemed to represent at its first appearance. Wagner himself never specified that the theme first sung by Alberich itself represented 'the renunciation of love'. It can be interpreted simply as connected with the idea of love: a force that is sometimes rejected, sometimes denied, and one that would reasonably be uppermost in Alberich's mind as he made his fateful decision. This makes Siegmund's use of this theme at this crucial moment of his own life entirely logical.

By invoking the 'Valhalla' and 'Alberich' themes from *Das Rheingold* in Act I of *Die Walküre*, Wagner not only supplies information and deepens the emotional resonance of key moments, he also binds together two stories that could easily seem disparate in a much more powerful way than could be achieved by text alone. Needless to say, though, he does not normally restrict himself to recalling one motif at a time. As *Die Walküre* continues, Wagner increasingly juxtaposes and combines multiple themes, creating scenes of extraordinary richness – such as Act II, scene 2, in which Wotan reveals his deepest feelings to Brünnhilde, the beloved Valkyrie daughter he has fathered with Erda.

Wagner did not originally intend this scene to be so long or complex. The first prose draft for *Die Walküre*, probably from October 1851, indicates simply that Wotan should reveal his distress at having to ensure Hunding's victory in the impending battle with Siegmund, and that he should command the reluctant Brünnhilde to carry out his wishes. By the time of the final prose draft in May 1852, however, the emphasis of the scene has moved towards narration of past events, recounted by Wotan to Brünnhilde to explain his state of mind: alongside much of the plot of *Das Rheingold*, there are further stories from both earlier (what compelled Wotan to make his fateful contract with the giants) and later (why he fathered Brünnhilde with Erda; how Alberich, too, has fathered a child by a mortal woman). This accumulation of narrative makes this scene a pivotal moment not just in *Die Walküre* but within the entire *Ring*. It is both the fullest account Wotan ever gives of his state of mind, and the first occasion on which he reveals his ardent desire for 'das Ende': for death, and the destruction of all he has ever striven to create.

Wagner writes music both for the start of scene 2 and for the start of the long narration from Wotan that lies at its heart that is almost shockingly bare, as if to suggest that the events the god will recount predate not only the start of *The Ring* but the beginnings of music itself. Characters sing in plain recitative, accompanied only by long-sustained single notes from bass instruments.

A questioning figure from the cellos, beginning with a distinctive flourish of grace-notes, punctuates the discourse: this motif has already been much used in the previous scene, in association with Wotan's growing realisation of the limits of his power. Fragments of melody – those associated in *Das Rheingold* with the Rhinemaidens, with Alberich's ring, with Valhalla and with Erda – briefly surface as Wotan's narrative gathers pace and he passes their places in the story.

As the narration continues, Wagner uses previously heard material with ever greater frequency, allowing motifs to morph into one another rather than preserving their distinct identity. Themes such as those associated with Erda, with Alberich's curse and with the ring itself are extended, distorted and combined, paralleling Wotan's attempts to convey the consequences of what he has learned for his own destiny. In this scene, Wagner demonstrates for the first time the sophistication, both musical and psychological, of which his system of leitmotifs is capable. His themes are far more than aural signposts pointing back to previous events or non-verbal means of conveying information to the audience, though both those functions remain important throughout the cycle. Here they stop being the tools of an omniscient narrator and start to become a means through which a character himself expresses his deepest feelings, adding immeasurably to what can be conveyed in words. Wotan himself has seized control of the narrative, even as he realises his inability to keep control of the world.

* * *

Perhaps even Wagner himself is surprised by the way in which his system of leitmotifs evolves as he composes. *Opera and Drama* sets out his intention to use 'reminiscence motifs', a technique used since the late eighteenth century (operas by Mozart, Méhul and Grétry contain interesting examples) to remind listeners of important characters or ideas from earlier in a work. Wagner (the theoretician of 1851) anticipates that his own dramas will contain many more such motifs than these earlier operas, and that they will play a more integral role in the musical substance of the work, but he expects that they will always first appear in the melodies that characters sing, only then passing into the orchestra. Wagner (the composer of 1853 onwards) proceeds rather differently: some of his most important themes initially appear in the orchestra, and refer to objects or characters that have not yet appeared on stage, or in some cases have not even been mentioned. These are motifs not of reminiscence but of anticipation.

Towards the end of his peroration at the end of *Das Rheingold*, after welcoming the shelter that Valhalla offers from the approaching night, Wotan briefly stops singing; string tremolos sound a perfect cadence in C major, twisting round from the flat keys used for the rest of the final section of the piece; Wagner indicates in the stage directions that Wotan is 'firmly seized' by a 'great idea'; a fanfare-like theme, with a falling octave followed by a gradual ascent through the C major triad, rings out on a solo trumpet. He places nothing else in either the text or the original stage directions of *Das Rheingold* to indicate what Wotan's 'great idea' might be or what this striking new melody might signify (though Cosima's diaries indicate that during the rehearsals for the Bayreuth premiere Wagner changes his mind and decides that Wotan should brandish a sword discarded from the hoard by Fafner, to make the point clearer).

It is only in Act I of *Die Walküre*, in the passage where the eyes of the silent Sieglinde direct Siegmund to look at the tree where the sword has been placed, that the theme appears again – plaintive renditions on bass trumpet, oboe and cor anglais, drifting towards a minor key. Without a word being sung, the nature of Wotan's inspiration becomes clear: he will father a family of heroes who can regain the ring from Fafner, and will equip them with a sword capable of fighting off all enemies. From this tentative re-emergence in the dumb show, the 'sword' motif increasingly pervades the orchestra for the rest of Die Walküre's first act, blaring out triumphantly in C major from three trumpets as Siegmund pulls the sword he now calls 'Nothung' from the tree. Power passes from Wotan to the Volsung not through words but through music.

By restricting himself in Das Rheingold to a brief, wordless anticipation of Nothung, Wagner plants a reference that can only be understood in retrospect, or on repeated hearings of the music. By contrast, he introduces the stirring motif associated with Siegfried on several occasions in the final act of Die Walküre, almost always in association with words that explain what it means. This is a message that no audience member will miss, even on a first encounter with the drama. Wagner reveals the theme for the first time towards the end of the Ride of the Valkyries scene, as Brünnhilde flees the wrath of Wotan with the pregnant Sieglinde, anxious to ensure that she escapes with the shattered fragments of Nothung so that she can pass them on to her unborn son. Brünnhilde tells Sieglinde that this child will grow up to be the greatest hero in the world, and Wagner places the two rising intervals (of a minor third and a minor sixth) that make the melody instantly memorable on two key words – 'Helden' (hero) and 'Welt' (world). A few bars later, Wagner assigns the same intervals to the words 'Schwert' (sword) and 'schwingt' (swings), embedding the association between the future hero and the weapon he will wield, just before Brünnhilde announces that his name will be Siegfried. By presenting the theme in combination with these words on its first appearances, and by reprising it at several points during the remainder of the act, Wagner makes certain that Siegfried's place in the drama that is to follow is clear. When Wotan sings the same melody as he declares, in the drama's final words, that only a hero unafraid of his spear can rescue the sleeping Brünnhilde from the flames with which he has asked Loge to surround her, no listener will misinterpret who he means – though Wagner gives a final rendition of the theme to the orchestra just to be sure.

If Wagner underlines the importance of the 'Siegfried' theme to the drama from its first appearance onwards, then he takes longer – much longer – to reveal the significance of the melody that Sieglinde sings in immediate response to Brünnhilde's revelation about her child's identity: 'O hehrstes Wunder! Herrliche Maid!' (Oh noblest wonder! Radiant maid!). Wagner sets Sieglinde's outpouring of gratitude for the love that Brünnhilde has shown for her and her child to an ecstatic strand of melody lying towards the top of the singer's range, then after a mere eight bars moves on. He will not use this theme again until the end of *Götterdämmerung*: according to a letter written by Cosima, he intends it to represent the 'glorification of Brünnhilde', making it one of relatively few themes in *The Ring* for which Wagner seems to have committed himself to a definite meaning explicable in words. His decision to abandon such a promising melody so abruptly in *Die Walküre*, saving the opportunity to develop it for a moment that will come only some nine hours of music and eighteen years of work later, is an indication of his level of confidence – staggering but justified – in the musical design of his work as a whole.

Wagner completes the full score of *Die Walküre* on 23 March 1856, almost five years after noting down his first fragmentary ideas for its best-known scene, the Ride of the Valkyries, on a loose sheet of paper. The process of orchestration is more protracted than for *Das Rheingold*, due to the frustrating hiatus caused by the previous spring's conducting activities in London: when he returns to his sketches, 'I often sat before my pencilled pages as if confronted by hieroglyphics I was incapable of deciphering.' His work on the second and third acts, meanwhile, is coloured by his recent discovery of Schopenhauer, whose idea of renunciation – at least as Wagner understands it – parallels Wotan's willingness to relinquish power and wealth and to embrace 'das Ende'. Wagner is also increasingly struck by the parallels between himself and Wotan: having imagined himself in Act I as Siegmund, irresistibly drawn towards Sieglinde/Mathilde, he sees in Act II's bitter arguments between Wotan and Fricka a reflection of the state of his own marriage to Minna.

But despite his unhappiness and frustration, he pours into his music the love whose absence from his life he feels so keenly. And inspired by Schopenhauer's eloquent account of music's ability to convey the workings of the will itself, he composes with increasing freedom, shaking off *Opera and Drama*'s dogmatic doctrines about text and music's necessary unity and allowing purely musical material more time and space to unfold. Perhaps paradoxically, love and freedom are nowhere more in evidence than in the moments where Wotan punishes Brünnhilde's disobedience by imprisoning her on a rock: the last scene of *Die Walküre* contains some of the tenderest music that Wagner ever writes. Mathilde's golden pen has been put to good use.

Siegfried

ZURICH, 22 SEPTEMBER 1856. Wagner begins to sketch *Siegfried*, disappointed but not deterred by recent decisions from Breitkopf and Härtel (no contract for the scores of *The Ring*) and the King of Saxony (no amnesty). More mundane problems soon intrude: noisy neighbours practise the piano too loudly, and a tinsmith moves in over the road and starts hammering throughout the day. Wagner considers giving up in order to try and find quieter lodgings, until he has a moment of inspiration. He finds a theme he has been searching for, one that will convey Siegfried's rage at Mime's incompetent attempts to forge the fragments of Nothung back into a complete sword. Wagner's amusement at his own angry rendition of Siegfried's song – and perhaps also at the parallels between his domestic frustrations and those of his hero – persuades him to resume work.

The combative relations between the residents of Zeltweg are matched by those in Wagner's new drama, with much hammering in the score as well as on the street. In *Die Walküre*, love – however problematic it turns out to be – unites those who spend most time singing together (Siegmund and Sieglinde; Wotan and Brünnhilde), but much of *Siegfried* consists of arguments between characters who loathe one another. Mime and Siegfried; Mime and the Wanderer (the name by which Wotan goes in *Siegfried*); the Wanderer and Alberich; Siegfried and Fafner; Alberich and Mime – not until the Woodbird begins singing towards the end of Act II does any character exhibit any positive sentiments towards anyone else on stage. Not until the Woodbird's appearance, either, is a female voice heard (and perhaps not even then: though the Woodbird is usually sung by a woman, Wagner originally conceived the part for a boy treble, and occasional productions, such as Stefan Herheim's for the Deutsche Oper, cast it this way). If *Siegfried* as a whole is always a test of stamina for singers, due to the extraordinary demands of the leading roles and the relatively heavy orchestration, then the first act can (at least in a less than sympathetic production) also try the endurance of audiences, thanks to the wordy libretto, Wagner's unrelieved use of male voices and the largely confrontational character of the drama.

This is not at all how Wagner himself sees *Siegfried*. As his reference in his autobiography to the laughter that punctuates his composing makes clear, he still envisages it as the scherzo of *The Ring*, a light-hearted intermezzo separating the great tragedies of *Die Walküre* and *Götterdämmerung*. The character of its eponymous, dragon-slaying hero owes as much to fairy tales – the idea that he needs to be taught the meaning of fear derives from a story retold by the Grimm brothers – as to the mythological sources that inform the cycle as a whole. Wagner intends to bring this hero to life with music that will ensure *Siegfried*'s popular success and pave the way for the acceptance of *The Ring* as a whole. It doesn't work out quite that way, for a number of reasons. As composition proceeds, the imperative of connecting the story to the wider plot of *The Ring* means giving the more sombre scenes involving the Wanderer, Alberich and Erda a weight that counteracts the intended comedy of the Siegfried scenes. And by the time Wagner completes the full score in 1871, his entire understanding of the *Ring* project is so different that the original comic intentions for *Siegfried* recede into the past.

Perhaps the most fundamental reason that few listeners instinctively describe *Siegfried* as a comedy, however, is that the relationship between Siegfried and Mime is not as amusing as Wagner thinks it is. In Act I, at least, Wagner makes it difficult for the singer playing Siegfried to inject enough charm into the role to counteract the unpleasantness of his treatment of Mime. Of course, the story gives us plenty of reasons to feel sympathy for Siegfried: his questions about his father and mother suggest his distress at their absence – and especially at the possibility that his own birth caused his mother's death. And Mime can scarcely have been the most agreeable substitute as his foster parent. But not-withstanding these mitigating factors, aspects of Siegfried's behaviour towards Mime can seem so sadistic and contemptuous as to prompt some listeners to perceive the Nibelung as a caricature of Jewishness whose treatment embodies Wagner's antisemitism. While there is no evidence that Wagner intends this interpretation, the whining, wheedling melodies he allocates Mime are so redolent of *Jewishness in Music*'s notorious characterisation of 'Jewish music' that it seems plausible.

But whether or not Act I of *Siegfried* is actually funny, Wagner treats his new drama as a comedy by constructing the music in a very different way from *Die Walküre*. As in many comic operas, and in German *Singspiele* such as Mozart's *Magic Flute* or Weber's *Frei-schütz*, songs – self-contained, symmetrically constructed musical numbers with memorable melodies, which occur at points in the story where characters might sing even if this were a spoken drama – are central to the action. In scene 1, Wagner sets Mime's self-justifying account of how he has selflessly attended to Siegfried's every need since infancy to an insidiously catchy triple-time melody, with a light orchestration including pizzicato strings, as if to suggest a folk song accompanied by guitar. Sections of this 'starling song', as Siegfried calls it, recur throughout the scene, and at one point he quotes it sarcastically. Siegfried has songs of his own, too: his first speech of any length, when he tells Mime how he prefers the bear he has just found in the forest to him, is accompanied with music that is similarly regular and tuneful. The implication is that both characters are repeating sentiments they have expressed to each other many times before, rather than spontaneously voicing thoughts that have just occurred to them.

In scene 3, the songs that Wagner gives to Siegfried suffuse the musical texture, reflecting the hero's increasing dominance over his guardian. As he uses the bellows to stoke up the fire with which he will re-forge Nothung, Siegfried begins a triple-time song that swaggers confidently down a minor scale before bursting into an exuberant refrain ('Hoho! Hohei!'); Otto Wesendonck is impressed with this 'fearfully majestic music' when he hears it through an open window at the Asyl, where the Wagners take up residence in April 1857. Siegfried's final song of the act, sung as he hammers the sword into shape, is more jubilant still: so pleased is he with his handiwork that he brings the song back after Mime's surreptitious aside for a second verse, words changed but melody identical – a gambit commonplace in *Singspiele* but almost unique in mature Wagner. The songs that Wagner threads through this extended altercation between Mime and Siegfried – and the musical repetitions that feature in the elaborate question-and-answer session between Mime and the Wanderer that interrupts it – by no means suspend the development of the web of leitmotifs that he takes forward from *Das Rheingold* and *Die Walküre*: indeed, he adds several important new themes to the stack. But in this particular act, it is the songs – longer and more diffuse than leitmotifs, but nonetheless immediately recognisable – that more noticeably structure the experience of the music, their repetition orienting listeners in their passage through the story, and bringing the act to its triumphantly rough-hewn conclusion.

Anxious, perhaps, to avoid the difficulties in interpreting his own sketches that he experienced when scoring *Die Walküre*, for Act I of *Siegfried* Wagner experiments with creating the orchestration more or less as he goes along: he finishes a preliminary draft in January 1857 and a more developed version in February, then completes the full score on 31 March. He begins Act II in May, but on 28 June, he writes to Liszt to tell him that 'I have led my young Siegfried into the beautiful forest solitude; there I have left him beneath a linden tree and have said farewell to him with tears of heartfelt sorrow.' Part of the reason for this momentous decision lies in his frustration at the seeming impossibility of bringing *The Ring* to the stage, or even to publication. A more pressing consideration, however, is his desire to embark on *Tristan und Isolde*, for which he has already made some musical sketches even though he has not yet written the poem. The implications of that opera for the music that follows it will be seismic, and so Wagner may also feel he needs to explore them fully in order that he can take what he discovers into *Siegfried*'s psychologically complex final act. Despite his apparently definitive pronouncement to Liszt, however, Wagner is not quite ready yet to abandon Siegfried to the forest. He has stopped work at the point in Act II, scene 2 where Mime exits expressing the hope that Siegfried and Fafner will kill each other: an annotation in the draft reading 'When we will see each other again??' confirms that this, the first of two occasions on which Siegfried lies down in the forest, is the moment in the drama to which the letter alludes. A fortnight later, however, Wagner resumes work, and by 9 August he has completed two sketches of the entire second act.

He therefore writes down over three-quarters of an hour's additional music in less than a month, a rate of progress almost matching *Das Rheingold*, and all the more remarkable since he has already decided to set *Siegfried* aside for an unspecified period of time. He takes afternoon walks in the woods near Zurich, where he hears birds whose songs help enrich the soundscape of 'forest murmurs' with which he surrounds Siegfried; he proves to himself that he has not been 'scared away from the older work by any feeling of weariness'. The music Wagner drafts during this peculiar phase includes some of the drama's most memorable moments: Siegfried's slaying of Fafner and his acquisition of the ring and Tarnhelm; the revelation of Mime's true intentions towards Siegfried, his bloodthirsty declarations comically mismatched with genial and jaunty music; the Woodbird's annunciation of Siegfried's future union with Brünnhilde. With these extra few weeks of work, Wagner has brought his hero to a point where the way ahead is clear: Siegfried is freed at last from the malign influence of Mime, his eyes opened by the Woodbird to the beauty that surrounds him and to the love and joy that exist in the world. Wagner's way forward, by contrast, is much more tortuous, and much more surprising.

* * *

The 'Asyl', Zurich, September 1857. Wagner reads the recently completed poem of *Tristan und Isolde* to a small group of friends. The Wagners' guests include Otto and Mathilde Wesendonck, Hans von Bülow – in whose career Wagner takes great interest – and Liszt's nineteen-year-old daughter Cosima, married to Hans a few weeks previously. Mathilde is overwhelmed with emotion; Minna is angry; Cosima is unimpressed.

The Bülows depart after three weeks, but Wagner quickly embarks on setting his poem and Mathilde becomes ever more closely involved, visiting his workroom almost daily. She gives Wagner five of her poems and he sets them to music: two of these

Wesendonck Lieder contain themes soon to be developed in *Tristan*, and all share the new drama's rarefied atmosphere and daringly chromatic harmony. On 7 April 1858, Wagner rolls a score of the Prelude to *Tristan*'s recently completed Act I around a long letter and passes it to a servant to deliver to Mathilde; Minna stops the servant during the short walk to the Wesendonck villa and demands to read the letter. Much of it deals with Wagner's thoughts on Goethe's *Faust*, about which he and Mathilde have recently disagreed, but it contains phrases sufficiently impassioned – 'My soul rejoices in this love'; 'my longing to be with you'; 'these wonderful, hallowed eyes' – to convince Minna that Wagner and Mathilde are lovers.

Minna confronts Mathilde; Mathilde explains the incident to Otto, who already has a clear understanding of his wife's unusual attachment. Minna leaves to spend three months at a sanatorium; Otto takes Mathilde on a holiday to Italy. Immediate disaster is averted, but gossip spreads and relationships among the residents of the Wesendoncks' extensive park are never the same again. In August 1858 Wagner leaves for Venice – without Minna, but in the company of Karl Ritter, whose mother subsidises the trip.

He does not write to Mathilde during his seven-month stay, though he keeps a diary that he intends her to read later: early entries address her as 'du', in the same impassioned manner as the 'Morning Confession' that Minna intercepted in Zurich; by the end she is once more 'Sie', his respectably married patroness. Wagner will continue to protest his 'eternal love' for Mathilde in private for some years to come, though with decreasing frequency and fervour. Otto magnanimously continues his generous subsidy of Wagner's work, and both Wesendoncks support and visit the Bayreuth Festival even after Wagner's death, undeterred by Cosima's jealousy of the woman who was once her husband's muse.

Wagner completes Act II of *Tristan* in Venice in March 1859, and Act III in August in Lucerne. The opera's musical importance is incalculable, but it is scarcely the easy-to-produce moneyspinner he originally envisaged. With German royalties on his earlier works limited and uncertain, he needs success on a bigger stage. In September he leaves Switzerland for Paris, determined that now, unlike twenty years ago, he will at last conquer the Opéra.

This time he makes an early impact: in January and February 1860 he gives three concerts of his own music which, though financially disastrous, win him some important admirers, none more ardent than Charles Baudelaire, who describes the performances as the greatest musical pleasure he has ever experienced. The programmes include the first performances of the *Tristan* Prelude – perhaps the most influential ten minutes of music of the entire nineteenth century, thanks to the much-analysed opening chord and Wagner's avoidance of conventional cadential closure, an eloquent expression of the unsatisfied (unsatisfiable?) yearning of the drama's eponymous lovers.

In March, in what seems at the time like a lucky break, Princess Pauline Metternich, wife of the Austrian Ambassador, convinces Emperor Napoleon III to order a production of *Tannhäuser*. Wagner undertakes a thorough revision of the fifteen-year-old opera and composes some orgiastic new ballet music for the first act. Unfortunately, his defiance of the Opéra's iron rule that ballets always occur later on in the performance – certainly no earlier than the second act, so that patrons can get there in good time after dinner – combines with the unpopularity of Austria and its princess to make Paris's *Tannhäuser* one of the most spectacular scandals in musical history. Members of the notorious Jockey Club make so much noise at each of the three performances in March

1861 that the music is almost inaudible. Wagner's hatred of Paris is now implacable: it is perhaps as a perverse form of revenge that he spends some of his final weeks in the French capital working out the scenario for his most German work, *Die Meistersinger von Nürnberg*. At least a partial amnesty from King Johann means that, as long as he seeks permission in advance, he is now allowed to enter the territory of the German Confederation – though not yet Saxony itself.

Both personally and professionally, the next few years are the most unsettled of Wagner's never straightforward life. In February 1862, against his better judgement, he makes a final attempt to salvage his marriage as Minna, by now an invalid, comes to join him in Biebrich am Rhein. After ten days of arguing, and jealous recriminations from Minna, it is clear that the gulf between them is too great. Wagner suggests divorce, but realises this would put too great a strain on Minna's increasingly precarious health. She settles in Dresden on her own, with a vague understanding that he will visit occasionally – Johann has at last granted him a grudging pardon. Wagner visits Dresden in November, but never sees Minna after this, though he gives her a quarterly allowance for the rest of her life.

He has no shortage of female admirers. Seraphine Mauro, niece of the doctor of the Empress of Austria, at whose house he stays; Mathilde Maier, daughter of an employee of the music publisher Schott, who is showing interest in his work; Friederike Meyer, a singer who is also entangled with the director of a theatre where Wagner conducts *Lohengrin* – all these and others flit in and out of his life. In November 1863, Wagner visits the Bülows in Berlin. He and Cosima have become increasingly close since the previous summer: now, while Hans is rehearsing, they take a fateful carriage ride during which they confess their shared unhappiness and mutual love, and agree that they will henceforth 'belong to each other alone'. At least, this is how the incident is related in *Mein Leben*, the autobiography that Wagner dictates to Cosima a few years later – it may not have felt quite so clear-cut at the time.

Meanwhile, unsuccessful attempts to stage *Tristan* dominate Wagner's working life: there is interest first from Karlsruhe, then from Vienna – a much more prestigious prospect, so he bases himself there in the hope of making a breakthrough. But suitable singers cannot be secured, and the unperformed opera acquires a reputation as unperformable. Wagner returns to concert-giving, conducting his music across Europe – in Prague, Pest and, most profitably, St Petersburg. But the income he brings in is nowhere near enough to resource his luxurious Viennese lifestyle. Once again his creditors threaten to pounce, so in March 1864 he makes a hasty escape. He turns up near Zurich at the home of his old friends François and Eliza Wille, but after a month François makes the limits of their hospitality clear, so he heads off again.

By 2 May, Wagner has reached Stuttgart. Spending the evening at the house of the city's Kapellmeister, Karl Eckert, he is surprised to receive a visitor's card marked 'Secretary to the King of Bavaria'. He assumes that it is a ruse from one of his creditors, and hides in his hotel, but the mysterious stranger tracks him down. The king in question is the eighteen-year-old Ludwig II, who ascended the throne weeks earlier on the death of his father. Alongside German mythology, Wagner's work has been his principal passion since early adolescence, and he has committed several of his libretti to memory. He is well aware of the magnitude of Wagner's ambitions and of his equally immense need for financial support if they are to be realised. Forty-eight hours after the emissary's arrival, Wagner has his first audience with the king at the Residenz in Munich and the pair immediately strike up an extraordinary friendship. Ludwig pays off his most pressing debts, showers him with gifts and provides him with a villa on Lake Starnberg, fifteen miles outside the city. Each day Wagner travels into Munich in the king's carriage so that the new friends can figure out how he will present the rest of his life's work: *Tristan, Die Meistersinger, The Ring, Die Sieger, Parsifal* . . .

All he needs now is a companion. On 22 June he writes to Mathilde Maier to implore her to join him – she is the only woman who can redeem him, he assures her mother in a follow-up letter, notwithstanding his supposed vow to Cosima – but the invitation is rescinded almost as soon as it is sent. On 29 June Cosima arrives with her daughters, Daniela and Blandine; a few weeks later she becomes pregnant with another child who can only be Wagner's. Isolde von Bülow – of course all concerned maintain that she is Hans's – is born on 10 April 1865, two months before the premiere of the drama from which she takes her name. Due to the size of the orchestra, *Tristan und Isolde* is produced not in the exquisite little Cuvilliés theatre within the Residenz, as Wagner first hoped, but in the Court Theatre. At Wagner's insistence, Bülow conducts; the unprecedentedly demanding title roles are taken by the wife-and-husband team of Malvina Garrigues and Ludwig Schnorr von Carolsfeld – whose unexpected death three weeks after the final performance profoundly affects Wagner and creates an unhelpful stream of press speculation about the allegedly lethal character of his vocal writing. Despite the excellence of the interpretation, *Tristan*'s revolutionary musical idiom – which surely seems more bewildering still to audiences who have heard no Wagner more recent than *Lohengrin* – proves off-putting to many. Ludwig, however, is enraptured.

Unfortunately for Wagner, the delight that the king takes in his presence in Munich is not shared by his ministers or the public at large. By the time *Tristan* is premiered, the backlash is well under way. Wagner's high-handed behaviour and the king's lavish subsidy of his luxurious lifestyle cause alarm and resentment; so too does Wagner's plan that his old Dresden associate Gottfried Semper should design a festival theatre devoted to his own work, resourced by a new German Music School. In December 1865 – the month in which Wagner completes the full score of Act II of *Siegfried*, a year after beginning work on it – Ludwig's advisers make the gravity of the situation clear. The king's conspicuous generosity towards Wagner and the degree of influence that the composer is perceived to exert over state affairs are becoming politically dangerous. The king reluctantly acquiesces, and orders Wagner to leave Bavaria, though not without assuring him of his continued devotion and support.

Exiled once more, but this time with money in his pocket, Wagner yet again heads to Switzerland, where in January 1866 he receives the news of Minna's death in Dresden. A couple of months later, he and Cosima find their perfect home: a villa in Tribschen, just outside Lucerne, set in beautiful grounds on a promontory with magnificent views over the lake and the surrounding mountains. Ludwig generously responds to Wagner's request to enable him to secure the property, and on 22 May, Wagner's fifty-third birthday, he pays a surprise visit under the name of Walther von Stolzing, the hero of *Die Meistersinger*. Munich is outraged that Ludwig has missed the state opening of parliament in order to make this visit, and mutterings in the press about the state of relationships in the Wagner and Bülow households get louder. Ludwig still chooses to believe that Cosima visits Tribschen only as Wagner's much-needed secretary and amanuensis, and she tricks the king into signing a letter deploring the slurs cast on her family's reputation. Ludwig's dismay when he finds out the truth is profound, but as ever, his love for Wagner's music trumps his disgust at the composer's behaviour. At Christmas 1867, Wagner presents the king with the score of *Die Meistersinger*, and a production is planned at the Court Theatre for the following June. Bülow, by now installed at Wagner's instigation as the city's Kapellmeister, will conduct. The new drama chimes with the current rapid awakening of German national sensibility, and its musical accomplishment – less confusing to the ear than that of *Tristan* – is widely admired. The premiere on 21 June 1868 is Wagner's greatest triumph to date – though he still manages to stoke controversy by his presumptuous acknowledgement of the audience's applause from his seat in the royal box.

Wagner continues to assure Ludwig that his relations with Cosima are entirely proper, and she keeps up the pretence by residing at the Kapellmeister's lodgings whenever she is in Munich. But by July, the strain is too much, and she asks Bülow for a divorce; he – mindful of the effect such a scandalous decision would have on his career in Munich – refuses. Cosima and Wagner retreat to Tribschen with their children, Isolde and Eva, who was born in 1867; Cosima's elder daughters join them the following spring. It will be another eight years before Wagner sees Ludwig in person again, but the king's passion for Wagner's work once more prevails, and by February they are in correspondence again. On 1 March 1869, as he delightedly informs the king, Wagner begins work on Act III of *Siegfried*. In the dozen years since he completed Act II, he has composed two astonishing new music dramas, and substantially rewritten a third; more unexpectedly, he has fathered two children, and eagerly awaits a third. That child, his only son, is born on 6 June. His name – of course – is Siegfried.

* * *

Wagner's renewed sense of purpose as he resumes composition is palpable from the Act III Prelude's first bars. The themes he uses are a dozen years old or more, but the way he combines them feels utterly new. This Prelude shares the obsessive quality of the openings of *Das Rheingold* and *Die Walküre* – the galloping dotted-rhythm undercurrent first heard in the strings appears in all but six of its fifty-eight bars – but here many more layers of sound are piled up on top, creating an irresistible momentum. Motifs associated with Erda and Wotan – among many, many others – are heard simultaneously rather than successively, enabling Wagner to prepare the listener in little more than two minutes of music for the pair's momentous encounter.

The music that Wagner has composed in the period since completing Act II of *Siegfried* has developed his technique as a composer, in several different if not contradictory directions. In *Tristan und Isolde*, and in the new music for the Paris *Tannhäuser* he composed in *Tristan*'s wake, he postpones harmonic resolution for longer periods of time than any composer has ever done before, and creates sequences of chords whose chromaticism, whose remoteness from any idea of a 'home key', anticipate the first atonal compositions of Arnold Schoenberg, written half a century later. In *Die Meistersinger*, meanwhile, Wagner devotes himself to counterpoint – the craft of superimposing multiple melodies so that they each retain their individual integrity while combining to form a harmonically coherent whole – as never before. He demonstrates his new-found skill to virtuosic effect in the overture, packing a large number of the drama's musical themes into its nine-minute duration, sometimes enabling four or five of them to be heard simultaneously. If both the story and the musical innovations of *Tristan* require Wagner to create unbroken musical spans of ever greater length – he famously boasts to Mathilde Wesendonck, with specific reference to the second act, of the 'art of the most delicate and gradual transition' that enables him to ensure 'unity and clarity' while doing so – then in *Die Meistersinger*, the outlines of traditional operatic numbers such as arias, duets and ensembles are more evident, even if the divisions between them are more apparent than real.

Wagner's development since 1857 has been centrifugal rather than linear: he now has an expanded range of techniques with which he can achieve his expressive ends. This enables him to create, in Act III of *Siegfried*, a musical structure that is both diverse and coherent. As with Act I, the overall design is extremely simple: the act is a chain of three duets, of which the second and third each contain one character from the previous scene and one new character (Erda/Wanderer, Wanderer/Siegfried, Siegfried/Brünnhilde). This design reinforces the act's significance within *The Ring* as a whole as the point when the crucial transfer of power – from Wotan to Siegfried, from gods to mortals – is effected. Wagner underlines this musically with an expansive new theme, made up of a falling sixth followed by a gradual ascent up the scale, which passes from the Wanderer in scene 1 to Siegfried and Brünnhilde in scene 3. The importance of this theme is clear from the outset; Wagner will later say in rehearsal that 'it must sound like the proclamation of a new religion'. It is first heard in the orchestra as the Wanderer tells Erda that he now looks forward to the end of the gods' reign, the outcome he once dreaded; and again at the end of the scene as he tells her that 'the god will gladly yield his rule to the young'. Wagner does not reprise the theme in scene 2, as if to suggest that the bumptious, disrespectful, Brünnhilde-less Siegfried who appears in that scene is not yet a worthy recipient of Wotan's power. In scene 3, however, it returns on numerous occasions: it is first played gently on an oboe as Brünnhilde sings for the first time of her love for Siegfried; later – unusually for mature Wagner, as if he does not want anyone to miss its significance – the cello section, subsequently joined by first violins, play it in unison with Siegfried as he sings of Brünnhilde's wisdom and love for him. With this theme, among other less obvious devices, Wagner creates a sense of coherence across the span of the act, but there is also considerable diversity of style and approach between the three scenes: an emotionally wrenching dialogue, conveyed in music of brooding chromaticism; an almost improvisational intermezzo, in which an initially courtly exchange soon becomes distinctly aggressive; a grand love scene with an exhilarating and emphatically tonal C major conclusion.

Wagner's autobiography breaks off in 1864 at the point when he is summoned to Munich to meet Ludwig – its final sentence confidently declares that 'under the protection of my exalted friend the meanest cares of subsistence were never to touch me again' – but from 1869 Cosima replaces it with a much more detailed account, and one that she writes as events unfold. On New Year's Day Cosima begins a diary, making an entry almost every day until Wagner's death in 1883, though in the weeks around Siegfried's birth Wagner himself writes them. Though the diaries are ostensibly written for Cosima's children, in part to explain her actions in leaving Bülow for Wagner, they provide posterity with almost a million words of extraordinarily close, if necessarily partial, insights into Wagner's working life. Many of these are mundane, but some are highly revealing. On 12 March 1869, for example, Cosima records that when setting the Wanderer's final speech in scene 1, Wagner has decided not to 'introduce recitative', despite the 'great effect' it would produce, but to prioritise the 'flow of melody': 'music, he says, transfigures everything, it never permits the hideousness of the bare word.' The specific moment to which

Cosima refers is where the Wanderer sings 'Seit mein Wunsch es – will!' (Since my will desires it!), i.e. the downfall of the gods: comparing this richly scored passage with the much sparser texture of the dialogue in Act II of *Die Walküre* where Wotan first reveals to Brünnhilde his desire for 'das Ende' makes clear how far Wagner's approach and aesthetic have changed.

Cosima's diary entry from Christmas Day 1870 describes her astonishment at waking up to hear an orchestra playing from the staircase outside her room at Tribschen. This is the first performance of the 'Symphonic Birthday Greeting' – Cosima's birthday is actually Christmas Eve but she celebrates it the following day – now known as the *Siegfried Idyll*. Its first theme is the tender melody that Brünnhilde sings towards the end of scene 3 of Act III of *Siegfried*, as she realises (and at first resists) the implications of her love for the hero: the end of her life as a Valkyrie, protected by divine power; rebirth as a mortal woman. A further entry in Cosima's diary, from 30 January 1871, describes this as 'the theme which had come to him in Starnberg (when we were living there together) and which he had promised me as a quartet'. This comment shows the need to treat Cosima's testimony with caution: though Wagner does indeed invent this theme in the first months of their relationship, the first sketch dates from 14 November 1864, after he leaves the Starnberg villa for an apartment in Munich, and despite the best efforts of musicologists, no evidence of any intention to compose a string quartet has been unearthed. It is more likely, despite the romantic story that Wagner spins to Cosima, that he drafts the theme for *Siegfried* itself, finally believing that it will be staged: he writes it down a month after signing a contract with Ludwig to complete the entire cycle.

Another theme that Wagner uses both in the *Idyll* and in the closing moments of *Siegfried* comes from even further back in his sketchbooks. This is the joyful sequence of fourths first played by the horns as Brünnhilde bids farewell to Valhalla, then quickly taken up by both the lovers to convey their sense of eternal joy. On 9 July 1859, Wagner writes to Mathilde Wesendonck from Lucerne that as he is working on the final act of *Tristan*, 'there suddenly occurs to me a turn of melody that is still more jubilant . . . I was about to reject the whole thing when I finally realized that this tune does not belong to Tristan's shepherd, but was Siegfried incarnate.' When he checks the libretto, he is delighted to realise that the new melody exactly fits some words he has already allotted to Brünnhilde. As usual – particularly when writing to Mathilde – Wagner's account of his creative processes has a self-congratulatory tone, but the anecdote nonetheless reveals two important things: firstly, that even long after supposedly abandoning Siegfried to his fate in the forest, the drama that bears his name is never far from the surface of Wagner's consciousness; and secondly, that he has an acute awareness of the different soundworlds and harmonic idioms of the various works he intends to write. The theme he finds in Lucerne would indeed have been out of place in *Tristan*, but its brash exuberance – echoing that of the horn call with which the hero first appears in Mime's cave – perfectly caps *Siegfried's* compelling conclusion. The assurance with which Wagner integrates material originally conceived long ago into a score of this complexity is astonishing.

He completes the draft of Act III in exactly fifteen weeks, finishing on 14 June, eight days after the birth of the boy who shares the new work's name. He does not begin the orchestral score until 25 August, exactly four weeks before the premiere of *Das Rheingold* at the Court Theatre in Munich. Wagner is not there: he does not approve of this enterprise – this is not at all how he imagined his greatest work reaching the stage – but the terms of the contracts he has signed with the King make him powerless to stop it. He is similarly unhappy about the premiere of *Die Walküre*, which takes place in Munich the following June. At least he can prevent a similar fate befalling *Siegfried*, by the simple means of refusing to complete it. Despite Ludwig's constant enquiries as to his progress, it is not until February 1871 that the full score is complete, by which time the danger of an unwelcome and premature premiere has been averted.

Götterdämmerung

TRIBSCHEN, 30 SEPTEMBER 1869. Cosima reports that 'R. appears to be sketching out *Götterdämmerung.*' The first page of sketches, dated two days later, begins with the First Norn's opening line: 'Welch' Licht leuchtet dort?' (What light is shining down there?) Not until more than three months later does Wagner draft the orchestral introduction with which the drama ultimately begins: the numbering of the other pages has to be altered to accommodate the change of plan. The opening as Wagner eventually conceives it yokes together one of *The Ring*'s most recent events (the first two bars of *Götterdämmerung* repeat the striking harmonic progression used in *Siegfried* to depict Brünnhilde's awakening on the rock, albeit a semitone lower) with the earliest (the bars that follow unmistakably echo the start of *Das Rheingold*, though again in the unusual key of C flat major). The freedom with which Wagner treats beginnings and endings is in keeping with *Götterdämmerung*'s paradoxical status as the first story in *The Ring* to be written, but the last to be set to music.

Wagner continues the disconcerting play with beginnings and endings in the Prologue's first scene by allowing the Norns to narrate events that occur both before *and* after anything that has yet been seen: the storyline is not so much continued as exploded. At the start of the scene, the First Norn tells of how Wotan tore a branch from the World Ash Tree and used it to make a spear, a rupture with nature that precedes the start of *Das Rheingold* and retrospectively helps to make sense of Wotan's behaviour in that drama. Towards the end of the scene, meanwhile, the Third Norn tells of how the remaining wood from the World Ash Tree that Wotan has ordered to be cut down will be used to set Valhalla on fire. The events related in this short scene encompass the entire history of the world of *The Ring*. At its end, as if to symbolise the end of that history, the Norns' rope breaks; singing over a sustained dissonance in the orchestra, they acknowledge that their influence over the events of the world is at an end. Only very rarely in *The Ring* thus far has more than one singer sung at once, and hardly ever have multiple singers sung the same notes: by reserving unison for this moment, Wagner ensures that its significance is registered.

If the Prologue's first scene is both a beginning and an ending, then the second is a beginning made to sound like an ending by Wagner's extraordinary music. As Siegfried prepares to set out on his adventures, he gives Brünnhilde the ring that he took from Fafner, as a symbol of his devotion; they sing of their mutual love and their indissoluble union. Like the opening of *Das Rheingold*, this scene's exhilarating climax is in E flat major: an apt connection, since both passages depict a state of untroubled joy briefly experienced before the malign intervention of a Nibelung (Alberich in *Das Rheingold*, his son Hagen in *Götterdämmerung*). And like much of the final act of *Siegfried*, this scene is in Wagner's most advanced, post-*Meistersinger* style, the various love themes combined with such dexterity that the music almost overflows with melody. Wagner imbues this scene with so much contrapuntal richness, composing with such flexibility and apparent spontaneity, that the opening of the interlude in which he depicts Siegfried's journey along the Rhine seems shockingly plain by contrast, with its Mendelssohnian lightness, regular four-bar phrases and simple texture (just one main melody: a version of Siegfried's horn call). Once again time seems to travel in two directions at once: Wagner's music goes backwards – at least momentarily – to an earlier, simpler idiom, even as his story moves forwards.

* * *

Götterdämmerung – Siegfrieds Tod, as it was originally called – is the only one of the four *Ring* libretti substantially written before the radical rethinking of his practice that Wagner undertook in *Opera and Drama*. It contains numerous situations and plot devices familiar from earlier operas, in general character if not precise detail: journeys; formal greetings to honoured guests; magic potions; sudden declarations of love; pledges of allegiance; confusion caused by the assumption of a disguise. Such situations lend themselves to being set to music as formally distinct, strongly characterised sections whose style may reflect internal or external aspects of the situations concerned. In his later libretti, Wagner tends to avoid such 'set pieces' in favour of longer spans of dialogue that are more amenable to an elaborately symphonic musical treatment, but the story he tells in *Götterdämmerung* is too intricately bound up with the rest of *The Ring* for him to try and unpick it now.

It is not just the structure of *Götterdämmerung*'s libretto that distinguishes it from the rest of *The Ring*, but also its setting. By contrast with the locations for the earlier dramas in the cycle, which are either mythological (Nibelheim; Valhalla), open-air (a river; a forest; a rock) or isolated (Hunding's hut; Mime's cave), the Hall of the Gibichungs, where most of *Götterdämmerung* takes place, contains numerous people (this is the only drama that includes a chorus) arranged in a social hierarchy analogous to that of the royal courts with which Wagner himself is familiar. Because of the clearly defined ways in which they relate to one another, and the series of distinct interactions of which the libretto is comprised, characters at the Gibichung court (it is different when the action moves to the Valkyrie rock) behave towards each other with a formality mostly absent from the rest of *The Ring*. Wagner registers this with music that, initially at least, seems curiously archaic. At times it is almost as though he has returned to the world of *Lohengrin*, to the realm of King Henry the Fowler. For the first 149 bars of Act I, scene 1 – until Gunther rises from his seat, impatient with Hagen's apparently implausible suggestion that he can help him win Brünnhilde as his queen – the music scarcely deviates from the stately triple-time metre established as the curtain rises. This orderly progress is in marked contrast to the fluidity and frequent tempo changes found in the third act of *Siegfried* and in most of Wagner's other recent music, including *Götterdämmerung*'s prologue. The sense of decorum is underlined by the transparent orchestration, with trumpets prominent, the prevalence of quasi-baroque dotted rhythms, and the insistent repetition of certain melodic and rhythmic cells.

By far the most important of these is the pattern – in its essentials it is too abbreviated to be called a melody – that Wagner introduces in the second bar of Act I, scene 1. It consists simply of a short note on the first (strong) beat of the bar, followed by a lower note on the second (unstressed) beat: in the terminology of poetic metre, it is a trochee. By contrast with some of *The Ring*'s leitmotifs, this pattern is defined not by any specific intervals but by its rhythmic identity and its falling shape: so clearly does Wagner articulate it that he enables his listeners to recognise it whatever the specific pitches involved. This pattern becomes the musical signature of the Gibichung court, immediately conjuring up its oppressive atmosphere and used ubiquitously in connection with all the characters who live there. Wagner features it prominently in the orchestra as Gunther formally welcomes Siegfried to his court, for example, and again a few minutes later as Gutrune silently offers him the drink that will make him forget his love for Brünnhilde. Its constantly downward pitch trajectory makes it an effective musical symbol for the decadence of the Gibichung siblings, a pair too weak to advance their romantic or political interests except by using deceit, and therefore easy prey for Hagen's scheming. But Wagner also strongly associates the pattern with Hagen himself, often with the two notes separated by an augmented fourth: the tritone or so-called *diabolus in musica* that musicians since the Renaissance have regarded as a symbol of evil. As Hagen sits and monitors the hall after Siegfried and Gunther have left to claim Brünnhilde, Wagner slows the tempo and asks tubas and double basses to repeat the two-note pattern with tritone intervals, as if to reveal the depravity at the heart of Gunther's kingdom. The tempo, instrumentation and intervals of this passage will return at the end of the act, as the disguised Siegfried seeks to subdue Brünnhilde, even though Hagen is not physically present, underlining that it is his will that has dictated the actions of the hapless hero.

'Hagen's Watch' – to give the earlier passage the title by which it is known when extracted for concert performances – is a moment of truth-telling rare in the opening scenes of *Götterdämmerung*. For much of the act, characters play out their expected roles in predetermined rituals, set to music of comparable formality. In the passage, for example, where Siegfried and Gunther swear an oath of blood-brotherhood (Hagen conspicuously refuses to take part), Wagner uses all the tricks in the operatic book. Just as they might do in an opera by Wagner's exact contemporary, Verdi, the new allies throw similar phrases back and forth, take it in turn to produce ever higher notes, and show their unity of purpose by singing in thirds and sixths, then finally in unison (Siegfried very low in his register, tellingly anticipating the end of the act, when he has to imitate Gunther's baritone range to win Brünnhilde). But even in such seemingly conventional sections, Wagner draws on motifs from earlier in the tetralogy – by this point he has a huge number to choose from – to suggest alternative interpretations of his characters' behaviour. In the case of the blood-brotherhood passage, he punctuates Siegfried and Gunther's declarations with loud renditions of the theme previously associated with Wotan's spear. If a doggedly literal approach is taken to the relationship between theme and object, this reference is puzzling: Wotan does not sing in this drama and his spear has been shattered for good. But of course, by this point the theme has accumulated a much wider range of meanings: Wagner's use of it here may simply be intended to suggest the status of Siegfried's oath as a legal contract like those that the spear formerly guaranteed; it may also serve to remind listeners of the spear's shattering, the moment at which power symbolically passes from god to hero; alternatively Wagner may wish to alert listeners to the forthcoming chain of events that will lead from Siegfried's ill-fated alliance to Wotan's ultimate downfall. The multiplicity of possible meanings implanted by a single leitmotif ensures the rich ambiguity even of *Götterdämmerung*'s most apparently formulaic passages.

The section of Act I that owes least to operatic convention and most to the musical techniques that Wagner developed in his time away from *The Ring* is Waltraute's plea to her sister to return the ring to the Rhinemaidens – not coincidentally, this is also one of the passages where the libretto differs most from the 1848 version. In *Siegfrieds Tod*, all eight Valkyries visit Brünnhilde on the rock to reprimand her for her disobedience to Wotan and remind her of the life that she has lost – but they say nothing about Wotan's current state, nor do they say anything about the ring. When Wagner rewrites this scene after completing the libretti of the earlier dramas in the cycle, he both extends and greatly improves it. The version he sets vividly describes the gods' attenuated state, filling out the account already given by the Norns and acting as a vital bridge between their scene and Brünnhilde's final monologue. The information Waltraute imparts is crucial, too: although Brünnhilde does not respond to her plea at the time, it will ultimately help her to decide what to do with the ring. So eloquent is the music that Wagner gives to Waltraute that it arouses sympathy for the gods and perhaps a wish that Brünnhilde should act to save them, even though the drama's very title makes clear that this cannot happen. As in the third act of *Siegfried*, Wagner draws freely and extensively on motifs from previous acts to create a many-layered orchestral texture around the narration. Particularly telling are the references to the theme beginning with a flurry of grace-notes that pervades Wotan's scene with Brünnhilde in Act II of *Die Walküre*, since they instantly recall the agonising nature of the god's dilemma. Brünnhilde's ultimate refusal of her sister's request is articulated with the theme to which Alberich renounces love in *Das Rheingold*. This reference is doubly appropriate: like Alberich's gesture, Brünnhilde's decision denies the claims of the Rhinemaidens; but it also demonstrates her faith in the love she currently feels, just as Siegmund does when he sings this same melody at the end of Act I of *Die Walküre*.

* * *

Wagner finishes the orchestral sketch of Act I on 2 July 1870; he does not begin Act II until 24 June 1871. The year that passes between the acts is eventful, both for Wagner and for Germany. On 18 July 1870, Cosima finally obtains a divorce from Bülow; on 25 August, King Ludwig's birthday, she and Wagner marry in Lucerne's Matthäuskirche – a newly consecrated Protestant church, even though Cosima is still a Catholic (and will not convert for another two years). Wagner is now fifty-seven and Cosima is thirty-two; on 4 September the couple baptise their one-year-old son, Siegfried.

The day after Cosima's divorce is finalised, war breaks out between France and Prussia. On 1 September, France suffers a catastrophic defeat at Sedan; eighteen days later, Prussian forces lay siege to Paris, with appalling consequences. By contrast with 1866, when Bavaria took Austria's side in its disastrous campaign against Prussia, Ludwig now recognises that the strength of Prussia's troops cannot be resisted and commits Bavaria's army to fight alongside them. Paris eventually surrenders on 28 January 1871, ten days after the German Empire, with Wilhelm of Prussia as its Kaiser, is proclaimed in the Hall of Mirrors at the Palace of Versailles – a location chosen to humiliate the French as well as for its historical resonances. On 21 March, Otto von Bismarck is announced as the new Empire's first Chancellor.

Meanwhile, Wagner and Cosima, who have long since abandoned any thought of building the festival theatre for *The Ring* in Munich, continue their search for a suitable location. On 12 May 1871, Wagner announces his intention to build his Festspielhaus – literally, a 'festival play house' – in the small town of Bayreuth in the north of Bavaria. The couple cannot know how Ludwig – on whose financial support they continue to rely, and who retains ownership of the four *Ring* dramas – will react to this unilateral and unequivocal declaration of independence. On 24 June, the day Wagner begins Act II of *Götterdämmerung*, Cosima's diary records that 'we are expecting bad experiences with our Bayreuth venture, but at least it will show us where we stand'.

It is in this unsettled state that over the next five months – he finishes on 19 November – Wagner drafts possibly the most disturbing act he will ever compose. Part of this effect is down to the sheer sonorous impact made by the chorus, who feature here for the first time in the cycle – and the only time, discounting a handful of lines for the men in the hunting scene in Act III. As Hagen calls the Gibichung vassals to greet Gunther, who is returning home with his bride Brünnhilde, violins and violas pound out a middle C, the same note that Hagen sounds on a steerhorn and also repeatedly sings. Wagner's obsessive focus on this single note creates a potent musical symbol of Hagen's monomaniacal determination to acquire the ring for himself; the explosion of male choral sound that springs from his summons further amplifies his malignant message. Equally shocking are the distress and confusion that Brünnhilde experiences during her enforced entry into the Gibichung Hall, and the decision she takes in consequence to ally herself with Hagen and Gunther to bring about Siegfried's death. Like the blood-brotherhood duet in Act I, the conspiracy trio that ends Act II draws on a familiar operatic trope which nonetheless proves brilliantly effective in this unfamiliar context. Brünnhilde's willingness to be led into a music whose idiom is so remote from everything she has sung before is a measure of how effectively Hagen has manipulated the situation.

The two-note falling pattern associated with the Gibichung court pervades this act, too, appearing in several new guises. Gunther sings an ingratiatingly melodious version in scene 4 as he brings Brünnhilde to meet his 'noble friend' and 'lovely sister', oblivious to her distress. A celebratory variant with the upper and lower notes a fifth apart is introduced in scene 2 as a theme associated with Gutrune; it rings out from the horn section at the start of scene 3 and periodically recurs during that scene almost like a rondo theme; it returns with renewed vigour at the end of the act, as if to signify Siegfried's headlong rush to celebrate his marriage to Gutrune. Wagner increasingly associates Hagen, meanwhile, with a compressed form of the two-note cell in which the gap between the notes is reduced to the smallest possible interval of a semitone: D flats appear before the Cs as he begins to summon the vassals; falling semitones ominously return on trombones and horns after Hagen pronounces the dread words 'Siegfrieds Tod'; trombones blast it out obsessively in the act's final moments, as Hagen forces Brünnhilde to take Gunther's hand. Wagner's retention of the same basic falling shape for patterns whose musical character is otherwise very different – harmonious for Gunther and Gutrune; dissonant for Hagen – helps to unify the score, but also to supply the sense of inexorable momentum that makes this act such an overwhelming experience. This music is only going in one direction.

Act II's music is often aggressive and violent, occasionally crude or manic, but in the interstices between such sections Wagner also composes passages of great charm. Some of these moments are for orchestra only, such as the astonishing depiction of dawn over the Rhine between scenes 1 and 2, composed for eight horns in canon. Some are associated with memories of happier times, such as in scene 4, when clarinets and violins in thirds recall love music from *Siegfried* as Brünnhilde challenges Siegfried's assertion that Nothung has always kept him virtuously apart from her; or in scene 5, when despite the angry tone of her words, playful figures passed between woodwind and strings conjure up the love that made her use her magic to protect Siegfried's body (though not his back) from harm. These beguiling passages are important not just for the variety they inject into Act II, but also for the way they help set up Act III: although Hagen has succeeded in channelling Brünnhilde's desire for revenge towards the achievement of his own nefarious plans, by continuing to provide her with music of such beauty Wagner reminds the listener that love remains at the core of her being.

* * *

Tribschen, 4 January 1872. Wagner begins Act III of *Götter-dämmerung*. He and Cosima have just received a newly published book: *The Birth of Tragedy: Out of the Spirit of Music*, by the twenty-seven-year-old Friedrich Nietzsche, a frequent visitor to their home since his appointment three years earlier as Professor of Classics at Basel. The Wagners have seen an early draft of the book but are eager to know how Nietzsche has used his numer-ous conversations with Wagner at Tribschen. The couple read it together over three evenings; Wagner declares: 'This is the book I have been longing for.' Its thesis is that the potency of Greek trag-edy – a potency no subsequent genre has recaptured, at least until Wagner's music dramas – stems from its fusion of two contrast-ing impulses, named after Greek gods: the Apollonian, associated with clarity, reason and logic; and the Dionysian, associated with intoxication, emotion, ecstasy. Wagner's young acolyte is not the first to articulate this idea – the composer himself, among others, suggested something similar in passing in *Art and Revolution* – but Nietzsche develops it more extensively and compellingly than any previous author, with a keener sense of tragedy as a manifestation of collective imagination, notwithstanding his book's overblown, Wagner-soaked prose style.

Like Wagner, Nietzsche is a devoted follower of Schopenhauer, and his characterisations of Dionysus and Apollo owe much to Schopenhauer's concepts of will and representation respectively. Music, for Nietzsche, is inherently Dionysian, and it is through music – music like Wagner's – that he believes the spirit of tragedy can be reborn. Wagner is both flattered by his youthful admirer's panegyric and enthralled by his argument: Cosima reports that on the very day he begins reading, the composer 'calls me his priestess of Apollo – he says I am the Apollonian element, he the Dionysian, but we made an alliance, a pact, and from it came Fidi [the family name for Siegfried]!' It is a joke, but a revealing one: as Wagner's work on *The Ring* draws to a close, it is the Dionysian aspect of his creativity with which he increasingly identifies.

In the final act of *Götterdämmerung*, Wagner foregrounds the music – both metaphorically and, sometimes, literally. The act begins with a steerhorn and French horns instructed to play 'auf dem Theater' – on the stage itself, or in the wings, rather than in the orchestra pit – and Wagner supplements this marking with indications of where they should be in relation to each other and to the audience ('further away', 'on the opposite side', etc.). A little later, he also calls for four harps to play 'auf dem Theater', in addition to the two required in the pit; at the end of the first scene, horns play at the back of the stage and behind it. Coupled with some equally specific directions about where singers should be positioned (vassals begin off-stage in scene 2; Brünnhilde's movements from upstage to downstage before her final peroration are precisely indicated), these instructions suggest an idea of the orchestra as more than an accompaniment for the singers. Instruments and singers interact with precisely calculated geometry and on an equal basis; in this final act of *The Ring*, more than ever before, it begins to seem as if the orchestra actively shapes the course of events.

It is, of course, the abundant stock of leitmotifs that Wagner has gradually accumulated over *The Ring*'s previous scenes and acts that allows him to create this illusion. In scene 2, as Siegfried offers to 'sing' – the choice of verb is significant – the story of his life, the themes from successive acts of *Siegfried* that seamlessly flow through the orchestra seem to prompt his recollections, rather than the other way around. Through the association of melodies previously only heard separately, and aided by the antidote that Hagen gives him to Gutrune's draught of forgetfulness, Siegfried is at last able to understand the story of his own life, just as it is about to end. The most powerful of these recollections is also the simplest: as Siegfried is on the point of death, a single wind triad – restored to its original key of E minor after the flattened version that begins *Götterdämmerung* – brings back a memory of finding Brünnhilde on the Valkyrie rock. The orchestra conjures up her physical presence for him as he dies, or so Wagner makes it seem.

The moment at which Siegfried falls to the ground after being stabbed by Hagen is articulated in the orchestra with a new theme – two pairs of stabbing chords, followed by a flurry of chromatic triplets – which in turn becomes the 'leading motif' of the orchestral interlude that immediately follows his death. Siegfried's Funeral March tells the hero's story again, but this time beginning before his birth, with recollections from Act I of *Die Walküre* of the Volsung twins and the love that led to Siegfried's conception. The themes of Nothung and Siegfried himself follow, presented in the most splendid form imaginable, and then the interlude reaches its climax as the brass section play a harmonised and massively slowed-down version of Siegfried's horn call. As on so many occasions in *The Ring*, retelling a familiar story from a new perspective produces fresh understanding. The only difference here is that there is no one on stage telling the story: the perspective is that of the music itself.

And it is music itself that has the final say in *The Ring*. As his political and philosophical outlook changes, Wagner considers various ways in which he might allow Brünnhilde to convey the work's message in words, but he ultimately decides not to set the

'Feuerbach' and 'Schopenhauer' endings discussed and quoted on pages 87 and 90, arguing instead (in a footnote to the published libretto) that the 'meaning [of the verses he does not set] was already conveyed with the greatest clarity by the musical effects of the drama'. Perhaps he also realises that, for all the millions of words he writes about his own work, there are questions about this ending that he cannot satisfactorily answer in words. Why (as August Röckel famously asked him) do the gods have to die, given that Brünnhilde has returned the ring to the Rhinemaidens? Why does Brünnhilde decide to throw herself on the pyre, and why does she take her horse with her? Should the audience assume that Alberich survives the conflagration, even though he is not seen on stage at the end, since there is no mention of his death? Where does Brünnhilde believe she will be reunited with Siegfried, since there will no longer be a Valhalla to which she can take him? Does Wagner expect his audiences to leave *The Ring* with an optimistic or pessimistic view of the prospects for the future of humanity?

'It is only through the spirit of music', Nietzsche argues in *The Birth of Tragedy*, 'that we understand the joy in the annihilation of the individual', and Wagner seems to have agreed. In the final pages of *Götterdämmerung*, after Brünnhilde has stepped into the fire and Hagen has vainly attempted to grab the ring, Wagner draws together themes from across the entire cycle with a virtuosity and confidence unparalleled anywhere in his music. A quick glance at the full score reveals some unusual notation that shows how much is going on: some of the parts teem with activity and are divided up into numerous short bars; in others, melodies unfold spaciously across bars several times longer. Seven bars from the end, the tumult stops and the whole orchestra breathes together for a final ecstatic rendition of a theme that, until a few moments ago, has not been heard since Sieglinde's hymn of thanks to Brünnhilde in Act III of *Die Walküre*. Wagner makes it sound both familiar and new; both a spontaneous inspiration and the only possible way the cycle could have ended.

He completes the compositional sketch of Act III on 10 April 1872, little more than three months after he begins. Twelve days later, he leaves Tribschen for good and takes up residence at the Hotel Fantaisie in Donndorf near Bayreuth. Cosima and the children follow a week later; Nietzsche, distraught at the family's departure, turns up to help with the packing. Their personal relationship will never be the same again, and in time Nietzsche will violently reject Wagner's ideas, but *The Birth of Tragedy* remains a prophetic articulation of what music drama promises to the new and barely formed nation of Germany: an expression of collective identity.

On 22 May, Wagner's fifty-ninth birthday, he leads a group of his supporters up a hill in the rain to lay the foundation stone of the Festspielhaus. Later that day, he conducts a celebratory performance of Beethoven's Ninth Symphony in the Margravial Opera House, drawing singers and instrumentalists from all over Germany; his niece, Johanna, is the contralto soloist. The next months are filled with the relatively mundane tasks necessary to make the theatre a reality: networking, fundraising, making speeches, recruiting singers. In September Wagner and his family move into a rented house on Dammallee where they will live until their permanent residence is completed. It is not until 3 May 1873 that Wagner begins the full score of *Götterdämmerung*, taking another eighteen months to complete it. Finally, on 21 November 1874, at his splendid new home, Wahnfried, he writes the final notes, adding at the bottom, 'Ich sage nichts mehr!' – 'I say no more!' This is not quite how things turn out.

5
Selling the story

From book to building

L EIPZIG, APRIL 1863. The Swiss-born publisher Johann Jakob
Weber brings out the first edition intended for the general
public of the four *Ring* libretti as they currently stand. Wagner's
preface, written in Vienna, sets out with unusual brevity what he
thinks needs to happen next. A temporary theatre must be constructed, probably of wood, in a town where there is no competition from another major opera house, but with sufficiently good
transport links and tourist infrastructure to accommodate the
audiences that Wagner expects to gather from across Germany
and beyond. The theatre's design, on which Wagner has already
consulted the eminent Gottfried Semper, will make the orchestra
invisible to the audience, so that they will not be distracted by
gestures or sounds extraneous to the drama, and will experience a
perfect acoustic balance between orchestra and voices. The most
talented actor-singers available will be invited to spend the entire
summer at the new theatre, to avoid the distracting demands of
other operatic commitments; audience members, too, will be
encouraged to treat their time at the new festival as a vacation
from everyday life, so that they begin each performance in the
state of relaxed concentration that Wagner's new form of drama
will require, rather than arriving after work, exhausted and seeking only superficial diversion. Wagner hopes that the festival will
encourage younger composers and directors of other opera houses
to create work in which music and every detail of the action are

indissolubly fused, just as they are in *The Ring*. In this way, it will establish, for the first time, an authentically German school of musical drama, far removed from the triviality of the French and Italian opera that so sadly dominates Germany's theatres.

All that is missing from Wagner's plan is the funding needed to make it a reality. He sets out two possible scenarios for achieving this. A syndicate of wealthy music-lovers sympathetic to his cause might between them raise the funds – but Wagner is not sanguine about the chances of this happening. Alternatively, and more straightforwardly, a German prince might be persuaded to divert his current budget for an opera house to supporting Wagner's new enterprise. Such would be the contribution of this hypothetical ruler to Germany's cultural flowering that he would win immortal fame for himself, as well as for Wagner. But will such a prince be found, Wagner rhetorically and somewhat plaintively enquires.

The future Ludwig II reads Wagner's plea two months after the book is published, but at this point he is not yet king, and Wagner's audacious appeal to 'a prince' is certainly not written with Bavaria in mind – he knows nothing of Ludwig's fascination with his work. Wagner gives at least two of the specially bound editions of the libretti he requests from Weber's press to music-loving aristocrats of his acquaintance – Grand Duke Carl Alexander of Weimar, Liszt's long-standing patron, and Grand Princess Elena Pavlovna, aunt of Tsar Alexander II, whom he gets to know during a visit to St Petersburg – and these are unlikely to be his only targets. But these fruitless approaches are forgotten by the following year, when Ludwig ascends the Bavarian throne and almost immediately summons Wagner to Munich – a picaresque intervention that might have happened even without the preface's prompting, such is the king's veneration for the composer whose operas he has loved since childhood. He admits that helping Wagner, rather than governing Bavaria, is his most important purpose in life, his destiny; artist and monarch proclaim their shared ideals and mutual devotion in ecstatic terms. Even if Munich is scarcely the small and isolated town in which Wagner has imagined building his new theatre, a prince more precisely meeting the requirements he has set out could not have been found.

In October 1864, after his summer on Lake Starnberg, Wagner moves into a handsome house not far from the royal Residenz, found for him on Ludwig's orders and provided rent-free, with a substantial sum added for refurbishment. The king's purpose in meeting Wagner's material needs is to enable him to complete *The Ring*. According to the contract Wagner signs the same month, he will deliver the scores of each of the four operas within the next three years to the Cabinet Treasurer, Julius von Hofmann, and the work (and therefore the right to order its performance) will become the property of the king. In return, Wagner will receive 30,000 florins (a sum ten times the annual rent of the house), in addition to his annual stipend of 4,000 florins and his accommodation.

This contract is extraordinarily generous to Wagner, but the following August – perhaps emboldened by the success of the *Tristan* premiere – he asks the king for substantially more. So that he can rid himself for ever of the debt that constantly distracts him, he requests an immediate cash advance of 40,000 florins: this, the king should understand, would be a loan, to be repaid from his estate after his death, rather than a gift. He furthermore proposes that the Treasury should allocate a sum of 160,000 florins for his future needs, from which he will draw 2,000 florins in interest each quarter (effectively doubling his previous allowance). Ludwig grants the increased allowance – as a stipend, not as interest on ring-fenced capital – but equivocates over the cash advance, fearful that the 40,000 florins will be quickly spent only for more debts to emerge. After some confusing and ill-tempered communications with Franz von Pfistermeister – the Cabinet Secretary who located Wagner in Stuttgart, but now fears his excessive influence in Munich – the king finally relents on 18 October 1865. Cosima visits the Treasury to collect the money: the officials who meet her express their resentment by supplying some of it in the form of heavy sacks of coins.

Only seven weeks later, on 6 December, Johann Lutz, Pfistermeister's deputy, informs an astonished Wagner that the king wishes him to leave Bavaria immediately. Wagner's surprise is understandable: he and Ludwig have become the closest of friends, spending long periods alone together at Hohenschwangau, the royal castle near the Austrian border. The devastated king clings to the hope that Wagner will return quickly after the six months specified for his exile; his ministers determine to ensure that no such thing will happen. A number of factors motivate their plot to force Ludwig into this most unwelcome of decisions. Wagner has not helped his own cause with his imperious demands for financial support and his unwise forays into politics, publishing anonymous articles which everyone knows he has written and lobbying the king to replace his Minister-President. The man whom Wagner believes Ludwig should dismiss is Baron Ludwig von der Pfordten, who knows him of old: in 1848, as King Friedrich August's Minister for Public Worship and Instruction, he was unimpressed by Wagner's plan to reform the theatres and music schools of Saxony, and he has even less sympathy for what he has in mind for Bavaria. While Wagner's extravagance, political meddling and undue influence on the king have aroused the hostility of the press and the public, Pfordten, Pfistermeister and their colleagues are more concerned by the composer's longer-term aspirations. His plan to build a festival theatre in Munich devoted to his own work, resourced by a new school of music, threatens to derail the public finances of Bavaria for a generation.

The first step to establishing the school has already been taken: in July 1865, Ludwig issued a decree to close the Munich Conservatoire of Music after two decades of existence, clearing the way for a new institution to be founded following the principles set out by Wagner in a lengthy report submitted to the king earlier that year. This institution will train singers in the particular skills required to perform German opera, helping to establish a distinctive national style of vocal performance that Germany has thus far sadly lacked, by contrast with France and Italy. Although Wagner will no longer be in Munich to act as the new institution's figurehead, he remains determined to influence its work. In January 1867, writing from Tribschen, he insists that Hans von Bülow – currently living in Basel in an attempt to avoid gossip about the state of his marriage – returns to Munich as the school's first director. This demand is more controversial than it was two years earlier when Wagner first made it: the proudly Prussian Bülow will arouse hostility in a city chastened by Prussia's recent victory over the Austrian forces that Bavaria supported in the Seven Weeks' War. But Ludwig understands that Bülow, whose devotion to Wagner's music has remained miraculously intact throughout the extraordinary entanglement of their personal lives, represents the best means of ensuring that Wagner's artistic ideals will shape the new institution. On 16 July 1867, when he eventually issues the decree to establish the music school that October, Bülow is indeed appointed director, with full authority to choose his entire staff.

Wagner's commitment to the school (and to Bülow as prospective director) is remarkably unaffected by his departure from

Munich; towards the theatre the school is intended to serve (and towards Semper as prospective architect) his attitude becomes more equivocal once he is in exile. Until this point, Wagner and Semper, who have spent much time together both in Dresden and in Zurich, have generally taken a similar view of what is needed from a theatre. They share a veneration for ancient Greece as a model example of a society spiritually nourished by the arts, and the architect's research into the theatres of antiquity has shaped the composer's thinking about what his own festival theatre will look like. Almost as soon as Ludwig's patronage made a new theatre a realistic possibility, Wagner drew his old friend into the project, and from December 1864 onwards the three men start to engage in detailed discussions, though generally in secret – ministers issue categorical denials of Semper's involvement to the press – and without the architect ever being given a contract. Ludwig favours moving immediately to develop a permanent stone structure on the Gasteig hill (where a new cultural centre for Munich was built in the 1980s); Wagner and Semper suggest instead trying out their ideas in a provisional theatre within the Glaspalast, a huge glass exhibition centre in the city's Old Botanical Garden (modelled on London's Crystal Palace), which opened in 1854 and will be destroyed by fire in 1931. Whether the theatre is permanent or temporary, it is essential that the orchestra pit should be large, deep and invisible to the audience, so that nothing distracts from the illusory world conjured up on the stage.

Uncertainty over which plan the king really favours mars Semper's progress, but during the course of 1866, he presents him with models for both. Ludwig is enthusiastic, but his ministers find excuses to prevent the scheme from proceeding; Wagner, by now settled at Tribschen, disloyally does nothing to help. By March 1868, Semper reluctantly accepts that neither theatre will ever be built, and submits an invoice to the Bavarian Treasury for the three years of fruitless work he has undertaken, along with a letter expressing his disappointment. Not until January 1869 is he paid a single thaler for his efforts.

Wagner's sudden loss of interest in the theatre where he had until recently imagined *The Ring* being brought to life is due in part to his disillusionment with Munich and its political machinations. Whatever he tells Ludwig, he knows that he will never again be a permanent resident of the city – apart from anything else, he can scarcely live openly there with a woman still married to a senior Court employee – and so his ability to influence the work even of a theatre constructed according to his own specifications will be limited. However, his change of heart also reveals his rapidly changing understanding of the politics of Germany as a whole and of what his own place in the new Empire whose emergence seems inevitable might be. In 1865, he expresses his loathing of Prussia in typically paranoid and antisemitic terms – too many French, too many Jews – and disparages Bismarck; the following year, in the middle of Bavaria's disastrous military campaign against Prussia, he urges Ludwig to stand firm and put aside any thoughts of abdication, describing him as the enlightened ruler that Germany needs; but by 1867, he sees not only the inevitability but also the advantages of Prussian dominance, and urges Ludwig to form an alliance that will secure Bavaria's position in the new Germany. That autumn, he writes a series of articles for Munich's *Süddeutsche Presse* which celebrate the impending arrival of a German commonwealth, led by Prussia: though Ludwig approves of the earlier articles, which focus on the artistic potential of the new Germany, the pan-German sentiment and crass anti-French diatribes in the later contributions become so offensive to him that he orders the editor to spike the last two.

Although Wagner is more than happy to continue accepting Ludwig's financial support, their views are increasingly divergent. By 21 June 1868, when they sit together at the premiere of *Die Meistersinger* – Wagner's greatest triumph in Munich, perhaps anywhere – they have very different opinions on what form the Germany whose art the opera celebrates should ultimately take.

* * *

The contract that Wagner signed with Ludwig II in October 1864 was not the first document that traded the prospect of future profits from *The Ring* against its composer's need for immediate cash. In his agreement with Otto Wesendonck, made just over a decade earlier, Wagner guaranteed his Zurich neighbour the fees he would receive from productions of future operas – including *The Ring* – as partial repayment of the loan Otto had advanced him. The moral rights to the score that this agreement conferred were consolidated in a further deal made in September 1859, whereby Otto agreed to purchase the right to publish each drama for a similar fee to that which Breitkopf and Härtel – after backing out of negotiations for *The Ring* – had recently agreed to give Wagner for *Tristan*. Otto advanced the composer 12,000 thalers for the two dramas he had so far completed, to which he added a further 6,000 the following spring for *Siegfried*, still a long way from being completed. But despite his repeated generosity towards Wagner, it is doubtful whether the composer ever seriously intended to pass any payments over to him, if and when he succeeded in finding a publisher for his vast undertaking.

Discussions with Breitkopf over *The Ring* sputtered on until late 1859, but eventually foundered when Wagner realised that the firm would never agree to support him in the style he believed he deserved until the unspecified point at which all the scores would be completed. Around the same time, however, he was offered an unexpected alternative when the Viennese Kapellmeister Heinrich Esser told him that Franz Schott – grandson of the Mainz music publisher Bernhard Schott and current owner of the firm that bore his name – was interested in his plans. Wagner duly wrote to Schott on 11 December 1859 and boldly demanded the same amount (10,000 thalers) for each of the four dramas as Breitkopf had proposed to pay for the entire cycle. Schott unsuccessfully attempted to beat Wagner down, but eventually paid him the agreed amount in January 1860 for the full score and piano reduction of *Rheingold*, with the understanding that he would be given first refusal on the rights to the remaining dramas.

Wagner signed this first contract – and all his subsequent contracts with Schott, negotiated with increasingly extravagant demands that threatened almost to bankrupt the publisher – without any reference to his prior agreement with Wesendonck. Nor did he make any attempt to repay his benefactor from the funds he received from Schott. Instead, he used his *Rheingold* fee to pay for his financially disastrous concerts in Paris, though he did at least acknowledge his debt to Wesendonck later in 1860 when he disingenuously suggested that his benefactor should treat the money that he would eventually have paid him for *Götterdämmerung* as a repayment of his own debt for *Rheingold*.

It was unlikely that Otto, knowing Wagner as he did by this point, ever expected him to honour the agreement he had made concerning the rights for *The Ring*: both men probably regarded it as a convenient fiction. Indeed, in 1864, when both Wagner's financial situation and *The Ring*'s prospects of performance seemed bleak, he wrote to Otto to tell him that he should regard the advances he had made to him as lost; in July 1865, once Ludwig had transformed his situation, he wrote again, this time to ask that Otto should acknowledge the king's superior claims to the *Ring* dramas, relinquishing not only his theoretical ownership of the work but also the autograph full score of *Das Rheingold* that Wagner had given him as a gesture of good faith. Otto agreed to this request with better grace than Wagner deserved; Ludwig was pleasantly surprised to receive the manuscript on 25 August as a present to mark his twentieth birthday.

Although Wagner continued to press Schott for financial support throughout his work on *The Ring*, publication was only one of the means by which he proposed to disseminate its music in advance of a production. The full score of *Das Rheingold* would not be published until 1873, with *Die Walküre* following in 1874 (the year of Schott's death) and the remaining dramas in 1876 and 1877. But some of *The Ring*'s music had been introduced to audiences long before this point. Showing acute awareness of his new work's commercial potential, Wagner extracted some of the cycle's most striking passages for use in concert performances. He arranged the Ride of the Valkyries in 1862 for concerts in Vienna and Leipzig; over the next few years, he similarly uprooted sections including Siegmund's 'Winterstürme' aria and Wotan's Farewell (from *Die Walküre*) and Siegfried's Rhine Journey (from *Götterdämmerung*) for concerts in Munich, Berlin, Prague and elsewhere. He must have been aware that by carving out chunks, bleeding or otherwise, from his scores in this way, he contradicted his own clearly stated precept that they should be experienced only complete and in circumstances where their service to the drama as a whole could be perceived. That he nonetheless proceeded with the carving demonstrates the paramount importance to him of selling his story not just to a king but to the public at large.

Munich, 22 September 1869. The premiere of *Das Rheingold* takes place at the Munich Court Theatre, four weeks after Ludwig's twenty-fourth birthday, the auspicious date that is originally chosen. The performance is conducted by Franz Wüllner, a pianist and teacher in his mid-thirties who directs the choral programme at the German School of Music. According to Peter Cornelius, who reviews it for the *Neue Zeitschrift für Musik*, the scenic effects – the cause of much anxiety in recent weeks – generally work well. The music is reasonably well received, though many of the audience are perplexed by the novelty of the idiom and in particular the lack of memorable melodic lines for the singers. The most popular section seems to be Loge's narration from scene 2, whose ending is interrupted by spontaneous applause that would no doubt have horrified Wagner, had he been there.

His reasons for staying away are not as straightforward or as principled as he tries to maintain. Though he is happy for others to believe that he wishes *The Ring* to be performed only under circumstances of his choosing once the entire work is complete, this is not in fact the case. A letter written in February 1868 to Lorenz von Düfflipp, Pfistermeister's successor as Ludwig's Cabinet Secretary, makes clear 'that it would not be impossible, should his Majesty the King wish it' – as he is perfectly entitled to do, as the work's legal owner – 'for the separate parts of the cycle to be provisionally performed' in Munich. And in October 1869 – after the Munich premiere – he tells Schott that he is happy for a production of *Das Rheingold* on its own to take place in Vienna next year. His specific objections to the Munich production are not so much aesthetic as personal. Increasing public awareness of his adulterous relationship with Cosima has not only made it difficult for him to spend any time in Munich, it has also deprived him of one of only two conductors he trusts to render his scores to his satisfaction: Bülow resigns his post as Kapellmeister on 9 June 1869, tired of the continual gossip that he owes it to his peculiar status as the husband cuckolded by the object of the King's obsession.

Wagner's other favoured conductor is the twenty-six-year-old Hans Richter, who has spent a great deal of time at Tribschen over the last three years as copyist and assistant. The composer has already secured Richter an appointment as 'Musikdirektor' at Munich following his invaluable assistance to him and Bülow on the *Meistersinger* premiere, so after Bülow's withdrawal he becomes the obvious candidate to conduct *Rheingold*. He visits Tribschen in July to receive instructions from Wagner, who has no intention of involving himself in the preparations, but on 28 August Richter writes to the King to tell him that he cannot in good conscience take part in a production that will not respect the intentions of the work's composer. His abrupt resignation is shortly followed by that of Franz Betz, the baritone who created the role of Hans Sachs in *Meistersinger* and is now due to play Wotan. The objections to the scenic designs that Richter has cited are no more than a convenient excuse for a course of action that has been planned for some weeks: both men have been acting on instructions from Wagner, who seems to hope that by removing two such crucial figures at such a late stage he will force the King and the theatre's intendant, Karl von Perfall, to re-engage Richter on terms that will allow Wagner himself to dictate exactly what happens. A furious Ludwig has no intention of allowing himself to be manipulated in this way; on 1 September Wagner visits Munich to issue his demand for Richter's reinstatement in person, but returns, humiliated, the following day when the king refuses to see him. His maverick behaviour entrenches the hostility of Munich's Court, theatre and press.

Ludwig himself soon resumes his friendly correspondence with Wagner, but makes it clear that he still intends to produce *Die Walküre* the following year; he also ignores the composer's attempt to decree how it should be done. This time Wagner knows better than to risk sabotaging his own work, but he privately resolves to deny the King the opportunity to treat *Siegfried* in the same way. The *Walküre* premiere takes place on 26 June 1870, before an audience that includes Liszt and Saint-Saëns, Brahms and Joachim; Wüllner once again conducts, after Bülow declines the opportunity; the critical reaction is positive, so much so that Wagner feels compelled to explain that it has succeeded for the wrong reasons. Further performances are given of *Rheingold* and *Walküre* in sequence in July, but by this time Ludwig has more important matters to deal with.

On 15 July, as the inevitability of war between Prussia and France becomes clear, Ludwig orders the Bavarian army to mobilise in preparation to support Prussia. Two days later, his government asks the chamber of deputies to approve the allocation of a sum of 27 million gulden to the military effort, an amount that makes even Ludwig's support of Wagner seem modest. There is some opposition, but the vote passes. Despite his instinctive dislike of Prussia and his personal inclination towards neutrality, Ludwig is clear about the choice that needs to be made. Wagner, meanwhile, is exhilarated by the prospect of war: crassly disregarding the feelings of the group of French visitors who are staying at Tribschen at the time – Camille Saint-Saëns, Henri Duparc, Auguste Villiers de L'Isle-Adam, Catulle Mendès and Judith Gautier – he eagerly anticipates the bombing of Paris. The city's siege the following year inspires one of his most unpleasant and worthless pieces of writing: *Eine Kapitulation* purports to be a 'farce', though no one other than its author seems to find its mockery of the Parisians' suffering funny. Perhaps Wagner is trying to ingratiate himself with Bismarck, to whom he sends a poem dedicated 'To the German Army in Paris' and a *Kaisermarsch* which he hopes in vain will become the new Empire's national anthem. He has had Prussia's Minister-President in his sights for some time as a possible benefactor for *The Ring*: two years earlier Cosima only narrowly prevented him from sending Bismarck's wife a copy of *German Art and German Politics* to pass on to her husband, fearful that Ludwig would think Wagner disloyal if he found out. In May 1871 he meets the newly proclaimed Chancellor in Berlin and is 'enchanted with the genuine charm of his character', according to Cosima. Nothing suggests, however, that Bismarck has any interest in supporting Wagner's enterprise, though this does not prevent the composer from making various approaches in his direction over the next few years.

Against this backdrop, Wagner and Cosima continue their search for a suitable location for their festival theatre. With the Semper project in Munich now definitively abandoned, Wagner's original preference for a small town isolated from urban distractions resurfaces. He has been thinking about Bayreuth since 5 March 1870, when he and Cosima looked it up in the famous encyclopedia published by Brockhaus, the family firm of Wagner's two Leipzig brothers-in-law: 'to our delight, we read in the list of buildings of a splendid old opera house!' Bayreuth is near the northern border of Bavaria, but between 1791 and 1807 it was part of Prussia: though Bismarck has no interest in reclaiming it, its territorially chequered history may be a factor that appeals to the composer as he seeks to appeal to both states simultaneously. It occupies a central position within Germany as a whole, a feature of symbolic importance to Wagner. Importantly for the purposes of enabling future visitors to reach a festival, it also enjoys good rail connections: there has been a spur from the main Bamberg–Hof line since 1853, making it one of the oldest tracks in Germany, initially financed by Bayreuth's enterprising town council then leased back to the Bavarian state.

It is not until 16 April 1871 that Wagner and Cosima first visit Bayreuth together. It is immediately obvious that the baroque Margravial Opera House will not meet Wagner's requirements, despite its beauty and huge stage, so a new building – which is what he has always really wanted – is once again in prospect. Plans develop fast: Wagner quickly befriends the chairman of the town council, Friedrich Feustel, who usefully happens to be a distant relative of Wagner's Brockhaus brothers-in-law. As well as offering personal financial support, Feustel persuades the town council – as public-spirited and far-sighted now as they were when planning the railway two decades earlier – to make available to Wagner free of charge any site that he deems suitable for his purpose. Various options are investigated: an attractive location in the gardens of the former Margravial Palace is ruled out because of its poor drainage, and another prospect is lost due to a dispute between its owners, but in January 1872 the town council acquires the plot of land where the Festspielhaus now stands and presents it to Wagner.

Meanwhile, the composer has shamelessly written to Düfflipp to ask him to send Semper's now redundant plans for the new theatre in Munich, though he emphasises that he will only make use of those ideas that he considers to be his own. Wagner's treatment of Semper has been such that he can no longer consider approaching him for his new project, and besides, Semper is now fully occupied in Vienna, where he will later build the Burgtheater, the Kunsthistorisches Museum and other important buildings on the Ringstrasse. Instead Wagner invites Wilhelm Neumann from

Berlin to develop a design, but he proves slow and uncommunicative; Wagner replaces him with Otto Brückwald, an architect from Leipzig in his early thirties. The design team grows to include Carl Brandt, a brilliant stage technician from Darmstadt, Carl Runkwitz from Altenburg, who assists him, and various master craftsmen from Bayreuth. Despite the complexity of the operation, Wagner emphasises that the building will be 'provisional' – not because it will be burned down after the performances, as he had idealistically imagined in Zurich, but because it will eliminate anything that is not essential to its function. 'Therefore economize here, economize – no ornamentation,' he writes to Feustel in April 1872. 'With this building we are offering only the outline of our idea, and handing it over to the *nation for completion* as a monumental edifice.'

By now, 'the nation' means something very different from what it did in 1862, when Ludwig first offered his support, let alone in 1848, when Wagner first conceived *Siegfrieds Tod*. At the ceremony on 22 May 1872 to mark the laying of the foundation stone, toasts are raised both to Ludwig and the Kaiser. This ostentatious even-handedness, unfair though it is to the King who has financed Wagner for the last decade, reveals the composer's determination to demonstrate his allegiance to the multiple locations of power in this rapidly changing Germany – and also, perhaps, that he still does not know quite where the rest of the money is going to come from.

* * *

Wagner announced his intentions with regard to Bayreuth to the general public in a notice issued on 12 May 1871 – just over a year before the laying of the foundation stone, and less than four weeks after he and Cosima first visited the town together. The festival

182

would take place in summer 1873, Wagner declared, giving him scarcely two years to raise the 300,000 thalers he estimated would be needed to pay for the theatre itself, plus the costs of the production and the expenses of everyone involved. He proposed to generate these funds in a manner unlike anything previously seen in theatrical history. He had adumbrated the basic principle in his preface to the 1863 publication of the libretti, when he speculated that a group of patrons sympathetic to his ideas might between them generate the funds he needed, but at that stage he could not envisage the mechanism that might make this happen; and in the event the timely appearance of the alternative solution – a wealthy prince – relieved him of the immediate need to do so.

The scheme that would turn Wagner's vague aspiration into hard cash was devised by the pianist Carl Tausig, together with his pupil Marie von Schleinitz, a wealthy Berlin socialite. Tausig himself was a star student of Liszt, who had introduced him to Wagner in 1858 when he was still a teenager. He was one of several German Jews who played crucial roles in the establishment of the Bayreuth Festival, despite its founder's antisemitic diatribes; Hermann Levi, the first conductor of *Parsifal*, was another. Tausig quickly became devoted to Wagner's music, and the composer enlisted his help in creating and performing piano transcriptions as a means of publicising his new works. Tausig and Schleinitz proposed to Wagner that a Patrons' Association should be created, and that its members should each purchase a certificate of patronage at a cost of 300 thalers. In return, they would be allotted a seat without further charge at each of the three cycles of *The Ring* that Wagner planned for the first festival. Should three patrons wish to share the cost of a certificate – which represented a considerable outlay – then each could be admitted to a single cycle. If all the thousand certificates that Tausig proposed to issue were sold, then the costs of the festival would – at least in theory – have been met. Wagner set out the details of these arrangements in a further notice issued on 18 May, six days after the first.

Wagner's announcement made an immediate impact. Three days after the publication of the first flyer, Emil Heckel, an instrument manufacturer and music publisher based in Mannheim, wrote to express his enthusiasm for Wagner's music and his interest in his plans; Wagner put him in touch with Tausig and the two men met in Berlin. From this meeting came the idea of the 'Wagner Society': a group of enthusiasts in a particular location who would share the costs of a single certificate, and who would decide on the lucky recipients of the seats at performances by drawing lots. Heckel himself founded the first Wagner Society in Mannheim on 1 June, skilfully harnessing the patriotic sentiment ubiquitous in the first few months of the new German Empire by describing it as a 'Society in Support of the Great National Undertaking'. By the end of 1871, Wagner Societies had also been founded in Leipzig, Munich and Vienna; the following year, they proliferated all over Germany and were founded in London, New York and Pest. The constitutions of these new societies, and of the similar groups that sprang up in the next few years in locations as far afield as Riga, Cairo and Boston, committed them not just to the financial support of Wagner's enterprise in Bayreuth but also to promoting the public understanding of his work in their own regions.

Unfortunately for Wagner, this welcome evidence of enthusiasm for his work across the world did not produce the financial outcome for which he was hoping. The news from Leipzig of Tausig's sudden death from typhoid in July 1871, at the age of only twenty-nine, dealt him a severe blow, depriving him not just of a close friend but also of a key advocate whom he had already appointed as manager of the forthcoming festival. Meanwhile, the scheme that Tausig devised attracted considerable attention but few actual patrons. On Heckel's advice, Wagner began travelling to give fund-raising concerts in the various cities where Wagner Societies had sprung up, beginning in Mannheim in December 1871.

He and Cosima proceed to spend much of the next two years travelling across Germany, their visits taking in many of the places where Wagner has previously lived and worked: Würzburg, Magdeburg, Leipzig, Dresden. Their time is not wasted: their presence helps to spread understanding of what the festival will entail and raises the morale of the Wagner Societies they visit, and the performances they hear along the way help Wagner to identify (and rule out) possible singers for his own production. But their schedule is exhausting, and prevents Wagner from mak-ing the progress he hopes with the full score of *Götterdämmerung*. And their efforts do not generate anything like the financial rewards they expect. Despite a few generous high-profile back-ers – Liszt; the Sultan of Turkey; the Khedive of Egypt – the patronage scheme has stubbornly failed to catch the imagination of the public at large. Nor do members of any other royal houses in Germany come forward to join Ludwig in supporting the pro-ject. It soon becomes clear that the timetable set out so boldly in Wagner's announcement is unrealistic: the date of the inaugural festival is put back first to 1874 (in 1872), then (in 1873) to 1875.

By April 1873, of the 1,300 patronage certificates that Wagner now hopes to sell – the total number has been increased to match the rise in projected costs – only about two hundred have been purchased. A month short of his sixtieth birthday, Wagner is exhausted and demoralised. Even the elaborate celebrations that Cosima has secretly planned for the day – which begin with sing-ers hidden in his garden serenading him with a chorus from *Die Meistersinger*, and end with performances in the Margravial Opera

House of music that he himself wrote so long ago that he can scarcely recognise it – cannot entirely dispel his gloom.

* * *

Bayreuth, 2 August 1873. The topping-out ceremony for the Festspielhaus takes place in the late afternoon sunshine. Cosima and her children tentatively make their way up to the top of the scaffolding. The processional march from Act II of *Tannhäuser* is played as the workmen hammer the final pieces of the structure into place. An uplifting hymn is sung: *'Nun danket alle Gott'* (Now thank we all our God). Liszt – reconciled at last to his daughter and new son-in-law after many years of estrangement – attends the ceremony and opines that this is the first time a theatre has ever been built to house an idea. That evening, a splendid firework display is held in the town. Cosima thinks with pride about how the children will remember this great day.

Behind this public display of confidence in the theatre lies a great deal of private anxiety about whether Wagner will ever be able to afford to mount a festival there. All that has been completed is the theatre's empty shell: the state-of-the-art stage machinery, which has always been the part of the project that Wagner imagines costing the most, still needs to be commissioned and procured. Shortly after the ceremony, going back on what he has promised, Wagner writes to Ludwig to request a loan; Düfflipp responds that the King's own building projects at the castles of Neuschwanstein and Linderhof preclude any further support of Wagner's. An advance from Schott on the yet-to-be-completed full score of *Götterdämmerung* generates some useful cash, but much more is needed, and Wagner's other fundraising ideas – mailshotting booksellers across Germany with an impassioned appeal from a Dresden literature professor; asking other German theatres to support his new enterprise with benefit performances – draw a complete blank. By the end of the year, the situation seems desperate.

Just as happened ten years earlier, an intervention from Ludwig turns everything around. On 25 January 1874, he writes to Wagner to tell him that, notwithstanding everything he has said previously, he *will* help to salvage his festival: he cannot do anything else, so deeply invested is he in his work and his vision for revealing it to the world. Wagner writes back immediately to express his gratitude for the fact that, even if the new German nation has sadly failed to recognise the importance of art that expresses the German spirit, the King of Bavaria has remained steadfast. By the end of February, a new contract has been signed. The Bavarian Court will advance a loan of 100,000 thalers to enable the fitting-out of the theatre to be completed in time for a festival that everyone still expects to happen the following summer. All outstanding debts will be repaid in full in eighteen months' time from the proceeds of the first festival. In the meantime, any further income generated from patronage certificates and half of whatever Wagner raises from fundraising concerts will pass straight to the Bavarian Treasury as partial repayment of the loan. Some of these clauses are unrealistic: in October Wagner confesses that it will not be possible to hold the first festival until 1876, meaning that the loan will not be repaid until then at the earliest; the following September, after much wrangling, he negotiates an amendment to the clause about patronage certificates, arguing that the income they bring is needed to complete items such as costumes.

Meanwhile, Wagner and his family have taken up residence at Wahnfried, a luxurious new villa on a plot adjoining the gardens of the former Margravial Palace. They move in on 28 April 1874 after two years of building works. Wagner explains the villa's name in a verse couplet that is inscribed over the main door:

'Here, where my illusions found peace [*Wähnen Frieden fand*] / Wahnfried shall this house be named.' He pays most of the construction costs using a gift of 25,000 thalers from Ludwig, of whom he places a twice-life-sized bronze bust – also a gift – in a prominent position in the front garden.

By the summer of 1875, the theatre – or the stage area at any rate – is near enough completion to be used for rehearsals. On 24 July, Wagner for the first time experiences the acoustic of which he has dreamed, as members of the cast give a rough rendition of the opening scene of *Das Rheingold*. Rehearsals progress through the summer, with singers and an orchestra whom Wagner has persuaded to work for only notional remuneration. Despite some unwelcome changes of cast, the portents for next summer's festival are promising, artistically at least – financially, things remain precarious.

In September Wagner reluctantly petitions Kaiser Wilhelm I for emergency assistance (he had initiated a similar approach the previous January, but was saved from having to follow through with it by Ludwig's unexpected change of heart). On this occasion the Kaiser himself initially seems sympathetic, but his ministers rebuff Wagner: they suggest that he asks the newly assembled Reichstag, an idea Wagner treats with contempt. However, he is not without useful supporters in the Prussian capital: Botho von Hülsen, intendant of the Hoftheater, secures him some retrospective royalties on thirty years of Berlin performances of *The Flying Dutchman* and persuades the Kaiser to donate the income from the premiere of a new *Tristan* production to the Bayreuth fund, all of which generates helpful cash for the fast-approaching festival. At this stage every contribution, however small, is gratefully received: even by February 1876 Wagner has only sold 490 of the projected 1,300 patronage certificates. But the money he generates in Prussia is only a tiny fraction of what he has received from Bavaria, and more specifically from its king. Whatever he might have expected to happen in the heady days after Prussia's victory over France, and whatever the vicissitudes of their personal relationship, it is Ludwig's unfailing faith in Wagner's artistic vision that has almost single-handedly enabled the festival to become a reality. A few weeks before it is due to open, the king agrees to yet another stop-gap loan to ensure that it can go ahead.

Ludwig's dearest desire has long been to witness *The Ring* in the theatre – but on his own, free from any obligation to mix with the subjects, dignitaries and fellow monarchs who make his life as king so miserable. On 6 August 1876, his wish finally begins to come true. Accompanied only by two aides, he arrives in Bayreuth by train at one in the morning. Wagner greets him with a carriage ready to take him to the Eremitage palace: it is the first time the two men have met in person since the premiere of *Die Meistersinger.* That evening, Ludwig attends the 'general rehearsal' – effectively a private performance – of *Das Rheingold,* with only Wagner for company: the pair sit in the royal box whose inclusion in the design is a last-minute concession to tradition. The composer persuades the king that the acoustic of the theatre will be improved if there is a proper audience present for the next three dress rehearsals, and issues free tickets, but these other attendees remain in darkness and do not diminish Ludwig's enjoyment. Twelve years and many hundreds of thousands of thalers after first meeting Wagner, he has at last experienced the artwork that without him might never have come into existence. He responds not with pride but with gratitude. 'Fortunate century', he writes to Wagner, 'that saw this spirit arise in its midst! How future generations will envy those to whom fell the incomparable happiness of being your contemporaries.'

6
Staging the story

From casting to curtain-up

BAYREUTH, JUNE 1874. An opera company from the nearby city of Coburg is performing in the Margravial Opera House. Hans Richter – who has recently agreed to conduct the first production of *The Ring* in two years' time, despite the demands of his new position as Director of the Pest Opera and some heavy-handed negotiating tactics from Wagner – attends performances of *Don Giovanni* and *William Tell* and identifies a promising soprano among the cast. He invites her to meet the Wagners at Wahnfried, and on 9 July, Friederike Sadler-Grün sings some excerpts from *Tannhäuser* to them. Cosima records in her diary that 'in Frau Grün from Coburg we have made a real discovery: the voice is lovely and her whole character reveals a good musician and a fine woman.' Their next encounter, twelve days later, is more awkward: 'Frau Grün again comes over from Coburg; she sings "Brünnhilde's Awakening," which causes a certain amount of embarrassment, since she cannot sing Brünnhilde.' A more suitable Brünnhilde is soon identified in Amalie Materna, a Viennese soprano still in her early thirties; on 26 August, meanwhile, Sadler-Grün's husband writes to Wagner to tell him that his wife '*would be inclined* to take over the part of Sieglinde!!' – Cosima's italics and exclamation marks make clear what she and Wagner think of that idea. The matter is finally resolved on 5 November: 'Frau Grün . . . comes to our house; it is settled that she will sing Fricka.'

Similarly tortuous sets of discussions will be required in order to resolve most of the other forty-eight casting decisions required for the first *Ring*. Personal issues intrude: Wagner is keen that Therese Vogl should play Sieglinde, as she did in the Munich production of 1870, but worries that her husband Heinrich will not let her do so unless Wagner also allots him one of the cycle's principal tenor roles – Siegfried, or at the very least Siegmund. Herr Vogl took the latter role in Munich, but Wagner has no intention of letting him reprise it here; he is pacified with the part of Loge, which he played in Munich in 1869, but provokes an unwelcome last-minute casting challenge with his announcement of his wife's pregnancy. Wagner resolves this problem with only qualified success by recruiting the Munich singer Josephine Schefsky to replace her as Sieglinde.

Wagner has a singular set of requirements. Above all, he wants singers who can not only master the formidable vocal challenges of the music he has written, but also act convincingly. This emphasis on verisimilitude – one that places him at odds with almost every other opera producer of his day – also dictates his concern that his singers should be more or less the right age for their parts. That criterion affects his thinking about the casting of Sadler-Grün, who will be forty by the time of the production, and also rules out an obvious candidate for Siegfried: the Berlin singer Albert Niemann, who sang Tannhäuser in the infamous Paris production and has appeared as Walther in *Die Meistersinger*, but who will be in his mid-forties by 1876 – too old, in Wagner's opinion, to play the callow hero. Wagner has always had Niemann in mind for Siegmund, but the prickly singer, conscious of his pre-eminence in the profession, sees no reason why he should not also take on Siegfried. This idea is anathema to Wagner, who believes that his audiences will lose their belief in the story if they see the same singer in different roles in successive evenings, but he will not rule it out before being sure he has another tenor capable of taking the role of Siegfried in the last two dramas.

Wagner has always known that Siegfried would be the hardest role to cast. He has sometimes lamented his own tendency to write his most demanding parts for the tenor voice, but he has been lucky with his tenors in the past. He holds such fond memories of Josef Tichatschek in the roles of Rienzi and Lohengrin that in 1867, when Ludwig asked him to mount *Lohengrin* in Munich, he conquered his own preference for age-appropriate casting and chose his old Dresden friend for the title role; unfortunately the King was unable to suspend his disbelief in this sixty-year-old Knight of the Swan, and replaced Tichatschek with the youthful Vogl for the public performances. Wagner holds even fonder memories of his first Tristan, Ludwig Schnorr von Carolsfeld, whose death at the age of only twenty-nine deeply affected him, and whose widow Malvina disrupted the domestic harmony of Tribschen in bizarre fashion in 1866, when she claimed to be channelling her late husband's voice in an effort to help Wagner escape the baleful influence of Cosima. He feels sure that Schnorr von Carolsfeld would have become his ideal Siegfried had he lived; now, ten years later, he struggles to find a worthy successor.

Wagner's first choice is Franz Diener, a twenty-five-year-old tenor from Dessau with whom he works for some weeks in Bayreuth, but his shortcomings soon become clear. Richter proposes his mother's former singing pupil: Franz Glatz, a young Hungarian lawyer with no stage experience whatsoever. Wagner works with him, too, but it becomes clear that despite his powerful voice, Glatz has neither the stamina nor the technique to cope with the role. In April 1875 Wagner offers the part to Hermann Schrötter, whom he sees as Tannhäuser in Braunschweig, impressed by his voice if not by his acting; Schrötter accepts, but two weeks later withdraws when the theatre director in Braunschweig makes his displeasure at Wagner's invitation clear. Eventually, and in some desperation, he turns to Georg Unger, a tenor from Mannheim in his late thirties whom he has already cast as Froh.

Like Schnorr von Carolsfeld, Unger is of huge physical stature, matching the Siegfried of Wagner's imagination. Wagner casts him on potential rather than achievement, but believes that with appropriate guidance he can grow into the role. His lack of obvious credentials antagonises Niemann, who still believes that he should play Siegfried as well as Siegmund; Niemann threatens to resign from the production altogether, and Franz Betz – the Berlin baritone who withdrew from his role as Wotan in the Munich *Rheingold* and is cast as Wotan/the Wanderer here – weighs in on his colleague's side, hinting that he too will leave as a gesture of solidarity. Faced with this dual threat, Wagner considers giving up his strongly held opposition to casting Niemann in both roles – and writes a report for Ludwig that reveals that he remains undecided on the matter as late as August 1875 – but he eventually trusts his hunch about Unger. He draws up a programme of work that involves the singer giving up his post in Mannheim and rebuilding his technique under the guidance of Julius Hey, a singing teacher Wagner knows and trusts, who is willing to take leave from his post at the Munich School of Music to dedicate himself to the task. Wagner himself, meanwhile, works on Unger's acting, building the physical confidence and exuberance that are essential to his conception of the part. In September 1875 Unger tries out some passages from the third act of *Siegfried* on the Festspielhaus stage, and surprises both Hey and Wagner by how well he does. Provided that he withdraws from the contract he holds for the winter in Düsseldorf and continues to devote himself to his studies, he now seems likely to succeed.

Wrangling over the rest of the cast continues into 1876 as the production draws near. To secure Materna's leave of absence from her contract at the Hofoper, Wagner reluctantly accepts the Viennese theatre's demands: on 19 April Cosima notes, with even more exclamation marks than usual, the arrival of a letter from Franz Jauner, the theatre's intendant, 'delighted to get *Die Walküre* for Vienna (condition for Frau Materna!!!), intends to start on scenery right away'. Wagner's negotiating position is scarcely strengthened by the minimal fees he is able to offer his singers. He tries to secure their loyalty by dangling promises of better remuneration for festivals in 1877 and 1878 where much less rehearsal time will also be necessary. Some of his cast may suspect, correctly, that this year's likely losses will prevent any further festivals from taking place in the foreseeable future, but most nonetheless accept Wagner's conditions. A crucial cast member who does not is the celebrated Austrian bass Emil Scaria, who is due to play Hagen. In January he makes financial demands well beyond what Wagner can agree to, not least because of the ill-feeling it would cause among the rest of the cast if Scaria were singled out for special treatment. Unfortunately, Wagner soon realises that Josef Kögel, the singer from Hamburg whom he has cast in Scaria's place, suffers from stage-fright and will not be able to learn the part in time. He pleads with his original Hagen to return, offering him more than he initially asked for, but receives no reply. Fortunately for Wagner, his next choice – Gustav Siehr from Wiesbaden – proves excellent.

* * *

Bayreuth, 1 July 1875. Just over a year before the premiere is scheduled to take place, the cast begins to rehearse at the piano. Most of the sessions take place at Wahnfried while building works continue at the Festspielhaus: they last for two hours in the morning, and then everyone resumes from late afternoon until 7 p.m. *Répétiteurs* are drawn from a small group of devoted acolytes who become collectively known as Wagner's 'Nibelung Chancellery': they include his Hungarian-born amanuensis Anton Seidl, who has already lived at Wahnfried for three years, and the Russian-Jewish composer-pianist Joseph Rubinstein; both are still in their twenties. Wagner himself works with the singers with a vigour and level of detail never previously seen in an opera house, inventing the modern profession of 'opera director' as he goes. He rarely gives praise: only Karl Hill as Alberich earns his consistent approval, and on the rare occasions he compliments another singer – as when he tells his Brünnhilde, Amalie Materna, that one of her phrases from the *Götterdämmerung* Prologue was 'beautifully done' – everyone knows he is genuinely impressed. Occasionally he will let his singers simply run a scene without passing comment – particularly in the later parts of the cycle, where the score gives more detailed instructions, and especially in scenes involving Alberich, such as his dialogues with Mime in *Siegfried* and with Hagen in *Götterdämmerung*. But more frequently, he thrusts himself energetically into the action, showing by example how he would like each of the parts to be sung: he is, by all accounts, a brilliant actor, and convincingly inhabits characters of all ages, genders and species. When he recites the words that Brünnhilde sings at the height of her emotional turmoil following her awakening by Siegfried, he does so with 'the intensity of a flash of lightning, thrilling the spectator to the marrow'.

That memorable description comes from the recollections of Heinrich Porges, a Czech-Austrian writer and choral conductor whom Wagner has far-sightedly engaged to record his work in rehearsal: so specific are Porges's descriptions of Wagner's requests that subsequent producers treat them as canonical supplements to the scores. Another observer who provides helpfully detailed recollections is the choreographer, Richard Fricke, whom Wagner has engaged after being deeply impressed by his work on Gluck's *Orfeo* in Dessau: he is particularly keen for his help in making the movements of the Rhinemaidens in the opening scene of *Das Rheingold* convincingly aquatic. Fricke joins rehearsals from 12 July and becomes a close friend of the Wagner family, giving dancing lessons to the children at Wahnfried. Both Porges and Fricke subsequently publish their recollections in books that convey the unprecedented intensity of the rehearsal process.

True to the principles he set out in lengthy treatises decades earlier in Zurich, Wagner demands that his singers at every point serve the drama: musical accuracy is an essential prerequisite, but never an end in itself. He demands complete clarity – 'there was nothing he hated so much as blurred, indistinct words, notes or gestures' – and tempi are chosen with this in mind. In the most complex passages, such as the Ride of the Valkyries, this means adopting a relatively restrained tempo whenever dialogue is in progress and reserving faster tempi for choral outbursts and orchestral passages. Forceful singing is not just a matter of volume: it also requires attention to all the shorter notes, as in Siegfried's Forging Song, which once again sometimes means reducing the tempo. Elsewhere, however, Wagner encourages faster tempi: he insists that Waltraute's plea to Brünnhilde should at no point drag, so that the audience senses her 'fear and feverish haste'.

He warns against any of the histrionics associated with conventional operatic acting: for the scene between Siegfried and the Wanderer in the final act of *Siegfried*, for example, he asks for a plain, naturalistic style, though it is a naturalism that always keeps in mind the elevated, heroic qualities of the characters. Gentle vibrato is permissible as a means of colouring particular words, but the exaggerated tremolando found among many contemporary singers is not. Wagner is particularly insistent that his singers should always keep in mind their immediate on-stage relationship to other characters, even during rapturous melodic outpourings such as that with which Sieglinde greets Brünnhilde's announcement of her pregnancy: 'even in passages of lyrical abandon the singer should not adopt the bad old operatic habit of addressing the public but always keep the head turned in profile'. An impassive rather than an overly demonstrative style of delivery is often what he requires, as in the first scene of *Rheingold* when Woglinde delivers the information that only someone who renounces love will be able to take possession of the gold.

Alongside constant awareness of their responsibility to the drama, Wagner demands that his singers understand the relationship of their individual parts to the musical fabric of the cycle. In Act II of *Götterdämmerung*, for example, Gutrune's jealous interrogation of Siegfried when he returns from the Valkyries' rock can only be delivered effectively 'if she has an instinctive feeling for the harmonic structure of her short melodic phrases . . . the notation of melody linked to words presents only the surface of emotion; it is the harmony that reveals the underlying roots of thought and feeling.' Singers must appreciate how their parts relate to the cycle's web of leitmotifs, and also that leitmotifs should not be played or sung in the same way or at the same tempo each time they appear. The motif that depicts Valhalla, for example, needs to be performed 'slowly and broadly' if it occurs in conjunction with an actual event on stage, such as Wotan's invitation to Fricka and the other gods to join him there at the end of *Rheingold*; but if it is used to clarify characters' reminiscences about past events – as in Act I of *Die Walküre*, where it reveals the identity of the figure who placed the sword in the ash tree – Wagner asks that it is delivered at a faster tempo and in a less emphatic way, 'in the throwaway style of an experienced actor delivering an interpolated sentence'. Precise co-ordination between orchestra and stage is often necessary when a leitmotif in the former casts light on an action in the latter, as in Act III of *Die Walküre* when a distorted version of the 'Ride' motif accompanies the shriek of the Valkyries as they realise the humiliation that Wotan has in mind for Brünnhilde. Throughout these weeks of preliminary rehearsal, and those that follow the next summer, Wagner tries to tease out for his singers every possible nuance and implication of their words, music and actions, so that their individual performances make sense within the drama as a whole.

At the end of the rehearsal process, Wagner distils his advice to his cast into a few sentences which he writes out and fixes to the stage door with the date of the first *Rheingold* performance, 13 August 1876, at the bottom:

<u>Last Request</u>
to my dear comrades
<u>!Clarity!</u>
The big notes will look after themselves; the small notes and your text are the main object.
Never speak directly to the audience, only to each other; in monologues, look down or up, but never straight ahead.
<u>Last Wish</u>
<u>Be true to me, you dear ones!</u>

Wagner has done everything he can to help his performers understand the new and extraordinary type of acting he demands – now it is up to them.

The space into which Wagner's singers step has been designed to give the festival's audiences the impression that they are observing a mythical world entirely separate from the mundane realities of the present day. No lights are left on in the auditorium during the performance; the orchestra and conductor are concealed from the spectators, eliminating the risk that witnessing the musicians' labours in the pit will shatter their belief in the illusion being created on stage; the absence of side boxes and central aisle minimises the likelihood of distraction from other audience members. The sense of the stage as a self-contained universe is enhanced by its massive size, by the double proscenium that frames it and creates the illusion of still greater depth, and by the evenly spaced wooden columns on either side of the auditorium. From the back seats, these create a sense of an infinite series of arches that draw the spectator's gaze irresistibly towards the stage as they recede.

Wagner has always hoped *The Ring* would make a visual impact as overwhelming as that of his words and music. This can only be achieved with set designs quite unlike anything found in a conventional opera house, but Wagner knows that, however extravagant his range of talents, he does not have the skills as a draughtsman to create these for himself. After considering a number of possible designers, in summer 1872 he approaches the Viennese artist Josef Hoffmann, who is primarily a landscape painter but whose superbly detailed sets for the Vienna Hofoper's productions of *The Magic Flute* and *Der Freischütz* have attracted much admiration. When Hoffmann shows Wagner his sketches in November 1873, the composer is generally delighted at how well they suggest *The Ring*'s heroic character, though he feels that the artist sometimes prioritises landscape over drama, and would prefer a less fussily detailed approach to a number of scenes, particularly those in Hunding's hut and the Gibichung Hall.

Hoffmann is originally engaged by Wagner with the expectation that he will paint the sets himself, but it becomes clear the following year that this will be too big an undertaking for the artist, who has neither assistants nor a studio of an appropriate scale and does not wish to give up his work in Vienna to base himself at the Festspielhaus. Carl Brandt, now Bayreuth's technical director, who is widely regarded as the cleverest theatre technician in Germany, comes up with an alternative solution: Hoffmann's designs should be handed over to Max and Gotthold Brückner, two brothers who are doing a roaring trade as scenic designers in nearby Coburg, and a studio should be erected in Bayreuth to enable them to produce the scenery on site. But Hoffmann refuses to make the compromises necessary to turn his sketches into practical pieces of stage machinery. By autumn 1874, he and the Brückners have fallen out, and Wagner is unable to mediate. Brandt takes the brothers' side; Hoffmann is paid off and in turn surrenders his right to influence how his designs are realised. When he finally sees the sets in the theatre, he is deeply disappointed: they are so much more conventional, less magical than he had imagined.

No photographs survive of the sets the Brückners actually realise for the first production, and for more than a century the only inkling of how it looks is provided by a series of fourteen black-and-white photographs taken by Victor Angerer of Hoffmann's original sketches – three apiece for *Rheingold* and *Walküre*, four for each of the other two dramas. At the encouragement of Hoffmann, keen to make some further money from the time he has invested in an enterprise of which he is no longer part, reproductions are offered for sale to Wagnerian devotees in a handsome leather-bound port-folio. It is not until 2005 that the small oil sketches from which the photographs are taken are rediscovered in Munich, revealing the vibrant palette of colours that Hoffmann envisages, though it is a moot point whether the limited lighting technology available in the Festspielhaus would adequately convey his vision even were he there to articulate it. From the 1990s onwards, meanwhile, a series of much larger canvases by Hoffmann of scenes from *The Ring*, many of which he sells to King Ludwig, is rediscovered in locations across Germany: he paints these not for any practical purposes connected with the production, but to generate further income, and perhaps also as a means of assuaging his disappoint-ment at being removed from Wagner's project by suggesting what might have been.

Hoffmann's frustration is privately shared by Wagner, though he is careful to keep his feelings to himself. Cosima puts a positive spin on the situation, describing the scenery for Act II of *Siegfried* as 'outstandingly beautiful . . . Herr Brandt has once again worked wonders.' Due to the excellent relationship she establishes with Max Brückner, the older of the two brothers, he will go on to enjoy a long-lasting connection with Bayreuth. His studio will provide all the festival's designs and sets between 1896 and 1911, and his work provides the basis for the 'Bayreuth style' that is sub-sequently imitated in *Ring* productions all over the world.

Wagner ends up being no more satisfied with the costumes for the first *Ring* than with the sets: perhaps he bears some of the responsibility for this, as it is one of the few aspects of the pro-duction to which he has given relatively little thought. It is not until 17 December 1874 that he makes contact with a costume designer – Carl Emil Doepler, who studied in Munich, worked for six years in New York and is now based in Berlin – and sends him the libretti. Wagner's letter makes clear what he does *not* want the costumes to look like – they should not resemble the familiar illustrations with which artists such as Peter von Cornelius and Julius Schnorr von Carolsfeld (father of the singer) have adorned editions of the *Nibelungenlied*; nor should they imitate more recent artists who have represented Nordic deities as modified versions of Greek and Roman gods. But he is much vaguer about what he actually has in mind. Apart from an interesting passing comment that 'references to the costumes of the Germanic peoples in Roman authors who came into contact with these nations do not appear to have received the attention they merit', Wagner gives no guidance on how Doepler should represent characters 'from a period of culture not only remote from our own experience but having no association with any known experience'.

In the absence of more specific suggestions from the composer, Doepler conscientiously embarks on extensive research in various German and Danish museums and produces 500 or so designs that represent his best guess at what Wagner's mythical characters might have looked like, complete with bear-skins, drinking horns and horned helmets. Like Brückner's sets, Doepler's costume designs – which he later publishes as a portfolio of lithographs – are the model for an entire generation of *Ring* productions across the world, but they entirely fail to satisfy the touchy composer and his even touchier wife, who famously likens them to the outfits of 'Red Indian chiefs'.

The assorted non-human and semi-human characters in *The Ring* are brought to life with varying degrees of success. Grane, Brünnhilde's horse, is played by a real-life nine-year-old stallion – Cocotte, a gift from King Ludwig – who behaves impeccably. The dragon in *Siegfried* causes more problems. It is being manufactured in England, but it arrives late and in separate consignments:

the tail appears first, in July 1876; the head does not appear until mid-August, uncomfortably close to the first night; the neck that is supposed to join them never materialises (it may have been sent to Beirut rather than Bayreuth), so the stage managers have to find an impromptu solution for the performances, a shortcoming not lost on Wagner's more hostile critics. There is more success with the contraptions designed for the opening scene to create the illusion that the Rhinemaidens are swimming. Each of them lies down in a cradle attached to a trolley that is wheeled around under the stage, invisibly to the audience; with this device, and three assistants for each Rhinemaiden, they can be lifted up and down as well as back and forth. There is great anxiety when the machinery is first tried out, but after much rehearsal and careful choreographic input from Fricke, the effect is very convincing.

Despite the dedication of Brandt and his production team, some technical issues continue to create problems right up until the festival. An unforeseen issue arises in the interludes of *Das Rheingold*, when the steam that is used to conceal the movements of scenery necessary to effect the transformations enters the orchestral pit and causes the six harps to go out of tune. The orchestra complains of being cold: to his chagrin, Wagner himself has to traipse round the Festspielhaus in search of the offending open window. And the very last scene of the cycle causes a bitter dispute between Brandt and Fricke: the technical director insists that the mechanism he has designed to achieve the collapse of the Gibichung Hall must be used as he intended, but the choreographer argues that the effect is underwhelming and prevents him from manoeuvring his actors around the stage in the way he wishes. Brandt wins the argument when Wagner is forced to arbitrate – a reminder, perhaps, that despite the composer's reputation as an idealist, one who will stop at nothing to see his most elaborate visions turned into reality, he is also always ready to take a pragmatic decision if it will enable the performance to proceed.

* * *

Bayreuth, 24 July 1875. Music is heard in the Festspielhaus for the first time, during a technical rehearsal to try out some of the scenery. Lilli Lehmann, her younger sister Marie, and Minna Lammert, who play the three Rhinemaidens, mount the stage to sing their trio; Karl Hill adds Alberich's lines from the wings. 'Splendid sight, magnificent sound; R. greatly moved,' Cosima succinctly records. The acoustics are as good as Wagner has hoped: the series of columns on each side of the auditorium help the ear as much as they do the eye, by scattering the sound in the same way as the horizontal fronts of the numerous balconies do in an opera house such as La Scala. Audiences thus receive a complex combination of direct and diffused sound, providing an exceptionally warm and well-blended experience of the voices on stage. Many attribute this to the wood they see in the auditorium, though in fact this makes little difference: to save on costs, timber has been used only for the frame, which has been infilled with brick in the same way as a warehouse building.

A week later, on 1 August in the late afternoon, the orchestra assembles in the theatre for the first time. They cheer the composer and his family as they enter their Valhalla, and Franz Betz sings Wotan's paean from scene 2 of *Das Rheingold*: 'Finished is the eternal work . . .' The acoustics prove to be just as good for the orchestra as they are for the singers: 'heavenly sound, overwhelming impression, R. very moved'. The design of the orchestra pit is unique, with musicians arranged on six different levels descending steeply down from the conductor's desk. A cover curves over the front and top of the pit, originally intended to prevent light from escaping into the auditorium, but soon found to be helpful in limiting the volume of the orchestral sound and improving its blend; for similar acoustic reasons, a further cover will be installed at the back of the pit for the 1882 festival. Violins fill the first steps and some of the second, first violins on the conductor's right, seconds on the left: Wagner reverses the pattern used in every other orchestra so that the highest string notes are not projected straight into the cover of the pit. Violas occupy the next step, then cellos, basses and harps, all of which are split up so that their sound comes from both sides of the pit; the remaining steps are taken by woodwinds; by horns and trumpets; and finally – right underneath the stage – by trombones, tubas, timpani and percussion. Because only a small proportion of the orchestra's sound finds the pit opening and gets out into the audience chamber, singers can be heard without difficulty even in heavily scored passages.

The orchestra numbers 115 in total, almost twice as many as in most opera orchestras of the time, and includes 64 string players, led by the young violin virtuoso August Wilhelmj. Wagner has recruited most of the players from the best German opera houses, although a few come from much further afield: the American conductor and Wagner enthusiast Theodore Thomas, who has raised more than $10,000 for the festival, sends several members of his New York orchestra to take part. None of the players receives a fee, only travel expenses and subsistence. They rehearse for twelve days in 1875 – two sessions a day, the singers joining in the afternoons, covering an act each day – then assemble again on 3 June 1876. They are joined for *Götterdämmerung* by members of local choral societies who make up the chorus of Gibichungs.

While Richter conducts, Wagner sits at a small desk on the side of the stage, his score illuminated by a small petrol lamp.

He communicates what he wants not just through words, but also through his sheer physical presence: while the orchestra rehearses Siegfried's Rhine Journey from *Götterdämmerung*, for example, he says nothing, according to Porges, but 'his facial expression and characteristically eloquent gestures and hand movements were sufficient to spur the conductor to achieve the desired combination of plasticity, eloquent precision and perpetually forward-driving energy.' The shape of the Festspielhaus pit poses unique challenges for the conductor, who can scarcely hear the singers and must judge balance and ensemble by lip-reading and experience of the house; neither singers nor conductor ever experience the miraculous blend of sound reported by audiences. Felix Mottl, a member of the Nibelung Chancellery who will later become Cosima's favoured conductor, is terrified when Richter jokingly asks him if he would like to take charge. Numerous errors in the parts that most orchestra members are playing for the first time compound the difficulties: Richter impresses his players by calling out corrections instrument by instrument without stopping the rehearsal.

The relationship between Wagner and Richter has been much more strained of late than in the Tribschen days, when the conductor lived practically as part of the family. Still in his early thirties but newly married and with a burgeoning career conducting both concerts and opera, Richter has started to assert his independence. Wagner is offended that his conductor does not arrive in Bayreuth until two weeks after the first piano rehearsals begin in 1875; when Richter leaves the pit at the end of the last rehearsal for the year on 12 August, Wagner is mystified at the ovation the orchestra gives him: 'Oh Richter, I nearly forgot all about you!' After Richter's departure, Wagner is enraged by press reports that suggest that the conductor has been bad-mouthing him; Cosima, too, makes her frustrations felt, and angry letters fly between Bayreuth and Vienna, where Richter has recently been appointed as music director of the city's Philharmonic Orchestra. But Richter's underlying loyalty, and the composer's awareness of how much he needs the conductor to make his project succeed, ensure that the rift is repaired, even if things will never be quite the same as they were before: in December, Wagner and Cosima agree to serve as godparents to the Richters' first child, a girl whom they tactfully name Richardis Cosima Eva.

The following summer, as everyone returns to Bayreuth and the first performances loom, Wagner remains concerned that Richter does not intuitively find the tempi that he would like, that his conducting lacks flexibility and that he is insufficiently aware of the needs of the drama. He attributes much of the difficulty to Richter's continuing failure to attend enough of the piano rehearsals, which is where Wagner himself establishes the tempi with the singers. This sometimes leads to problems when the orchestra arrives, as in the passage from the last act of *Walküre* where Wotan is searching for Brünnhilde and Wagner tells Richter that 'you are bound too much to beating crotchets, which always hinders a tempo'. But Wagner is mindful enough of company morale to keep his reservations largely to himself, and more often than not, Richter's diaries for the rehearsals that proceed through June and July 1876 record that the Master is satisfied.

Both men know, of course, that Wagner will not be deterred from intervening whenever he thinks it necessary: he devotes the same attention that he has already lavished on the singers to getting exactly what he wants from the orchestra, and to securing precisely the right tempo for each passage. Players need to be aware of what happens on stage: for example, when introducing the exultant C major theme at the very end of *Siegfried* – marked

'Lively, but strong and without hurrying' – the horn players need to consider how Siegfried and Brünnhilde will each later sing it, so that it expresses 'sublime joy . . . a celebration of life'. Wagner's concern that listeners should recognise and subsequently remember new themes often dictates tempo, too: for the first appearance of Siegfried's famous horn call, Wagner gives the 'absolutely definite instruction: "not fast and above all establish the theme"'. The introduction of an important new theme does not always imply a slow tempo, however. Wagner requests that the 'proclamation of a new religion' theme in the third act of *Siegfried*, first heard after the Wanderer declares that he now cheerfully embraces the downfall of the gods, should be taken slightly faster than the previous bars. It may seem paradoxical that a theme of such weighty significance should not be played slowly, but Porges points out that 'taken a shade faster the effect of the sudden illumination by which Wotan himself is overwhelmed is all the more powerful'. What Wagner wants from each choice of tempo is very subtle and sometimes difficult to achieve, as when he demands that the dialogue between the Wanderer and Mime in Act I of *Siegfried* 'should combine the forward movement of an andante with the repose of an adagio'.

Informed interpretation of instructions regarding dynamics and close attention to balance – within the orchestra as well as between orchestra and stage – are equally important means by which instrumentalists can help to convey the drama. The Ride of the Valkyries requires careful treatment if the orchestra is to make the spectacular effect required by the piece's role in the drama while also meeting Wagner's demand for absolute comprehensibility of the words. Wagner asks that the orchestra does not play at full strength until the rousing change into the major key, and that players pay close attention to accents, becoming immediately quieter as soon as the necessary notes have been emphasised, since it is through careful phrasing rather than sheer volume that this passage should make its impact. Of course, there are sections of the score where Wagner wants the orchestra to take the lead – in the passage after Brünnhilde sinks on Wotan's chest, towards the end of *Die Walküre*, he asks for the strongest possible crescendo, and for the timpani to be particularly prominent – but most of his requests are for quieter playing. In the Wanderer/Erda scene in Act III of *Siegfried*, whose orchestral parts are densely populated with leitmotifs, he asks for these to be played in restrained, 'ghostly' fashion, setting out the principle that motifs 'of reminiscence or premonition should always be treated as subordinate to the events actually happening'; at the end of Act II of *Götterdämmerung*, he asks the orchestra to remember that Amalie Materna, playing Brünnhilde, is 'straining her physical and mental faculties to the limit', and therefore not to play too loudly. Wagner's final message to the orchestra, which he pins on the wall of the pit behind Richter, emphasises the need for delicacy, belying the reputation he has unjustly acquired for bombast: 'Piano pianissimo – then all will be well.'

* * *

Bayreuth, 13 August 1876. A crowd gathers outside the Festspielhaus for the first festival performance of *Das Rheingold*. At 7 p.m. – two hours later than originally planned, due to the heat – a group of trumpets plays an arrangement of 'Heda, heda, hedo', the rousing theme that Donner sings as he swings his hammer and clears the mists from the sky. This signal for the audience to take their seats has been chosen by Richter, who has selected similarly arresting fanfares to summon spectators to their seats for each act of the remaining dramas: the sword motif for *Walküre*, Siegfried's motif for *Siegfried*, the Valhalla motif for *Götterdämmerung*. Five minutes later, with everyone in the theatre, the fanfare is played again. Much else about the start of the performance surprises the audience. The curtains part in the middle rather than rising from the stage, a novelty admired by Alfred Pringsheim, future father-in-law of Thomas Mann. The gas lights in the auditorium are taken right down, if not completely extinguished, as some report. As the audience gets used to the unaccustomed darkness, the eight double basses play their first E flats.

Many celebrated composers are in the theatre for this and the further two cycles of *The Ring* that follow this first run: Liszt (of course), Bruckner, Grieg, Saint-Saëns, Tchaikovsky, Stanford. So too are numerous royal personages, including Grand Duke Vladimir of Russia and Emperor Dom Pedro II of Brazil, who earns himself a minor place in Bayreuth folklore by entering his profession as 'Emperor' in his hotel's visitors' book. Kaiser Wilhelm I arrives by train: as he greets Wagner, who is waiting at the station along with the entire orchestra and cast, he tells him that he never imagined he would manage to bring his festival off. Ludwig II is so entranced by his experience of the dress rehearsals that he conquers his own dislike of crowds to attend the final cycle, having been assured by Wagner that all his fellow kings and princes will have left Bavaria by then. He sits quietly with the composer in the royal box, but before the start of *Götterdämmerung* the lights go up and Friedrich Feustel gives the King a vote of thanks from the stage for all he has done, asking the audience to join him in raising three cheers.

Despite the support of Feustel and his fellow councillors, Bayreuth is not really prepared for the huge insurgence of visitors – including large numbers from the United States – that the festival has brought. Hotel accommodation is in short supply, and Tchaikovsky complains about how difficult it is to get a meal in town after the performances, with some visitors having to go without food altogether. The heatwave adds to the air of discomfort: Richter conducts in his shirtsleeves – a black cloth is pinned behind him so that the performers can see him – and many of the orchestra dispense with their jackets, too. 'This is where my musicians have to sweat,' Wagner tells the Kaiser as he shows him the pit during a tour of the building. It is not the last time that people complain about the heat in the Festspielhaus.

Almost every aspect of the audience's experience is different from that in every other opera house. The theatre is strikingly and deliberately plain. Its seating layout is modelled on that of a Greek amphitheatre: each of the 1,345 seats in the main body of the auditorium has a good view of the stage, thanks to the careful planning of the radius and rake of the seating. There are no boxes in the conventional sense of the term, though there is a 'princes' gallery' accommodating around one hundred people with a so-called royal box at the front of it. A further gallery seating around two hundred people is intended for artists and their families. The prohibition of applause during performances also surprises many spectators: after some enthusiastic audience members clap Vogl's performance as Loge during the first night of *Rheingold*, Wagner quickly manufactures placards to ensure that the offence is not repeated during *Walküre*. There are no curtain calls until the last night of *Götterdämmerung*, for which the entire cast and orchestra come out on stage, though Wagner does improvise a speech at the end of the first *Götterdämmerung* performance during which he ham-fistedly manages to offend audience and performers alike by inadvertently suggesting that there is not yet any real art in Germany.

A few technical blips mar the performances, particularly during the first night of *Rheingold*: a backdrop is raised too soon, giving audiences an unintended view of the back wall of the theatre and some stagehands; Betz mislays the ring as Alberich is cursing it and has to run into the wings to retrieve it. Some audience members carp at the pantomime-like appearances of the dragon, the bear, and the toad into which Alberich transforms himself; others are disconcerted by the covered pit and complain that the orchestra is not loud enough, not clear enough or not brilliant enough. But the overall response from audiences at all three cycles is overwhelmingly positive, and the applause is prolonged and rapturous.

Sixty music critics attend the festival and write hundreds of thousands of words of copy about every aspect of their experience. One of the most insightful accounts comes from Grieg, who notes – as few do at the time, though many will in years to come – the disparity between the subtle and allusive quality of much of the music and a staging so 'realistic' and 'obvious' as to 'jeopardise the drama': he would have preferred that more was 'left to the onlookers' imaginations instead of being openly displayed on the stage'. But despite his reservations, he praises Wagner as 'a true giant in the history of art, comparable in his innovation only to Michelangelo'. The coverage in the United States is extraordinary, helped by new cable technology that enables reports to be transmitted across the Atlantic at unprecedented speed. The conductor Leopold Damrosch files a series of articles for the *New York Sun* arguing that 'a new epoch in art has arisen'. John R. G. Hassard in the *New York Tribune* describes the festival as 'the most remarkable [experiment] that has ever been made either in music or in any of its sister arts'. And the *New York Herald* devotes four entire front pages in succession to the festival, each of them featuring a blown-up reproduction of a page of the score. It is the story of the century.

Financially, the festival is much less successful than Wagner expects. The total costs, including the theatre's construction, are 1,281,000 marks; the total income is only 1,133,000 marks, leaving a deficit of 148,000, in addition to which Wagner also owes 216,000 marks to the Bavarian Treasury from the loan Ludwig agreed in 1874. The practical result of these losses – as he soon realises, though he pretends for a few weeks that it is otherwise – is that he cannot proceed with his plan to stage another festival the following summer. As it turns out, the Festspielhaus will not open its doors again to the public for another six years.

But damaging though this outcome is to his self-esteem, it is much less crushing than his own nagging feeling that the festival has not been the success he anticipated. Everything was wrong about it, he tells Cosima over and over again: the singing, the conducting, the staging, the design, the organisation – even some of the music. In his worst moments he fears, as he confides to Ludwig some years later, that he has perpetrated something that is merely ordinary: an ordinary opera, an ordinary piece of theatre. It is scant consolation that the rehearsal methods he has introduced have changed the art of opera production for ever. And the fact that within a few years *The Ring* will sell out theatres across Europe – and that within a few more, half the world's writers, artists and musicians will come under its spell – does little to assuage his sense of regret that it could all have been so much better. It is a triumph whose failure will haunt him for the remaining seven years of his life.

7
The story retold

NEW YORK, 4 MARCH 1889. At the city's Metropolitan Opera House, opened only six years previously and located on Broadway between 39th and 40th Streets, Anton Seidl begins to conduct the first *Ring* cycle ever mounted in the United States. Brünnhilde is played by Lilli Lehmann, leading lady both here and at Berlin's Imperial Opera, who appears in New York by special permission of Kaiser Wilhelm II; like Seidl, she brings to this *Ring* the experience of working with Wagner while still in her twenties on the original production, in which she took roles as Rhinemaiden, Valkyrie and Woodbird. Compromises are made. To keep each drama under four hours Seidl concedes significant cuts, particularly in *Götterdämmerung*, which loses the Norns, Waltraute, and Alberich's dialogue with Hagen. Scenery and costumes are based on those at Bayreuth, but are judged as tatty and old-fashioned, failing to match the impact of the rest of the production. The quality of Seidl's conducting is not questioned, however: critics praise his intimate knowledge of the text, the sounds he draws from the orchestra and his flexible tempi, comparable to those of the Master himself. Nor is the production's commercial appeal in doubt: as in all the 'German seasons' the Met mounts between 1884 and 1891 – seasons in which *everything* is sung in German, even Italian opera – Wagner performances outnumber those of all the other composers put together, and they sell many more tickets and generate greater profits despite the higher costs of staging them. By the middle of May, Seidl and his company have toured the country, presenting complete cycles to capacity crowds in Philadelphia, Boston, Milwaukee, Chicago and St Louis.

America's embrace of *The Ring* has not come from nowhere. All four dramas have already been separately premiered in New York: *Siegfried*, *Götterdämmerung* and *Rheingold* at the Met under Seidl, the last only in January; *Die Walküre* as early as 1877, first in an unsatisfactory realisation at the Academy of Music, and then, in 1885, in a triumphantly successful production at the Met, with Amalie Materna, Wagner's Brünnhilde, taking the same role under Leopold Damrosch. This *Walküre* production is the centrepiece of the Met's first 'German season', a change of emphasis decided upon by the new house's Board of Directors after the opening season's diet of French and Italian opera proved financially disastrous. The Board's choice of the German-born Damrosch as General Manager and chief conductor is propelled by his enthusiasm for Wagner, which they expect to shape the company's repertoire for many years, but Damrosch dies unexpectedly only sixteen days after the first *Walküre* – many blame it on overwork. The fact that the Met's Wagnerian aspirations do not die with him demonstrates the resilience of the American public's interest in this novel form of opera, an interest only heightened by the composer's own death in Venice in February 1883, eight months before the Met first opens its doors.

The new theatre itself is a tangible sign of the rapid social change taking place in New York. The city's first dedicated opera house was founded in 1833 by Mozart's librettist Lorenzo da Ponte as a home for his short-lived company, but most of New York's opera performances since 1854 have taken place at the 4,000-seat Academy of Music opened that year on East 14th Street and Irving Place. Many of the nineteenth century's most important operas received their first American performances there, including Verdi's *Rigoletto, Il trovatore* and *La traviata*, all of which were heard in the 1850s, only a couple of years after their European premieres. Most of the city's wealthiest families own boxes at the Academy and hand them down through the generations; the problem is that there are only eighteen such boxes, meaning that families who acquire their wealth later in the century as a result of their industrial or financial activities – the Vanderbilts, Morgans, Goulds and Rockefellers, for example – are unable to secure them. The frustration of such families propels them in 1880 to establish the Metropolitan Opera Company, in which they can purchase stock that will guarantee a right to one of the new theatre's seventy-three boxes (five are eventually allocated to the Vanderbilt family alone).

The theatre's design is controversial: some complain that it is simply too large; others that so much of the prime space has been allocated to boxes that the acoustics are poor for anyone who has to sit anywhere else. But such criticisms die down once the German seasons get under way, and particularly when Seidl assumes the musical directorship after Damrosch's death. So successful is Seidl's musical offering – which includes the US premieres of *Tristan, Die Meistersinger, Siegfried* and *Götterdämmerung*, alongside other works including *Carmen* and *Aida*, all sung in German – and so popular does the Metropolitan become as a gathering place for the new Manhattan elite, that in 1886 the Academy cancels its opera season altogether, and in 1888 it turns its attention to vaudeville. By this point, with three of the four dramas already in the repertoire, the complete *Ring* of 1889 seems a natural next step. The cycle is not only the Metropolitan Opera's supreme musical achievement to date; it can also – with its depiction of an old order giving way to a new – be seen, from a certain viewpoint, as dramatising the very forces that bring the new house into being.

It will still be another seven years before *The Ring* is seen again in its original home of Bayreuth, four thousand miles away. Wagner had originally hoped to revive it in 1877, the year after the premiere, but he was thwarted by the first festival's disastrous financial outcome. When he finally mounts another festival – in 1882, a few months before his death – the work that he produces is not *The Ring*, but *Parsifal*, his final drama, which he describes as *ein Bühnenweihfestspiel* (literally, a 'stage-consecrating festival play'). He is determined that *Parsifal* should be staged only at the Festspielhaus, and his stipulation is largely honoured – despite unauthorised performances at the Met, in Amsterdam and in Buenos Aires – until his family lifts the edict in 1914. *The Ring* is a very different matter. Although Wagner had intended, for most of its lengthy gestation, that it should be performed only under festival conditions, he starts to take a more pragmatic view as the financial implications of running a theatre become clear to him. In 1878 he authorises Angelo Neumann, a Jewish-born impresario and former singer, to mount a cycle in Leipzig; three years later, he attends Neumann's production in Berlin, and is pleased to find it closely modelled on his own. A year later, he grants Neumann rights to the cycle for a season and sells him scenery and equipment from Bayreuth, which the impresario uses to give *Ring* premieres first in London and then in twenty-five cities across Europe. Neumann charters a special train to transport his company: the sets and costumes alone occupy twelve wagons. The orchestra – of just sixty players, compared with Bayreuth's 115 – is conducted by none other than Anton Seidl.

By the end of this tour, Wagner is dead. His coffin is transported back by boat and train from Venice to Bayreuth. Cosima, for a while, is paralysed by grief: she asks her daughters to cut off all her hair and places it in a cushion that she rests on Wagner's chest; she climbs into his grave and lies down on his coffin. But soon enough, the forty-five-year-old widow accepts her responsibility to safeguard Wagner's legacy in Bayreuth and to promote the performance of his work. In 1883 and 1884, only *Parsifal* is produced, but at subsequent festivals, Cosima gradually adds earlier operas – *Tristan* in 1886, *Die Meistersinger* in 1888, *Tannhäuser* in 1891, *Lohengrin* in 1894 – and earns justified plaudits for the skill with which she directs them. Not until 1896, however, does she return to *The Ring*, and when she does so, her aim is to replicate exactly what her husband wanted twenty years ago. Cosima commissions Max Brückner to produce new sets and costumes to replace those that have been sold to Neumann. He once again uses Hoffmann's paintings as a basis, but if anything adheres still more closely this time to the instructions set out in Wagner's libretti: Cosima praises his 'conscientious, affectionate regard for every detail of the poem'. Siegfried Wagner – who is now twenty-seven, and preoccupied by the need to conceal his homosexual liaisons – conducts some of the performances.

The long absence of *The Ring* from the repertoire of the Festspielhaus, and the lack of any new ideas about the cycle in Bayreuth once it does eventually return, opens up space for other interpreters to approach the four dramas in different ways, to join their own stories to those that Wagner writes. Intentionally or not, Anton Seidl's *Ring* at the Metropolitan Opera tells several such stories: of the Gilded Age's mercantile elite, whose new-found prosperity propelled the construction of the new opera house and who now seek to establish for it a distinctive identity; of the wave of German immigrants to the United States, attracted by the chance to celebrate their native culture in their new home; of the optimistic world-view that finds in Brünnhilde's closing peroration not a lament for what has been lost but a celebration of the better life still to come. While Cosima and Siegfried – mainly the latter from 1906 onwards, after a heart attack prevents Cosima from taking such an active role in the festival – try to preserve the Master's original conception in every detail, *The Ring* itself begins to make its way across the world, attracting new audiences and accumulating new meanings as it goes.

* * *

Bayreuth, 31 July 1951. Seventy-five years after the first festival and eighteen years after the last new production of *The Ring* was premiered, the curtains open on a brand-new *Rheingold*. The conductor is Hans Knappertsbusch, musical director of the Bavarian State Opera until the Nazi regime revoked his contract in 1936; the stage director is the thirty-four-year-old Wieland Wagner, oldest of the four children of the late Siegfried Wagner, and Richard Wagner's oldest acknowledged grandchild. (Cosima denied that Isolde was Wagner's child so that Isolde's son Franz Wilhelm Beidler, fifteen years Wieland's senior, could have no claim on the family.) Only two days previously, the Festspielhaus has opened its doors to the public for the first time in nine years, with a performance of Beethoven's Ninth Symphony conducted by Wilhelm Furtwängler, followed on 30 July by Wieland's new staging of *Parsifal*. After such a long gap, no one knows quite what to expect from these new productions, but everyone is aware of how much depends on their success. The prominent support given to the festival before and during the war by the Nazi Party and by Hitler himself has caused immense, perhaps irrevocable damage to its reputation – and by extension to that of Wagner's work. To Wieland falls the heavy burden of salvaging it.

Others involved with the festival may be able to claim that they had little to do with the Nazi regime, but this is not an option for Wieland. Hitler had been a regular visitor to Bayreuth since 1923, the year of the failed Munich Putsch: drawn there by a love of Wagner's music that went back to his experience of seeing *Lohengrin* as a twelve-year-old in Linz, he quickly found congenial companions around the festival, including the British-born Houston Stewart Chamberlain – husband of Wagner's daughter Eva, prolific writer and notorious antisemite. Hitler visited more frequently after 1930, when Cosima and Siegfried died within a few months of each other and Siegfried's thirty-three-year-old widow Winifred took over as festival director.

Born in Hastings in Sussex, orphaned at an early age and raised in Germany by distant relatives – her adoptive father Karl Klindworth was a conductor who prepared the vocal scores of many of Wagner's operas – Winifred first visited Bayreuth at the age of seventeen, and was seized upon by Siegfried's family, who were desperate that he should settle down and produce an heir before the scandal of his homosexuality became widely known. Now aged thirty-three, Winifred was determined but inexperienced; Hitler cast himself – or was cast by her – as her protector. Their obvious mutual affection led to rumours of an affair, even an impending betrothal, but the terms of Siegfried's will – which bequeathed the festival to the four children once they were of an age to take responsibility – precluded Winifred from remaining as director should she remarry.

Instead, Hitler settled into the role of 'Uncle Wolf', lavishing affection on the whole family but paying particular attention to Wieland – perhaps because he saw a reflection of his own youthful ambitions in the elder son's activities as a painter. When Wieland passed his driving test in 1935, Hitler gave him a silver-grey convertible Mercedes; he and his younger brother Wolfgang went to Munich to collect it, having dinner with the

Führer then staying the night on their own in his apartment after he left for Berlin. Two years later, Hitler personally intervened to reduce the length of the military service that Wieland was obliged to undertake, so that he could fulfil an invitation to design the sets for two of his father Siegfried's operas. Wieland remained on close terms with Hitler until December 1944, when he saw him for the last time at a private lunch at the Reich Chancellery where he was joined by his wife Gertrud, his younger sister Verena and her husband Bodo Lafferentz, a high-ranking SS officer. The visitors were all shocked at the Führer's tired appearance, but when he and Wieland took a walk on their own, Hitler expressed his enthusiasm for what he imagined as the first Bayreuth Festival of peacetime, and his personal wish – at least according to what Wieland later tells Winifred – that he should take on its artistic leadership.

After the war, Wieland entirely renounces any loyalty he has previously shown towards Hitler, shaken by what he has heard, and also – it seems, though he talks little of it – by the experience of working alongside prisoners-of-war in a Bayreuth camp. The same is not true of his mother, who is accused at her de-Nazification trial in 1947 of being one of Hitler's most ardent supporters and is classified after the evidence is heard as an 'activist', the second highest category. The following year, she successfully appeals this verdict, emphasising her limited personal involvement with the Nazi Party, and gets herself reclassified as a category three 'lesser offender', though she is barred from taking any future part in the leadership of the Bayreuth Festival and agrees to relinquish control to her sons. In private, however, she is entirely unrepentant about her friendship with Hitler, inviting friends to celebrate his birthday with the coded message '88' (H is the eighth letter of the alphabet, so '88' means 'HH' or 'Heil

Hitler'). In 1975, in the course of a five-hour documentary film made by Hans-Jürgen Syberberg, she notoriously reveals – as if there is nothing to be ashamed of – that if Hitler were to return to visit her she would greet him just as warmly as she ever did.

Ironically, the personal support that Hitler gave the festival – not only by attending, but also through regular and substantial private donations and through the public subsidy of tickets for military servicemen that enabled it to remain in operation during the war – freed Winifred to take a more liberal artistic approach than other organisations that depended on maintaining the good-will of Reich bureaucrats. The appointments she made from 1930 onwards were scarcely designed to secure Nazi Party support – a sure sign of Winifred's confidence that, due to her unique position of influence with the Führer, she did not need to do so. As artistic director she chose Heinz Tietjen, director of the Prussian State theatres, who had achieved distinction both as conductor and pro-ducer; she and Tietjen then chose Emil Preetorius as their princi-pal stage designer. Both men were in their late forties at the time of their appointment to Bayreuth; both had been active in the Social Democratic Party; and Tietjen in particular had expressed hostility to the Nazis before they came to power. Together with the new music director, Wilhelm Furtwängler, they managed to keep Jewish singers involved in the festival for much longer than at any other German opera house.

Artistically, too, Tietjen and Preetorius courted the disap-proval of the Reich's cultural commissars by moving the Bayreuth style away from Cosima and Siegfried's stultifying orthodoxy and reducing the superfluous detail the productions contained, whether in the scenery or the actors' movements. Although the *Ring* that Tietjen and Preetorius created in 1933 – the first at Bayreuth not produced by a Wagner – by no means abandoned

naturalism, its visual aesthetic aspired to classical simplicity, drawing out the connections with Greek tragedy to which Wagner
himself ascribed such importance. The story's symbolic resonances were suggested by subtle lighting effects, devised in collab-
oration with Paul Eberhardt, whom Tietjen brought to Bayreuth
as technical director and who subsequently played a crucial part in
Wieland's productions. The modestly progressive character of the
Tietjen *Ring* does not cancel out the bombastic interpretations of
Lohengrin and *Meistersinger* that Hitler loved, nor erase the familiar images of swastika-lined streets and of the Führer socialising
with the Wagner family, but it contributes to a more nuanced picture of Bayreuth during the Third Reich than is often presented.

It was on Tietjen's 1937 production of *Parsifal*, at the age of
twenty, that Wieland achieved his first credit at the Bayreuth
Festival. His set designs were highly accomplished but largely
traditional; even their modest departures from Wagner's instructions for the original production were enough, however, to earn
him a reproach from his aunt Daniela, Cosima's eldest daughter.
This incident helped to convince him to develop his skills as a
designer and director away from Bayreuth, where his position as a
Wagner descendant imposed a unique and inhibiting set of expectations. Opportunities were hard to come by in wartime: Tietjen
suggested that he serve an eight-year apprenticeship with him in
Berlin, but Wieland's growing suspicion of the man on whom his
mother increasingly relied – and with whom she was romantically involved, at least for a while – led him to reject this offer. He
assisted on productions in Munich and Nuremberg, then in 1943
– with the help of Joseph Goebbels – he was offered a position as
opera producer in Altenburg, a small city south of Leipzig. The
Ring that Wieland produced there over the next year anticipated
many of the features that would make his Bayreuth productions

so distinctive. Partly in response to the small size of the Altenburg stage, partly as a result of his study of modernist theatre designers such as Adolphe Appia and Gordon Craig, Wieland radically simplified his set designs and minimised the number of objects on stage, placing much greater emphasis on the role of lighting in characterising the individual scenes and the transitions between them.

Though Wieland has not produced an opera for seven years when he begins work on the productions that will reopen Bayreuth, his understanding of his grandfather's work has deepened, thanks to intensive musical studies under the guidance of the conductor Kurt Overhoff. The interpretation of *The Ring* he unveils in 1951 is uncompromising in its rejection of almost everything from the Bayreuth tradition. He comprehensively jettisons Wagner's original stage directions, regarding them as irrelevant to the essence of the story. There is nothing in his own designs to suggest that the action is taking place in Germany, past or present: almost everything happens on a plain sloping rectangle, starkly but strikingly lit. The destruction of Valhalla and the flooding of the Rhine are evoked with lighting rather than scenery, as if to suggest they take place within the characters' imaginations. The general reaction among the seasoned Wagnerians of Bayreuth is outrage: Wieland has distorted and disfigured everything they revere about the Master's work for his own misguided ends, and the fact that he is a Wagner makes matters worse. One of the principal detractors is Winifred, who is seen in the theatre with her back to the stage and confesses to a scornful Preetorius that she regards her son's innovations as 'nonsense', though she tries to remain loyal for the most part.

The production changes significantly over the eight years in which it remains in the festival's repertoire. Wieland quickly feels that despite all the controversy, his innovations of 1951 do not go

far enough, and tries to prevent photographs of these first performances from being circulated. He gradually removes almost
everything from the stage that suggests specific locations – huts,
halls, mountains, caves – and moves ever further from naturalism in his direction of the singers. In 1953 he introduces a huge,
slightly sloping circle in the centre of the stage, on which most of
the action takes place. There is much speculation as to what this
shape might mean – an obvious answer is that it symbolises the ring
itself – but its origins lie in the 'orchestra' or dancing space of the
Greek theatre that so inspires Wieland, as it did his grandfather.

In 1965, after Wolfgang has taken his turn at *The Ring*, Wieland
produces his second cycle for the festival. He invites Henry
Moore to design the sets and costumes – a surprising choice,
given that he has always designed his own productions and the
sculptor has scarcely worked in the theatre, but one that reveals
his increasing desire to find abstract, monumental forms with
which to convey his understanding of Wagner's music, informed
as it is by his increasing interest in Freudian and Jungian psycho-
analysis. Moore declines the invitation; Wieland himself devises
shapes described by Patrick Carnegy as 'pitted, honeycombed,
geological'; to accommodate the action, he designs a smaller disc
than before which is raised above the stage floor, helping to focus
the audience's attention. For all the abstract qualities of his production, however, Wieland by no means ignores *The Ring*'s resonances with recent history: he describes it as 'the most topical
and modern of living dramas' and asks Kerstin Meyer, who plays
Waltraute, to imagine Valhalla as the Reich Chancellery in 1945.
It seems as though now, twenty years after Hitler's death, he is
finally able to confront his feelings about the man with whom his
family's history has been so closely entwined.

The old-school Wagnerians who deplored Wieland's first

Bayreuth *Ring* have not quite disappeared, but they are now in the minority. Although controversy is aroused by a few of Wieland's decisions – such as his omission of the short scene in *Götter-dämmerung* where Gutrune awaits Siegfried's return from the hunt, which he finds uninteresting and superfluous – the critical response to the 1965 production, conducted by Karl Böhm, is more positive than it was in 1951. The acclaim this new *Ring* receives helps to consolidate Wieland's already flourishing reputation across Europe as a director of opera – not only those of Wagner.

In April 1966 Wieland directs Alban Berg's *Wozzeck* in Frankfurt; the conductor is Pierre Boulez, with whom he forms an instant rapport. He immediately invites Boulez to conduct that year's Bayreuth production of *Parsifal*, a work that both men think needs to be 'secularised' – treated as a piece of theatre rather than as a religious ritual. Boulez and Bayreuth are hardly an obvious fit – the Frenchman has a reputation as a fiery iconoclast, thanks in part to his facetious suggestion of blowing up opera houses – but he proves an inspired choice, who will return to the festival to conduct *Parsifal on* three more occasions and play a crucial role there a decade later. Wieland himself scarcely has a chance to work with him, however: he is diagnosed with inoperable lung cancer during rehearsals for *The Ring* and dies on 17 October 1966. Wolfgang assumes sole control and tries to distance himself from his brother's legacy, destroying his models, dismissing his colleagues and effectively evicting Gertrud and her children from Wahnfried. But Wieland's influence is not so easily suppressed: the theatrical revolution he has inspired in Bayreuth means that no one will think of *The Ring* in quite the same way again.

* * *

Vienna, 24 September 1958. The Vienna Philharmonic Orchestra begins to make the first ever complete studio recording of *Das Rheingold*. The conductor is the forty-five-year-old Hungarian-born Georg Solti, musical director of the Frankfurt Opera; the cast includes the Norwegian soprano Kirsten Flagstad, the greatest Brünnhilde of her generation. Now in her mid-sixties, she has agreed to sing the role of Fricka for the first time after much persuasion from Decca Records, who know how much her involvement will add to the credibility of this risky undertaking. The sessions take place in the Sofiensaal, a dance hall in the residential Landstrasse district originally built as a steam bath, whose high, vaulted ceiling and massive underground cavity, once a swimming pool, provide an unusually suitable acoustic for recording. The producer is the thirty-four-year-old Englishman John Culshaw, who has assembled a team of engineers whom he believes ingenious enough to solve the unique problems this work poses.

The idea of making the entire *Rheingold* commercially available has been made possible by two recent developments in the recording industry: the introduction of the long-playing record in 1948, which makes it possible to listen to longer spans of music than the five or six minutes available on a 78rpm disc; and the evolution of stereo technology, invented as long ago as 1932, to the point where it can be used in commercially viable mass-produced recordings. The first of these appear in 1957, only a year before Culshaw records *Rheingold*, and it is the breakthrough for which he has been waiting. Now, for the first time, opera recordings can do much more than simply document a production: a skilful producer can create the illusion for those listening at home that characters are singing from different places, and that they are moving across the stage and from off-stage to on-stage.

Culshaw's ambitions have been stoked by his experience of attending Wieland's first Bayreuth *Ring* in 1951: like many

audience members, he was disturbed by the production's apparent lack of interest in Wagner's stage directions, and also found it
visually dreary, a problem he ascribed to a limited budget. In this
period of post-war austerity, he believes that a recording has the
potential to offer a more authentically Wagnerian experience, a
more complete realisation of the composer's intentions, than anything likely to be offered on stage, despite – or perhaps because
of – its lack of visual information.

The project's foundation is the excellence of the musicians that
Decca has assembled on the Sofiensaal's stage: Culshaw believes
that he has found in Solti the greatest Wagner conductor of his
generation, and Solti in turn credits the Vienna Philharmonic
with a Wagner sound more beautiful than that of any other
orchestra. But Culshaw makes it his own business to realise with
the utmost precision and vividness every sound that he believes
Wagner wants but that cannot be produced by conventional
orchestral resources. He procures the eighteen anvils of different
sizes needed for the interludes and arranges them according to
instructions in the score that seem to anticipate the invention of
stereo; the orchestra is horrified by the resultant noise, but when
the recording is released the anvil ensemble becomes many hi-fi
salesmen's favourite means of demonstrating the quality of their
equipment. Culshaw devises a special box in which to record
Alberich during the section when he is invisible, so that his voice
can be modified and moved around the sound picture, creating
the same aural confusion in the listener that the terrified Mime
experiences in the story; he recruits forty Viennese schoolchil-
dren to produce the scream let forth by the Nibelungs as Alberich
shows them his ring and they disappear into the mines. The most
spectacular sound effect is saved for the end: the thunderclap that
allows the gods to see the rainbow bridge to Valhalla is produced

here not by Donner's hammer but by a twenty-foot sheet of steel brought in from Linz, shattering all previous preconceptions about the amount of sound that can be accommodated on a gramophone record.

Culshaw is desperate to record the entire *Ring* with Solti, but the expense of this will be such that Decca will only contemplate it if *Rheingold* is a commercial success. It is: ecstatic praise from critics and prizes from all over the world help to make the three-LP set the highest-selling opera recording of all time, at one point outselling Elvis in the US charts. Even so, it is not until 1962 that the human and financial resources necessary to make another recording can be marshalled. *Die Walküre* is ruled out of the reckoning for the moment, as it is already relatively well represented on disc: Furtwängler conducted it for EMI in 1954 as the first instalment of what would have been the first complete studio *Ring* had he not died two months later; Decca has already recorded Flagstad singing Act I with Hans Knappertsbusch and Act III with Solti himself. Rather than compete with those versions, Decca now moves on to *Siegfried*, which like *Rheingold* has never been recorded in the studio.

The biggest challenge of *Siegfried*, of course, is finding a Siegfried. Culshaw contracts a young but unproven *Heldentenor* whom he tactfully leaves unnamed in his book *Ring Resounding* but who has subsequently been unmasked as Ernst Kozub: his inability or unwillingness to learn the music properly wastes precious recording time and threatens to destroy the whole project. The veteran Wolfgang Windgassen graciously agrees to step in at the last moment, joining Birgit Nilsson (Brünnhilde), Gerhard Stolze (Mime) and Hans Hotter (Wanderer), currently unrivalled as exponents of these roles; in a piece of audacious luxury casting, Culshaw persuades Joan Sutherland to sing the Woodbird, a part she has previously taken at Covent Garden before becoming famous as Donizetti's Lucia. Once again, much painstaking attention is devoted to producing sounds more precise and dramatic than anything that could be achieved in the theatre: Fafner (Kurt Böhme) is recorded in a separate hall with a very resonant acoustic so that he will sound appropriately monstrous as the dragon; the complex rhythms that Wagner asks Siegfried to bang out on the anvil in Act I are played by a separate percussionist so that Windgassen can concentrate on his role's vocal demands.

By the time Decca begins to record *Götterdämmerung*, two years later, the historic significance of the entire undertaking is clear. The BBC and Austrian Television join forces to make a documentary, *The Golden Ring*; Humphrey Burton's final voiceover hails Culshaw and his colleagues as 'high priests of flawlessness'. The encomium acknowledges not just the dedication of the 'Decca Boys' but also the degree of artistic control that Culshaw exerts: for example, his preference for a faster tempo for Siegfried's Funeral March holds sway over Solti's instinct to take it more slowly, as a good-humoured altercation captured on camera after the conductor announces a brief *Zigaretten-Pause* makes clear. The footage also reveals the demonic energy that Solti brings to every bar of the score: in his sweat-soaked polo shirt, he seems to belong in a different era to the gentlemen of the orchestra (they are all men, apart from the harpists) in their suits and ties. Dietrich Fischer-Dieskau, whom Culshaw boldly casts as Gunther even though he will never take on the role in the theatre, speaks eloquently about the character's often-overlooked nobility and his own view of *Götterdämmerung* as a family tragedy. The differently shaped steerhorns that Culshaw has commissioned from an instrument-maker near Bayreuth to play the clashing pitches (C, D flat and D) heard as Hagen summons the vassals – the trombones generally used make too smooth a sound – are shown being moved into the perfect position. Not shown in the documentary is the technical wizardry deployed to alter the timbre of Windgassen's voice so that he sounds like a baritone at the point where Siegfried is disguised as Gunther; Culshaw justifies this by pointing out that the libretto requires Siegfried to sing with a 'rougher, deeper voice', the implication being that this is a device Wagner would have used had the technology been available to him.

Decca completes its pioneering cycle the following year with *Die Walküre*: Solti completes the final take of Wotan's Farewell with Hans Hotter at precisely 5.30 p.m. on 19 November 1965. The twenty-LP set, released the following summer, receives countless accolades and is still regularly described as the greatest classical recording project of all time. Remastered editions appear at frequent intervals, in 1984, 1997 and 2012; in 2022 Decca issues a 'high-definition transfer', for which their engineers go back to the thirty-eight original two-track master tapes and repair those that are in poor condition by baking them; it remains to be seen whether this is the final version. Although numerous other recordings of *The Ring*, made both in studios and in live productions, appear in the meantime, the Solti/Culshaw version continues to enjoy a special cultural status. This is not purely because it is the first such recording, and certainly not because it is necessarily the best: Wagner enthusiasts will never agree about something so contentious. Perhaps uniquely, however, Culshaw's recording is not merely an interpretation but a realisation of *The Ring*, or at least of one of its aspects. His visionary understanding of the technology at his disposal enables him to tell Wagner's story in sound better than anyone else – including Wagner – has thus far managed.

* * *

Bayreuth, 24 July 1976. A hundred years after the start of the first festival, audiences assemble once again to hear *Das Rheingold*. Wagner's grandson Wolfgang – who has been in sole charge of the festival since Wieland's death ten years ago – has commissioned a new production to mark the occasion. Wolfgang has directed two previous Bayreuth *Ring* cycles himself, but it is six years since the second of these was premiered, and this *Jahrhundertring* will be very different. The director is Patrice Chéreau, a thirty-one-year-old Frenchman with a growing reputation in the spoken theatre, but who has only previously directed two operas – Rossini's *Italian Girl in Algiers* and Offenbach's *Tales of Hoffmann* – and who himself saw *The Ring* for the first time only at the previous year's festival.

Wolfgang has engaged Chéreau – after Ingmar Bergman declines the opportunity – on the recommendation of the new *Ring*'s musical director, Pierre Boulez. When Boulez conducted *Parsifal* under Wieland's direction in 1966 (and for three further runs thereafter), his performances were quicker than any previously heard, and far less pompous, delivering on the aspiration he shared with Wieland when they first discussed his grandfather's final work: to rid it of the quasi-religious aura that had surrounded it since its premiere. With *The Ring*, too, Boulez prioritises transparency over tradition: some of the orchestral players do not like his tempi, others are outraged at his refusal to let them play out as they are accustomed to do. A deputation is sent to complain to Wolfgang, who steadfastly supports his conductor. But if the orchestra is upset by Boulez, the audience is far more concerned by what Chéreau has done to the revered score, as the boos, howls and whistles that ring out at the *Jahrhundertring*'s first performances testify.

The new production shocks many in the audience even before

a note is sung. The curtains part at the start of *Das Rheingold* to reveal not a traditional view of the Rhine, nor the abstract shapes familiar from the Wagner brothers' productions, but a hydroelectric power station. Rhinemaidens dressed as prostitutes parade on the steel bridge that joins the massive concrete struts; Alberich clambers up from beneath the turbine. The implication is clear: this is a world that is already developed, already industrialised, already despoiled. The idea of interpreting *The Ring* as an allegory about the consequences of industrialisation is not new – it has been in circulation at least since 1898, when George Bernard Shaw published the first edition of *The Perfect Wagnerite*, which characterised Alberich as a rapacious capitalist and Siegfried as a revolutionary leader modelled on Bakunin – and it has informed previous productions, notably Joachim Herz's recent cycle for Leipzig, whose final part has been seen for the first time only five months previously. But this is the first time that the Industrial Revolution has so heavily influenced the visual language of an entire *Ring*, let alone a Bayreuth *Ring*.

Machines are everywhere in this staging. Nibelheim is a factory filled with steam and smoke. In the final scene of *Rheingold*, there is industrial machinery in the gods' abode, as if to suggest that their wealth has been acquired through exploiting the labour of others. In *Die Walküre*, a huge engine overshadows Hunding's hut – actually an impressive mansion. For most of the second act, a gigantic Foucault pendulum – invented in 1851 to demonstrate the earth's rotation around its axis – circles slowly of its own accord, until Wotan unforgettably seizes it as he anticipates 'das Ende'. *Götterdämmerung* seems to take place in a decaying industrial landscape: a factory is visible in the distance from the Gibichung Hall; Hagen carries out his watch from between two iron pillars and summons the vassals from a steel jetty; Siegfried encounters the

Rhinemaidens at the same dam that is seen in *Rheingold*, though the river has now dried up and it has ceased to function.

However, the set designer Richard Peduzzi reserves the most spectacular mechanisms for *Siegfried*. Mime's efforts to forge together the fragments of Nothung take place outside a factory: despite the forest setting, bricks and wrought iron dominate the design, with large engines in the background overshadowing the Nibelung's more homespun technology. A mysterious covered object appears at the back of the yard. In the final scene of Act I this is revealed to be a steam-driven mechanical anvil which is capable of putting Nothung back together all by itself – one way for Siegfried to avoid the problem of co-ordinating his hammering with his singing. The gadgets continue to appear in Act II: the Woodbird is a mechanical toy which Siegfried finds in a metal box; the dragon is a model on a wheeled cart operated by puppeteers, from which the Fafner of *Rheingold* emerges after he has been stabbed.

These devices are not introduced merely for their visual impact: Chéreau's notes in the festival programme explain that they are there to demonstrate that Siegfried – contrary to appearances, and to what Wotan might think – has no true agency. Mechanised anvil and pre-programmed bird are physical manifestations of the control that Wotan exercises over the actions of his 'free hero'. Siegfried – in Chéreau's interpretation – is conscious both of the limitations of his freedom to act and of the weakness in his character that results from his inability to fear; he is aware, Chéreau writes, of the 'swindle which presides over his existence and his life: a feeling of a lack which he harbours like an inward and secret wound'. Whether or not Chéreau's Siegfried is one that Wagner would recognise, he is a more interesting, nuanced and sympathetic character than most productions present.

The all-French artistic team of the *Jahrhundertring* is completed by lighting designer André Diot and costume designer Jacques Schmidt, whose outfits range in period from the eighteenth century (Donner and Froh look like foppish Mozarts in their powdered wigs and glittery frock coats) to the present day (the vassals could be workers in a 1970s factory, with Hagen as their shop steward). There is nothing schematic about Schmidt's choices – as with the set designs, plenty of room is left for playfulness – but the choices he makes reinforce the idea that the story is moving forward in history with each successive drama. Hunding is dressed like a nineteenth-century industrial magnate; Mime has a briefcase that an Edwardian office worker might carry; Gunther is a tycoon in a flashy dinner jacket – and in a brilliant touch, Siegfried copies his outfit as he prepares to marry Gutrune. Wotan, meanwhile, gradually modifies his dress as the drama proceeds – in *Walküre* he wears then ultimately casts off a deep-red house-coat of the type of which Wagner himself was fond – as if mirroring his ultimately futile attempts to maintain control of the world.

The story that Chéreau tells through this eclectic but effective range of visual references is one that connects Wagner's period to his own. If Wagner is concerned – as Shaw believed – to show the problems that result for humanity from the capitalist exploitation of the world's natural resources, then Chéreau shows that those problems continue into his own century. For Shaw, Alberich was the *Ring*'s arch-capitalist; but in Chéreau's telling of the story, Wotan, Hunding, Gunther and Hagen all demonstrate similarly acquisitive tendencies, refracted through the different social contexts in which they operate. The space that Chéreau allows himself to disregard the detail of Wagner's stage directions – a space he credits Wieland Wagner with opening up – enables him to connect Wagner's story to the preoccupations of the present day, more vividly and directly than any other production, certainly in Bayreuth, has so far managed.

Chéreau refuses his audiences the comfort of distancing their own lives from the story, which is perhaps partly why his telling of it proves so provocative: in the final moments of *Götterdämmerung*, the crowd that has been watching the distant conflagration of Valhalla finally turns towards the audience, as if to turn the question of what it all means back on them. Nor does he permit the viewer to indulge any sentimental attachment to an idea of a prelapsarian natural state that once existed (and to which we could return if things were different): in this *Ring*, the riches of the Rhine have already been exploited for financial gain before the drama even begins, and the bird sounds that are heard in the forests are the product of human design, not nature.

As audiences grow familiar with the production during the centenary festival and the four that follow, outrage and derision turn to adulation: the final performance of *Götterdämmerung* on 25 August 1980 receives over an hour's standing ovation. During the 1979 and 1980 festivals, the cast gives extra performances for the benefit of film cameras rather than live audiences: perhaps ironically, given its critique of the baleful effects of industrialisation on human existence, the production ultimately benefits from technological developments that enable it to become the first complete *Ring* shown on screen. Audience seats are removed for the filming, so that a wider range of camera angles can be achieved, but each act is recorded as a continuous whole to give the effect of a live performance rather than a studio recording. Some critics complain that the video director, Brian Large, relies too heavily on close-ups rather than conveying the overall stage picture and the singers' spatial distribution across it. But for most viewers, such objections are outweighed by the benefits of Large's approach: he sequences the shots in a way that is both imaginative and musically sensitive, drawing out the human intensity of the successive interactions and revealing the skill and detail with which Chéreau directs his cast. Many of the performances stand up brilliantly to the cameras' forensic gaze: above all Donald McIntyre's Wotan, successively tortured and imperious; but also Gwyneth Jones's humane Brünnhilde; Heinz Zednik's unusually funny Mime; Peter Hofmann and Jeannine Altmeyer's ardent Volsung twins . . . The films are shown in cinemas around the world and later televised in act-sized episodes, telling Wagner's story – and Chéreau's – to millions more people than have ever been able to experience it before.

* * *

Berlin, May 2024. I emerge from the Richard Wagner-Platz U-Bahn station in the affluent district of Charlottenburg. Its platforms are decorated with faded black-and-white images of Valhalla and other scenes from Wagner's music dramas, its name rendered in an ornate font I see nowhere else on the network: quiet tributes to the composer and his century. Posters depicting Chancellor Scholz and his rivals from other parties have appeared on every corner, reminders of the more than usually consequential elections to the European Parliament that take place in a couple of weeks and in which the United Kingdom, for the first time, will play no part.

I am returning to the Deutsche Oper to see Stefan Herheim's production of *The Ring*, currently being revived for the first time since I saw it almost two and a half years ago. I know that my impressions will be different this time. Every experience of *The Ring* is the product of the peculiar, unrepeatable alchemy between the audience, the production, and the moment at which it occurs.

I am different now. Leaving aside all the other myriad changes that life brings, the live encounters with *The Ring* that I have had in the process of writing this book – cycles of long-established productions in Leipzig and Dresden, the latter conducted by Christian Thielemann with a miraculous combination of spaciousness and celerity; Richard Jones's fitfully brilliant *Walküre* and *Rheingold* (in that order) at London's troubled English National Opera, intended as the first half of a cycle that it now seems unlikely will ever be completed; a revelatory historically informed *Rheingold* conducted by Kent Nagano at the Lucerne Festival; the intriguing first part of Barrie Kosky's new *Ring* for Covent Garden, which I experience in an Art Deco cinema in Leven on the Fife coast – make me a different listener. I now navigate my way through the experience with a better sense of the cycle's peculiar geography, of where the hidden peaks as well as the obvious ones lie; I notice more and more links between themes each time I attend a performance, so that by the end of *Götterdämmerung* almost everything seems connected to everything else, which is probably the effect Wagner intends.

The production will also be different, if only in subtle ways. Herheim's approach to the cycle involves treating the entire cast as an ensemble, with many actors on stage far more of the time than they would be in a traditional *Ring*, so the effects of introducing new Brünnhildes, Erdas, giants, Norns and Rhinemaidens will ripple out to alter the dynamics of many more scenes than those in which they sing. The first run of performances drew so much on the wealth of experience that Nina Stemme brought to her interpretation of Brünnhilde that I am intrigued to see how the two new singers in this role (Ricarda Merbeth in *Walküre* and *Götterdämmerung*; Elisabeth Teige in *Siegfried*, adding the part to that of Sieglinde which she played so successfully last time around) will change things.

And Herheim's production will play this time to a Berlin audience many of whose perceptions will have been changed by the experience of seeing an entirely different cycle at the city's Staatsoper, whose pink-and-cream building and glamorous location on Unter den Linden contrast sharply with the Deutsche Oper's understated 1960s edifice on Bismarckstrasse. Dmitri Tcherniakov's Staatsoper production, which has already had three runs of performances in the twenty-eight months since I was last in Berlin, has received mixed reviews, though the conducting of Thielemann (standing in for an indisposed Daniel Barenboim) and Philippe Jordan has been widely praised.

The world is different now, too. The fears aroused by the pandemic, if they have not entirely receded, have been supplanted by threats that seem still more immediate and dangerous. Horrific and seemingly intractable conflicts in Ukraine and in Israel/Palestine provide real-life examples of the abuses of power that *The Ring* identifies. The name 'Wagner' has acquired a sinister new resonance since I was last here, due to its adoption by a group of Russian mercenaries, commanded until his death last year by Yevgeny Prigozhin, a former ally of Vladimir Putin. The increasing frequency and devastating impact of extreme weather resulting from man-made climate change makes *The Ring*'s denunciation of the immoral exploitation of the world's natural resources seem ever more prescient. Meanwhile, the bizarre presidential election campaign that is unfolding, for the moment at least, in the United States – between two unprecedentedly elderly candidates, both of whom have already held the world's most powerful office and one of whom has this very week been convicted on thirty-four felony charges by a jury in Manhattan – invites comparison with the struggle between Wotan and Alberich. These global concerns, whose gravity could not have been predicted when this *Ring* cycle was planned, now become part of its story, and part of the experience of every audience member. Wagner's story of the nineteenth century also tells stories that could not be more relevant for our own.

As I enter the theatre, now thankfully free of the COVID protocols that made the process so peculiar in 2022, I wonder whether the production will make the same impact on me this time around. Was the intensity of my previous experience the result of having been deprived of live music for so long? I take my seat; the orchestra tunes. With the house lights still up, a crowd of people trudge across the empty stage, their clothing and battered suitcases identifying them as refugees. A tall figure in a hat – Wotan, as he turns out to be – opens the lid of the grand piano, the only item of furniture on stage, and plays a low E flat as the orchestra begins the Prelude. The entire company, transfixed with wonder, slowly begins to sway. Rhinemaidens, gods and giants emerge from the crowd to take on their roles. I need not have worried. Herheim's inventiveness, the individual performances of a uniformly strong cast and the stunning effects devised by lighting designer Ulrich Niepel and video designer Torge Møller combine in a way I find just as rich as before. Runnicles's musical interpretation strikes me as even more supple this time, still more finely attuned to the nuances of the production; the richness of the string sound and the deployment of extremely quiet dynamics are exceptional.

I am struck even more forcibly on a second viewing by the acuity of Herheim's insights and the wit and ingenuity with which he conveys them to the audience. In *Götterdämmerung*, for example, actors dressed as nineteenth-century ideas of what Norse gods look like, in costumes closely resembling those found in the first *Ring* production, spend much of the evening on suitcases ranged high above the main action. Their very presence makes the point – obvious but often overlooked – that the gods oversee and are affected by the events of this final drama, even though they do not sing a note. Meanwhile, their archaic appearance and stilted movements, so different from the contemporary style and fluid interactions elsewhere in the production, betray their impending irrelevance, while also both highlighting and complementing *Götterdämmerung*'s peculiarly traditional dramaturgy – that of a grand opera, in Shaw's disparaging description. During Brünnhilde's final peroration, these gods remove their costumes, armour, helmets, wigs, beards and other accoutrements of godhead, and place them in the piano alongside Siegfried's body, ready for immolation. Götterdämmerung is enacted before the audience's eyes.

Herheim also finds an effective solution to the tricky problem of Siegfried's disguise as Gunther, as ingenious as Culshaw's though without the same need for technological intervention. Clay Hilley (Siegfried) and Thomas Lehman (Gunther), men of very different physiques as well as voices, are dressed in identical white tie and tails and placed by Herheim on either side of Brünnhilde, where they sing alternate phrases, as if to symbolise the temporary merging of their personas. The disconcerting shifts of timbre and direction of sound produce the disorientation and distress in Brünnhilde that Wagner intends. If this sounds confusing in theory, such is the clarity of Herheim's direction that in practice it is anything but. Though his approach might trouble purists, because of its disregard of Wagner's precise instructions, it nonetheless feels true to the moment's deeper meaning.

The question of what sort of fidelity directors owe to the score that forms the basis of their work is one that Herheim explores throughout his production. Red, leather-bound scores emblazoned with the name of the drama concerned frequently appear as props. At crucial points in the story, characters make their way to the prompt box at the front of the stage where the scores are kept. They riffle anxiously through the pages to find out what is going to happen to them; they jab their fingers at particular bars to point something out to another character; sometimes they take a score to the piano and accompany other singers who self-consciously perform their music as if giving a lieder recital; occasionally characters start to conduct. Erda is represented as a music librarian who emerges from the prompt box, dowdily dressed, with glasses on a chain round her neck: she is the only person who knows exactly what is in the scores, and therefore what is going to happen.

The presentation is witty, but the point is a serious one. No character can be said to enjoy true autonomy when all are subject to a destiny that has already been written down for them by Wagner. The score is an object that none of them owns, and therefore a visual symbol of the limited power even of the mightiest of them. Characters seek to assert ownership of the score – and of their destiny – by clutching it to their body or going to the piano and starting to play, but such moments of control are only ever temporary. During Brünnhilde's closing soliloquy in *Götterdämmerung*, as she addresses Wotan and divulges his 'endless guilt', the actor who plays the nineteenth-century image of the god sits at the piano stool, but is unable to play. A more eloquent representation of his ultimate loss of power cannot be imagined.

The score of *Siegfried* makes a prominent appearance in the final scene of Herheim's production of this opera: both Siegfried and Brünnhilde, bewildered by a situation they have never encountered before, consult it intently for guidance as to what they should do. Gradually, and with the score's help, inhibition gives way to confidence. As the horns begin the exuberant melody in fourths whose discovery Wagner reported to Mathilde, the exhilarated Brünnhilde holds the score aloft, tears out its pages and throws them down to the other sets of lovers of all ages and orientations who surround the piano, ready to engage in orgiastic celebration.

The progress of Brünnhilde's relationship with the score from careful consultation to joyful abandonment strikes me as a perfect embodiment of what a healthy relationship to *The Ring* might look like. Voluminous though the instructions contained in the score's thousands of words and millions of notes may be, and essential though it is to ponder them deeply, they do not contain all the answers. The story of *The Ring* encompasses not only many loose ends, but also an ambiguous beginning (does it represent a state of natural innocence, or has corruption already begun?) and ending (is it optimistic, pessimistic, or both at the same time?). Interpreters of *The Ring* from Wagner himself to Stefan Herheim have tried to tell its story in a way that is meaningful for their own place and their own time, taking decisions for themselves where they feel it justified rather than attempting to replicate something from an imagined past. Paradoxically, given Wagner's enormous output of explicatory prose and his attempts to control every aspect of the presentation of his story, it is its very porousness, its responsiveness to multiple ways of being told, that guarantees its continuing relevance.

Over the century and a half since *Götterdämmerung* was first produced, the apocalyptic events with which it concludes have been represented in numerous spectacular ways: from the crashing boulders of Otto Schenk's highly traditional 1980s production for the Met to the tumbling cardboard boxes of Richard Jones's irreverent 1990s staging for Covent Garden. There is no shortage of visual excitement in Herheim's production, but the final bars of the score are played by the orchestra in front of an almost empty stage. The actors have all departed, the sheets and suitcases have been cleared away – only the piano remains. The lighting rig is lowered below the proscenium, ready for the get-out. A solitary cleaner sweeps up the remaining debris. As the final chord ends, she pauses on her way across the stage, closes the lid of the piano – mirroring the gesture with which the cycle began – and gives it a quick dust.

I find this image as moving as any I have seen all week. It reminds me that however much the spectacle we have just witnessed has enthralled the audience, and however deeply we have identified with it, it has been a piece of storytelling, created by women and men who are singers, orchestral players or theatre professionals, not gods or heroes. It reminds me, too, that the decades of individual effort that Wagner devoted to the creation of *The Ring* must be matched by a still greater collective investment of hours each time the work is mounted. But the cleaner's concern that everything is tidied away for the next performance also conveys her confidence that the story will begin again, and will continue to be told.

Chronology

1813   Wilhelm Richard Wagner born in Leipzig, 22 May.
Father (Carl Friedrich Wagner) dies 22 or 23
November (sources differ).

1814   Mother (Johanna) marries Ludwig Geyer, 28 August;
family moves to Dresden.

1821   Stepfather (Geyer) dies 30 September.

1826   Geyer family moves to Prague; Wagner left behind in
Dresden.

1827   Confirmation in Kreuzkirche, Dresden. At end of year,
Wagner leaves school to join family in Leipzig.

1833–4   Writes first complete opera: *Die Feen* (The Fairies).

1836   Second opera, *Das Liebesverbot* (The Ban on Love),
performed in Magdeburg; marries Minna Planer.

1837   Initially settles in Königsberg; in June accepts
conducting post in Riga.

1838   Begins the first detailed sketch of his third opera, *Rienzi*.

1839   Flees creditors in Riga by travelling by sea to London;
from there he proceeds to Paris.

1842   Leaves Paris for Dresden; conducts *Rienzi* there to
great acclaim.

1843   Appointed Royal Saxon Kapellmeister in Dresden
(jointly with Carl Gottlieb Reissiger); conducts fourth
opera, *The Flying Dutchman*, there.

1843–4   Reads Jacob Grimm's *Deutsche Mythologie*.

1845   Conducts fifth opera, *Tannhäuser*, in Dresden.

1846   Conducts Beethoven's Ninth Symphony for the first
time, in Dresden; publishes essay on it with citations

from Goethe's *Faust*. Submits 'Report Concerning the Royal Orchestra' (rejected the following year).

1846–8 Composes sixth opera, *Lohengrin*.

1848 Completes plan 'On the Organisation of a German National Theatre for the Kingdom of Saxony' (rejected immediately). Meets Russian anarchist Mikhail Bakunin. Writes first prose plan for *The Ring*: 'The Nibelung Myth as Sketch for a Drama', and libretto entitled *Siegfrieds Tod* (completed 28 November).

1849 Takes part in Dresden uprising; leaves Dresden on 9 May; arrest warrant issued 16 May. Escapes Germany on 24 May, arriving in Switzerland four days later. Banned from entering Germany for next eleven years. Settles in Zurich.

1850 Premiere of *Lohengrin* in Weimar (28 August), in Wagner's absence, conducted by Liszt.

1850–1 Publishes writings including *The Artwork of the Future* and (under a pseudonym) *Jewishness in Music*. Abandons composition of *Siegfrieds Tod* and writes libretto for prequel entitled *Der junge Siegfried* (The Young Siegfried).

1851–2 Decides to expand *Siegfried* project into a cycle of four operas; begins libretti of *Die Walküre* and *Das Rheingold*. Publishes *Opera and Drama* (Leipzig, November 1851).

1853 Private publication of fifty copies of *Ring* text; public readings at Hotel Baur au Lac in Zurich. Begins composition of *Das Rheingold* after apparently revelatory experience in La Spezia on 5 September.

1854 Completes composition of *Das Rheingold* and makes first musical draft of *Die Walküre*. Reads Schopenhauer's *The World as Will and Representation*.

1855   Orchestrates *Die Walküre*. Conducts concerts in London.

1856   Completes *Die Walküre* and begins composing
Siegfried. Begins to sketch *Tristan und Isolde*.

1857   Moves with Minna into the 'Asyl', a small house in
the grounds of a villa belonging to his benefactor Otto
Wesendonck. Abandons composition of *Siegfried* at end
of Act II in order to concentrate on *Tristan und Isolde*.

1858   Leaves 'Asyl' after quarrel with Minna about his
attachment to Mathilde Wesendonck.

1859   Completes *Tristan*. Sells publishing rights of *The Ring*
to Otto Wesendonck.

1860   Receives partial amnesty in Germany but still cannot
return to Saxony.

1861   Vocal score of *Das Rheingold* published.

1862   Amnesty in Saxony. Last meeting with Minna in
Dresden (November). Begins work on *Die Meistersinger
von Nürnberg*.

1862–3   Excerpts from *The Ring* heard publicly for the first time
in three concerts in Vienna.

1863   *The Ring* text published with an appeal to a German
prince to finance the work's production. Enters a
relationship with Cosima von Bülow – daughter of
Liszt, and wife of the conductor Hans von Bülow.

1864   Ludwig II ascends Bavarian throne and summons
Wagner to Munich. Wagner signs contract for
completion of *The Ring*, transferring all property and
performance rights to Ludwig.

1865   Birth of first daughter, Isolde von Bülow, on 10 April.
Premiere of *Tristan* in Munich on 10 June. Forced to
leave Munich in December because of scandal of his
relationship with Cosima von Bülow.

1866   Rents Villa Tribschen on Lake Lucerne.

1868   Publication and premiere of *Die Meistersinger* (21 June), conducted by Hans von Bülow.

1869   Composes *Siegfried* Act III and begins *Götterdämmerung*. *Das Rheingold* premiered in Munich against Wagner's wishes, and in his absence. Reissues *Jewishness in Music*, this time under his own name.

1870   Premiere of *Die Walküre* in Munich against Wagner's wishes. Marries Cosima in Lucerne.

1872   Wagner family leaves Tribschen for Bayreuth; Wagner lays foundation stone of new festival theatre in Bayreuth, 22 May.

1874   Preparations for performances of *The Ring* begin. Completes *Götterdämmerung*, 21 November.

1876   Premiere of *The Ring* at Bayreuth Festspielhaus, beginning with *Das Rheingold* on 13 August.

1882   Premiere of *Parsifal* at Bayreuth Festspielhaus, 26 July.

1883   Wagner dies in Venice, 13 February.

1889   First complete American production of *The Ring*, at the Metropolitan Opera House, New York, conducted by Anton Seidl.

1930   Cosima dies in Bayreuth, 1 April, followed by her son Siegfried on 4 August.

1951   Reopening of Bayreuth Festspielhaus (29 July) with performance of Beethoven's Ninth Symphony conducted by Wilhelm Furtwängler.

1966   Decca releases first complete studio recording of *The Ring*, conducted by Georg Solti.

1976   New production of *The Ring* at Bayreuth Festspielhaus, directed by Patrice Chéreau and conducted by Pierre Boulez, to mark the centenary of the first production.

The story itself

Synopses of each drama

Das Rheingold

Scene One

Three water-maidens – Woglinde, Wellgunde and Flosshilde – play in the dawn light on the bed of the river Rhine. Alberich, the Nibelung to whom the title of Wagner's cycle refers, emerges from a chasm. Immediately entranced, he tries his luck with each girl in turn; each briefly feigns interest then mockingly rejects him. A shaft of sunlight reveals a stack of gold; the Rhinemaidens sing its praises and tease Alberich for his ignorance of its powers. They recall their promise to protect it: if it were stolen, the thief could forge a ring that would make him master of the world. Fortunately, this will never happen, they reassure themselves: only someone who renounces love could obtain the gold, and no one would do this – certainly not the lascivious Nibelung. But to their surprise and horror, Alberich declares a curse on love, seizes the gold, and takes it with him as he disappears from sight.

Scene Two

As dawn rises over the mountains, Wotan awakens and congratulates himself on procuring the fortress of Valhalla for the gods of whom he is king. His wife Fricka complains that he has contracted them to surrender her sister Freia to Fasolt and Fafner, the giants who built it. Wotan counters that he never intended to keep that promise: he expects Loge to help him find a way out, but the demigod of mischief and fire is slow to appear. The giants enter and demand Freia: Fasolt desires her for her own sake; Fafner is more interested in depriving the gods of the golden apples that only she knows how to tend, thus removing their immortality. Froh and Donner – gods of spring and thunder respectively, and brothers of Fricka and Freia – ineffectually threaten the giants; Wotan holds out his spear to intercept Donner's attack, telling him to respect the contracts inscribed on its shaft.

Loge eventually appears, pessimistic about Wotan's predicament: he has searched in vain for a reward more valuable than a beautiful woman. He tells the gods about the stolen gold, which the Rhinemaidens have asked him to help retrieve, and which Alberich has now used to make a ring. Wotan is excited by the idea of acquiring the ring for himself; Fafner suggests that the Nibelung gold would be an acceptable substitute for Freia. The giants will return that evening to collect it; meanwhile they take Freia as surety. The gods become lethargic and start to age; only Loge is unaffected. Wotan asks Loge to accompany him to Nibelheim, Alberich's underground kingdom; they slip through a crevice in pursuit of the gold.

Scene Three

In his underground kingdom, Alberich finds his brother Mime with the Tarnhelm he has ordered him to make: a magical headpiece that can confer invisibility, transform its wearer into any shape or transport them to wherever they choose. Alberich accuses Mime

– accurately – of trying to keep it for himself. He dons the Tarn-helm, makes himself invisible and beats Mime to keep him at work. Other Nibelungs enter but scream and disappear in terror when Alberich tells them he has enslaved them for ever.

Wotan and Loge appear and quiz Mime about the Tarnhelm, and the ring that Alberich has made for himself. Alberich returns and boasts to the visitors about the power he has obtained. Loge asks him to demonstrate the Tarnhelm: Alberich turns himself into a dragon. Loge challenges Alberich to turn himself into something very small – a toad, perhaps; when he duly does so, the visitors cap-ture him and take him back with them to the mountaintop.

Scene Four

Alberich is furious at being tricked, but orders the Nibelungs to bring up the gold to purchase his freedom. He also gives up the Tarnhelm, but refuses to surrender the ring; Wotan tears it from him. Alberich casts a new and terrifying curse on the ring – it will be desired by everyone but enjoyed by no one, and anyone who wears it will die – then vanishes.

The giants return for their payment. Fasolt is reluctant to part with Freia and asks that the gold should completely hide her. The gods pile it up, throwing in the Tarnhelm too, but Fasolt says that he can still see Freia's eyes, and Fafner demands that Wotan gives up the ring to fill the crack. Loge states that it belongs to the Rhinemaidens; Wotan angrily resists both Loge's request to return it to them and the pleas of Fricka, Freia, Froh and Donner to surrender it to the giants.

As the impasse is reached, the earth goddess, Erda, appears. She reminds Wotan that she is the mother of the three Norns, conceived before the start of time, and that she sees all the events of the world.

She prophesies a dark day for the gods: everything must come to an end, including them. She advises Wotan to renounce the ring.

Deeply affected by Erda's words, Wotan gives the ring to the giants. They immediately fight about who should keep it and how to divide the gold. Fafner kills Fasolt; Wotan is stunned by this immediate demonstration of Alberich's curse. Filled with foreboding, he wants to follow Erda and ask for further advice. Fricka tries to improve his mood by suggesting that the gods enter their new home. Donner summons up a thunderstorm; from its clouds emerges a rainbow bridge. As evening falls, Wotan sings a grand encomium to Valhalla and invites Fricka to join him there. The other gods follow, but Loge does not – his association with the gods embarrasses him and he predicts that their reign will soon end, however strong they now feel. The Rhinemaidens are heard in the distance, lamenting their lost gold. The gods ignore them as they process across the bridge to Valhalla.

Die Walküre

Act I

The curtain rises on the dwelling of Hunding and his wife Sieglinde: it is dominated by the trunk of a huge ash tree, whose branches spread through the roof. A storm rages then dies down. An injured traveller enters; Sieglinde is surprised to see him, but brings him refreshment and tells him that she will offer him shelter. Hunding returns and greets the stranger brusquely. He asks him his name and about his journey; the traveller tells of his upbringing in the forest. One day he returned from hunting with his father, Wälse, whom he names as Wolfe, to find his home burned down, his mother killed and his twin sister gone. Father and son fled into the forest where for years they lived and hunted, but one day the father disappeared, leaving only a wolf-skin behind him. The traveller then tells how a woman whose brothers wanted to marry her to a man she did not love appealed to him for help; he killed the brothers, and their kinsmen now pursue him for revenge. Hunding reveals that he is one of those kinsmen: he has just returned from a fruitless search for the culprit, only to find him in his own house. The stranger may stay overnight, but in the morning the two men must fight. Hunding tells his wife to prepare his night-time drink and wait in their bedroom.

Left alone, the traveller remembers that his father, whom he now names Wälse, told him that he would leave a sword for him, to be used in times of need; he sees a glimmer from the ash tree, but this is surely the afterglow of the dazzling gaze of the beautiful woman who has greeted him. Sieglinde returns, telling him that she has given her husband a sleeping draught; she suggests that he escapes while he can. She tells him how during her unhappy wedding to Hunding, a mysterious stranger appeared with a sword which he planted in the tree, so deeply that none of the guests could remove it. She realised then that the stranger was her father, Wälse – who is really Wotan in disguise, though she does not know this; she starts to realise now that the traveller is her brother – the hero for whose use her father intended the sword. A door blows open and the moon shines in. Sieglinde asks who has left; the traveller tells her that no one has left, but spring has come in. They sing of their growing love for each other, and how each will be the spring the other's life has been lacking. Sieglinde names the traveller Siegmund and urges him to pull the sword from the tree; naming it Nothung, he does so. The couple begin to make love; the curtain drops.

Act II

Out together in a wild, mountainous region, Wotan asks his daughter Brünnhilde – one of the Valkyries who transport dead heroes to Valhalla – to ensure that Siegmund wins his battle with Hunding, who is pursuing him as he flees with Sieglinde. Brünnhilde exuberantly agrees, but warns Wotan that Fricka is angry with him. Brünnhilde leaves; Fricka appears and tells Wotan that Hunding has asked for her support, as goddess of marriage; she condemns Siegmund and Sieglinde's adultery and incest and compares their conduct to Wotan's own repeated infidelities. She demands that Brünnhilde does not protect Siegmund, and that Wotan removes the power from Nothung. After Fricka departs, Wotan tells Brünnhilde of his despondency at his inability to help his son, whom he planned should be the man free to do what the laws he is obliged to uphold prevent him from doing himself: to capture the ring from Fafner so that Alberich cannot reclaim it. He orders her to protect Hunding. Distraught at her father's abject state – for the first time, she has heard him look forward to his own destruction – she reluctantly agrees.

Meanwhile, Siegmund and Sieglinde have fled into the forest and reached a mountain pass. Sieglinde is overwhelmed by shame, and fearful of the revenge her husband plans to exact; exhausted, she falls asleep in Siegmund's arms. Brünnhilde discovers the couple and tells Siegmund of the glorious destiny that awaits him in Valhalla, but he refuses to go once he realises that Sieglinde will not be there. If Hunding is indeed going to kill him, he would rather kill his sister – and their unborn son, whom Brünnhilde reveals that Sieglinde is expecting – than allow death to separate them. Moved by his love and loyalty, Brünnhilde resolves to defy Wotan by protecting Siegmund.

The sound of horns alerts Siegmund to Hunding's arrival; they start to fight. Brünnhilde hovers over Siegmund and protects him with her shield, but Wotan uses his spear to shatter Nothung; Hunding stabs his now defenceless opponent to death. Brünnhilde lifts Sieglinde onto her horse and rides away with her. Wotan dismisses Hunding with a contemptuous wave: he falls down dead. But the god vows to make Brünnhilde pay for her disobedience.

Act III

At the peak of a rocky mountain, Brünnhilde's eight Valkyrie sisters congregate: each carries the body of a slaughtered hero on her horse. They realise that Brünnhilde is not with them and anticipate Wotan's anger at her absence. Brünnhilde appears in an agitated state, her horse Grane carrying not a hero but a woman: Sieglinde. Brünnhilde explains that Wotan is pursuing her to avenge her disobedience; she asks her sisters to lend her a fresh horse so she can carry Sieglinde to safety, but they refuse. Sieglinde accuses Brünnhilde of saving her life without her consent – she would rather have perished with Siegmund – but when Brünnhilde tells her that a child is growing in her womb, her despair immediately gives way to exultation, and she asks Brünnhilde to protect her. Brünnhilde tells her that she must summon up her strength to escape before Wotan returns. She gives Sieglinde the fragments of Siegmund's sword, which she retrieved from the battle, and tells her to look after them so that her son – whom she must name Siegfried – can one day reconstruct Nothung. On Brünnhilde's advice Sieglinde flees eastwards into the forest towards the place where Fafner, in the form of a dragon, guards the hoard of gold.

Wotan appears and vents his anger, asking the Valkyries where they are hiding their guilty sister. When Brünnhilde steps forward, he tells her that she is no longer a Valkyrie: he intends to expel her from Valhalla and to cast a spell to make her sleep until a husband comes to take her. The other Valkyries plead with Wotan not to inflict this disgrace, but he is implacable: they should regard her fate as a warning.

Alone together, Wotan and his favourite daughter analyse the events that have led him to banish her for ever. She tells him that by protecting Siegmund she was acting on what she knew were his true wishes; he tells her she should have realised this could bring him no pleasure. He has been torn apart by the conflict between his own will and the necessity of acting against it; since she does not understand this, they can have no more to do with each other. Realising that Wotan will not retract his decision, Brünnhilde implores him not to dishonour her by leaving her prey to any man who happens to come along: will he protect her with a fire to deter all but the bravest? Deeply moved by her plea, he agrees. Bidding the Valkyrie a tender farewell, he places her under a pine tree, closes her helmet and covers her with her shield; he then summons Loge and asks him to surround Brünnhilde with a ring of fire. Only a hero who knows no fear will be able to awaken her.

Siegfried

Act I

In a forest cave, Mime is sitting at an anvil, struggling to forge a sword sturdy enough to resist the strength of his young charge, Siegfried. If only he could find a way of welding together the shattered pieces of Nothung, that would do the job: with it, Siegfried could conquer Fafner and Mime could win Alberich's

ring for himself. Siegfried enters with a bear and taunts the terrified Nibelung, whom he hates; Mime complains of Siegfried's
ingratitude, after all he has done for him: he sings a song about
how he brought him up from infancy and tended to his every
need. Siegfried is mystified that, unlike every other creature he
sees in the forest, he looks nothing like his supposed parent – also,
where is his mother? Mime starts to argue that he is both father
and mother to Siegfried, but when this fails to convince the boy
he tells him the truth. He encountered Sieglinde when she was
about to give birth; despite Mime's efforts to help, she died in
labour, passing on the fragments of the sword for her newborn
son as she did so. Struck by these revelations, Siegfried demands
that Mime restore Nothung to him so that he can leave and never
have to see his foster-father again. He runs into the forest.

Wotan enters Mime's cave, dressed as a Wanderer in a long
coat and broad-brimmed hat. He suggests that Mime asks him
three questions, volunteering to surrender his life if he cannot
answer them. Mime asks him what race lives beneath the earth
(Nibelungs), on the earth's surface (giants) and in the clouds
above (gods). Conceding that the Wanderer has given satisfactory
answers, Mime asks him to leave, but the stranger demands to
ask some questions in return. Which race does Wotan love the
most? The Volsungs. What is the sword that Wotan gave this
race? Nothung. But who will forge its fragments back into shape?
Conscious of his own inability to do this, Mime flounders. The
Wanderer departs, passing up his right to claim Mime's life – but
he tells him that it will nonetheless soon be taken, by someone
who knows no fear.

Siegfried returns, and Mime identifies him as the fearless hero
whom the Wanderer has described: the Nibelung has failed to
teach his young charge what fear is. Siegfried is curious, and

Mime proposes a trip to Neidhöhle, the cave where Fafner – now in the form of a fearsome dragon – guards the gold. If anything can inspire Siegfried with fear, Fafner will. Siegfried declares his impatience at Mime's inability to restore Nothung and takes his place at the forge. Mime realises that Siegfried will indeed be able to forge the sword and defeat Fafner with it, but he reassures himself that by preparing a potion that will send the boy to sleep, he will be able to kill him and claim the gold and the ring for himself. Singing as he works, with the forge at maximum heat, Siegfried successfully welds the pieces of Nothung together and hammers it into shape; Mime busies himself with preparing the draught. As Siegfried brandishes the sword and demonstrates its strength by smashing Mime's anvil, both are convinced that they will soon emerge triumphant.

Act II

Outside Neidhöhle, Alberich keeps watch. The Wanderer joins him, and they argue: Alberich complains about Wotan's theft of the ring and accuses him of plotting to help Siegfried to reclaim it. The Wanderer denies this: he plans that Siegfried should rely on his own strength, unaided by the gods; he recommends Alberich worry more about Mime, since he – unlike Siegfried – has designs on the gold. The Wanderer proposes to rouse Fafner so that Alberich can warn him about Siegfried's impending arrival, but the dragon refuses to listen to the Nibelung and the Wanderer departs.

Mime and Siegfried approach Neidhöhle: Mime attempts to make Siegfried afraid of Fafner, but Siegfried is unmoved and sends the dwarf away. Left alone, he stretches out under a linden tree and thinks about what his mother might have been like. A Woodbird sings to him, but Siegfried cannot understand its song;

he attempts to respond, first by playing a pipe cut from some reeds, and then, more successfully, with his horn. Fafner appears, they fight, and Siegfried stabs him in the heart with Nothung. As he dies, Fafner warns Siegfried that Mime plans to kill him. Unperturbed, Siegfried absent-mindedly tastes the blood of the dying dragon, and realises that he can now understand the Woodbird's song: inside the cave is a ring that will make its owner master of the world.

Siegfried goes inside the cave; Alberich and Mime emerge from their hiding places and start to quarrel about which is the gold's rightful owner. Alberich hides as Siegfried leaves Neidhöhle with the Tarnhelm on his belt and the ring on his finger. The Woodbird warns him not to trust Mime, and tells him that thanks to the dragon's blood he will be able to understand exactly what the dwarf is thinking. Mime inadvertently reveals his plan to drug Siegfried so that he can kill him and take the gold and the treasured items; Siegfried declines the drink that Mime proffers, and strikes him with Nothung. The dwarf drops dead, to the delight of the hidden Alberich, and Siegfried places his corpse alongside Fafner's at the entrance to Neidhöhle. Reclining again under the linden tree, he listens as the Woodbird tells him about Brünnhilde; Siegfried sets out to find her.

Act III

At the bottom of the mountain where Brünnhilde lies sleeping, the Wanderer awakens Erda, keen to hear her advice. He seems to be doubting his entire plan, asking Erda whether the rolling wheel he has set in motion can be stopped. Baffled by his visit and resentful at being disturbed, she asks why he does not seek help from the Norns, her three daughters, who watch over the world while she sleeps, and weave a rope that determines its fate; or from Brünnhilde, the daughter she bore Wotan. Distressed to hear of Brünnhilde's banishment, she accuses the Wanderer of hypocrisy; setting aside his earlier doubts, he tells her that he no longer fears the downfall of the gods, since Siegfried's kiss will awaken Brünnhilde and allow her to redeem the world. Erda returns to her slumber.

Siegfried enters and encounters the Wanderer: he has no idea who he is, but asks him for directions. He tells the Wanderer about his adventures and plans; the Wanderer asks him who made the pieces of Nothung, and teases him when he does not know. Siegfried mocks him in return; annoyed by the young man's bumptiousness, the Wanderer tries to bar his way with his spear. When he learns that this is the weapon that ended his father's life, Siegfried attacks the Wanderer, and Nothung easily breaks his spear. The Wanderer disappears, and Siegfried proceeds through the flames that surround Brünnhilde's rock.

As he reaches the summit he sees a horse and what he believes to be a sleeping soldier, but as he loosens the stranger's helmet and armour, he is astonished to encounter – for the first time in his life – what he realises must be a woman. He kisses Brünnhilde, and she awakens to greet the day and the long-awaited hero who has rescued her. He is confused – is she his mother? – but she gently explains that though his mother will not return, she herself has always loved him. He embraces her passionately, but she pushes him away, suddenly fearful; she explains that no one, not even a god or a hero, has dared touch her before, and now she no longer knows who she is. She asks Siegfried to leave her alone, so that he does not destroy her, but he continues to declare his love. Throwing herself into his arms as the curtain falls, she joyfully surrenders.

Götterdämmerung

Prologue

By the same rocky mountain where Brünnhilde lay sleeping, the three Norns discuss the story of the world. They begin by describing Wotan tearing a branch from the World Ash Tree to make his spear – a previously unmentioned event that predates everything depicted on stage. The Norns take the story into the future by anticipating a conflagration that will consume Valhalla and precipitate the downfall of the gods, but as they speculate about when and how this will happen, their rope breaks. Their power and knowledge are at an end.

Meanwhile, nearby, Siegfried prepares to set off on fresh adventures. He gives Brünnhilde the ring as a symbol of his love; she gives him her horse, Grane, to accompany him on his travels; they assure each other of their mutual passion and devotion.

Act I

At his palace near the Rhine, Gunther – son and heir of Gibich, the late king of the Gibichungs – and his half-brother Hagen discuss possible candidates to marry Gunther himself and their sister, Gutrune. Hagen – whom Alberich fathered with Grimhilde, mother of the royal pair – proposes that Gunther should marry Brünnhilde, and Gutrune Siegfried, but they will need Siegfried's help to claim Brünnhilde from the fire that surrounds her. Hagen proposes to give Siegfried a potion that will make him forget all other women and fall immediately in love with Gutrune, motivating him to win Brünnhilde on Gunther's behalf. At this moment, the sound of Siegfried's horn is heard from his boat on the Rhine; Hagen invites him into the Gibichung Hall.

Hagen's plan works as he had hoped: Gutrune offers Siegfried a drink, he raises it to his lips with a toast to his love for Brünnhilde, but as soon as he has drunk it he forgets her and is overwhelmed with desire for Gutrune. Gunther declares his willingness to allow Siegfried to marry his sister, and tells him of his own wish to claim Brünnhilde as his bride – if only he were strong enough to cross the fire that protects her. Showing no sign of recognising Brünnhilde's name, Siegfried offers to claim her on Gunther's behalf, using the Tarnhelm to disguise himself as the king; the two men seal the deal with an oath of blood-brotherhood in which Hagen declines to join them. As everyone else departs, Hagen remains on his own, keeping watch over the palace: his soliloquy reveals his hope that Siegfried will return not only with Brünnhilde, but with the ring that he intends to take for himself.

Brünnhilde's sister, the Valkyrie Waltraute, pays her an unexpected visit at the rock where she remains. She brings Brünnhilde desperate news of Valhalla: the Valkyries no longer ride out to collect bodies; Wotan has been bereft since Siegfried broke his spear; on his orders, the World Ash Tree has been chopped into logs that have been brought back to Valhalla as firewood. He has sent his two ravens into the world in the forlorn hope that they will return with news that will make him smile one final time. But he has revealed to Waltraute that Alberich's curse would lose its power and the gods might be saved if Brünnhilde were to return the ring to the Rhinemaidens – will she do this? For Brünnhilde, however, the ring represents Siegfried's love: she tells her sister that she will never give it up, whatever the consequences for the gods.

Shortly after Waltraute leaves, Brünnhilde hears the sound of Siegfried's horn. Her delight at his return turns to horror as she is confronted by a man she does not recognise. Disguised as Gunther, Siegfried insists that she accompany him as his bride; when she resists, he fights with her and forcibly removes the ring from her finger. As he goes to lie down with her, he announces that he will place Nothung between them as a guarantee of his chastity.

Act II

Outside the Gibichung Hall, Alberich interrupts Hagen's sleep to ask him to overpower Siegfried, so that they can take the ring and share its power. Hagen tells his father that he has already resolved to obtain the ring, but avoids offering him his loyalty.

As day breaks, Siegfried appears. The magic of the Tarnhelm has allowed him to return in an instant; Gunther and Brünnhilde will follow by boat. He tells Hagen and Gutrune how he won Brünnhilde on Gunther's behalf, and reassures Gutrune that despite spending the night with Brünnhilde he remained true to her. Gutrune is satisfied, and asks Hagen to order Gunther's vassals to attend court for the two impending weddings; she will invite the women. Hagen uses his steerhorn to summon the vassals, who are surprised by his aggressive tone and his request for weapons; these, he tells them, will be used to slaughter animals as a sacrifice to the gods, ensuring the success of the marriage. Excited by Hagen's uncharacteristic jollity and the prospect of a riotous wedding feast, the assembled company greets Gunther and Brünnhilde as they enter the hall.

Gunther announces the names of the two happy couples; Brünnhilde is stunned by the mention of Siegfried, and by seeing him with Gutrune – with the ring on his finger. She accuses Gunther of taking it from her and giving it to Siegfried; his stupefied silence makes her suddenly realise that it is Siegfried who has tricked her; Hagen steps in to accuse Siegfried of deceiving Gunther. Brünnhilde points to Siegfried and claims that he, not Gunther, is her true husband. Oaths are sworn on the point of Hagen's spear: Siegfried asks that it should kill him if he has betrayed his promises; Brünnhilde resolves that it will do just that. As he leaves with Gutrune, Siegfried reassures the company that the confusion generated by Brünnhilde's ill-temper will pass, and that soon all will be enjoying the celebrations.

Hagen approaches Brünnhilde and offers to carry out the revenge she wishes to exact by killing Siegfried. Brünnhilde responds that Hagen will surely be overpowered by Siegfried's legendary strength, unless . . . he could strike him in the back – she failed to protect that part of the hero's body with the magic she applied to the rest, as she assumed he would never retreat from an enemy. The devastated Gunther intervenes to complain of his own betrayal by Siegfried; Hagen tells him that only Siegfried's death will remove the shame he feels, and hints that he might enjoy the power conveyed by the possession of Siegfried's ring. Gunther overcomes his guilt at depriving his sister of the husband he has promised her, and joins Hagen and Brünnhilde in swearing an oath of revenge. As they conclude, they encounter a wedding procession leaving the Hall, led by Gutrune and Siegfried.

Act III

The Rhinemaidens emerge from the river by a forest and recall the innocent joy they felt when they still possessed the gold. Siegfried appears; the Rhinemaidens flirt with him in a vain effort to persuade him to give them the ring. He is initially enthralled by their beauty, but when they warn him of the ring's danger he declares that they will not frighten him into giving it up. The

Rhinemaidens depart, prophesying his death; he does not take them seriously.

Siegfried hears the sound of Hagen's hunting horn and answers it with his own. Hagen, Gunther and the vassals appear with the corpses of animals they have killed, and the party sits down to rest. Hagen gives Siegfried a drink and invites him to reminisce about his previous adventures. Siegfried talks about his upbringing with Mime and his slaying of Fafner, and then – thanks to the antidote to the forgetfulness potion that Hagen mixes with his drink – about his passionate love affair with Brünnhilde. The ravens that Wotan sent into the world to witness events that unfold in his absence appear from a bush and fly away. Hagen suddenly stabs Siegfried in the back, explaining to the shocked company that it is to avenge his lies. In his dying moments, Siegfried experiences a final vision of Brünnhilde's love. Gunther asks the vassals to carry Siegfried's body back to the Gibichung Hall.

Gutrune, tormented by bad dreams, waits for the hunting party to return. Hagen leads the procession into the hall: he tells her that Siegfried has been killed by a boar, but Gunther quickly corrects him. Hagen claims the ring; Gunther challenges him; Hagen kills his half-brother in a brief fight. As he tries to grab the ring from the dead hero's hand, it rises to prevent him. Brünnhilde calmly appears and tells Gutrune that she is the true wife of Siegfried, who loved her before he ever came to the Gibichung kingdom; Gutrune realises how Hagen has tricked her and collapses, distraught, over Gunther's body.

Brünnhilde asks the vassals to prepare a funeral pyre for Siegfried, proclaiming her love despite the way in which he betrayed her. She turns her attention to the gods, asking them to acknowledge their responsibility for her grief; hearing Wotan's ravens, she implores them to return to Valhalla to tell him that his reign is at an end. Brünnhilde then takes the ring from Siegfried's finger and invites the Rhinemaidens to retrieve it from the ashes of the fire that will purge it of Alberich's curse. Proclaiming the destruction of the gods, she sets the pyre alight, then mounts Grane and rides him into the conflagration. The Rhine bursts its banks; Hagen tries to retrieve the ring, but the Rhinemaidens prevent him. The water recedes and the Rhinemaidens play with the ring as they swim; Valhalla and the gods and heroes who sit there are consumed by fire.

Notes

List of abbreviations used

CWD: *Cosima Wagner's Diaries*, trans. Geoffrey Skelton, Vol. 1: 1869–1877, Vol. 2: 1878–1883 (London: Collins, 1978 [Vol. 1], 1980 [Vol. 2]).

Fifield: Christopher Fifield, *True Artist and True Friend: A Biography of Hans Richter* (Oxford: Clarendon Press, 1993).

ML: *Richard Wagner, My Life*, trans. Andrew Gray, ed. Mary Whittall (Cambridge: Cambridge University Press, 1983).

Porges: Heinrich Porges, trans. Robert L. Jacobs, *Wagner Rehearsing the 'Ring': an Eye-Witness Account of the Stage Rehearsals of the First Bayreuth Festival* (Cambridge: Cambridge University Press, 1983).

RWPW: *Richard Wagner's Prose Works*, trans. William Ashton Ellis. Eight volumes. Originally published in London by Kegan Paul, Trench, Trübner & Co. between 1892 and 1899, now reprinted in various editions. Also currently available online at www.imslp.com.

SLRW: *Selected Letters of Richard Wagner*, trans. and ed. Stewart Spencer and Barry Millington (London: Dent, 1987).

Chapter 1

6 *to league [himself] with Chaos*: 'Plan of Organisation of a German National Theatre for the Kingdom of Saxony', *RWPW*, Vol. 7, p. 322.

12 *in a whole variety of new ways*: quoted and translated in John Deathridge, *Wagner Beyond Good and Evil* (Berkeley: University of California Press, 2008), p. 246, n. 45; see Deathridge p. 12 for a discussion of the chronology of this essay and its significance for

Wagner's attempts to represent his own creative development.

13 *if the change [. . .] wholly indifferent hamlet*: 'The Wibelungen', *RWPW*, Vol. 7, pp. 267–8.

15 *that foremost vanquisher of Troy*: 'The Wibelungen', *RWPW*, Vol. 7, p. 283.

22 *noble concept*: *SLRW*, p. 141.

26 *eternal destroyer [. . .] thrifty burgher*: *RWPW*, Vol. 8, pp. 235, 234.

28 *shrapnels*: *The Diary of Richard Wagner: The Brown Book, 1865–1882*. Presented and annotated by Joachim Bergfeld, trans. George Bird (London: Victor Gollancz, 1980), p. 96.

30 *eyesore [. . .] temporary structure*: *ML*, p. 400.

Chapter 2

39 *never had more attentive listeners*: *ML*, p. 417.

42 *he receives thirty-seven Swiss francs*: figures taken from Chris Walton, *Richard Wagner's Zurich: The Muse of Place* (Rochester, NY: Camden House, 2007), p. 162.

42 *bacchanalian power*: 'The Artwork of the Future', *RWPW*, Vol. 1, p. 124.

44 *witnessed the applause at the end*: *SLRW*, p. 185.

44 *German! German!*: letter of 13 March 1849, quoted in Martin Geck, trans. Stewart Spencer, *Richard Wagner: A Life in Music* (Chicago: University of Chicago Press, 2013), p. 139.

44 *a yearly payment of 3,000 francs*: figures taken from entry on 'Ritter, Julie' in Nicholas Vazsonyi (ed.), *The Cambridge Wagner Encyclopedia* (Cambridge: Cambridge University Press, 2013), p. 504.

46 *an extraordinarily effective contribution to our domestic ease*: *ML*, p. 451.

48 *Nothing in it was complete*: *ML*, p. 260.

51 *purest human shape [. . .] a possibility that had not occurred to me*: 'A Communication to My Friends', *RWPW*, Vol. 1, pp. 358–9.

53 *whatever he later says about its composer*: the movement of *Das*

Paradies und die Peri whose main theme Wagner's sketch closely resembles is 'Chor der Genien des Nils', No. 11; another theme from No. 22 of Schumann's oratorio is identical to an important motif from *Die Walküre*. I will explore these links and their significance in a forthcoming article.

54 *unpleasantly foreign [. . .] forceful ejection of this destructive foreign element*: quoted in entry on 'Judentum in der Musik, Das', in Nicholas Vazsonyi (ed.), *The Cambridge Wagner Encyclopedia*, p. 225.

55 *fertilising seed*: *RWPW*, Vol. 2, pp. 235, 376.

56 *bound to go mad here*: quoted in Joachim Köhler, trans. Stewart Spencer, *Richard Wagner: The Last of the Titans* (New Haven and London: Yale University Press, 2004), p. 301.

57 *great plans*: letter of 7/11 October 1851, *SLRW*, p. 230.

57 *three dramas [. . .] erect a theatre*: texts of letters taken from Ernest Newman, *The Life of Richard Wagner*, Vol. 2: 1848–1860 (reprinted Cambridge: Cambridge University Press, 1976), pp. 265–6.

60 *a master builder from Giant Land*: Snorri Sturluson, *The Prose Edda*, trans. Jesse L. Byock (London: Penguin, 2005), p. 50.

63 *no longer existed in the booktrade*: letter of 12 November 1851, *SLRW*, p. 232.

Chapter 3

74 *the greatest poem I have ever written*: letter of 18 November 1852, *SLRW*, p. 275.

74 *total mistake*: comment reported to Wagner in a letter from Liszt, 8 April 1853. *Correspondence of Wagner and Liszt*, ed. Francis Hueffer, Vol. 1: 1841–1853 (Cambridge: Cambridge University Press, 2009; first published 1888), p. 276.

74 *I now feel that even my friends*: letter of 13 August 1853, *SLRW*, p. 289.

75 *poet [. . .] mere concoctor of opera-texts*: 'A Communication to My Friends', *RWPW*, Vol. 1, p. 308.

75 *found their own way in*: 'A Communication to My Friends', *RWPW*, Vol. 1, p. 300.

75 *sudden leap*: 'A Communication to My Friends', *RWPW*, Vol. 1, p. 308.

75 *mechanical reflex [. . .] traditional forms*: 'A Communication to My Friends', *RWPW*, Vol. 1, p. 368.

76 *alliterative verse*: 'A Communication to My Friends', *RWPW*, Vol. 1, p. 376.

79 *The musical phrases make themselves*: quoted in Robert Bailey, 'Wagner's Musical Sketches for *Siegfrieds Tod*', in Harold Powers (ed.), *Studies in Musical History: Essays for Oliver Strunk* (Princeton: Princeton University Press, 2015), pp. 469–504; p. 479.

81 *erring artist*: quoted in Ernest Newman, *The Life of Richard Wagner*, Vol. 2: 1848–1860 (reprinted Cambridge: Cambridge University Press, 1976), p. 437.

81 *the fugitive has returned and submitted himself to examination*: quoted in Ernest Newman, *The Life of Richard Wagner*, Vol. 2, p. 438.

81 *miserable presentation [. . .] continuing flow of income*: ML, p. 511.

89 *a commonplace, inane*: quoted in Bryan Magee, *The Philosophy of Schopenhauer* (Oxford: Clarendon Press, 1983), p. 273.

90 *found a sedative*: letter of 16? December 1854, *SLRW*, p. 323.

90 *I depart from the home*: trans. Stewart Spencer, in Stewart Spencer and Barry Millington, *Wagner's 'Ring of the Nibelung': A Companion* (London: Thames & Hudson, 1993), p. 363.

91 *pure cognition*: Arthur Schopenhauer, *The World as Will and Representation*, Vol. 1, trans. and ed. Judith Norman, Alistair Welchman and Christopher Janaway (Cambridge: Cambridge University Press, 2010), p. 224.

91 *a copy of the will itself*: Arthur Schopenhauer, *The World as Will and Representation*, Vol. 1, p. 285.

92 *only aggravate the verdict [. . .] they benefited me*: quoted in Martin Gregor-Dellin, trans. J. Maxwell Brownjohn, *Richard Wagner: His Life, His Work, His Century* (London: Collins, 1983), p. 544n.

93 *a monument [. . .] this most beautiful*: *SLRW*, p. 323.

Chapter 4

99   *kind of somnambulistic state*: ML, p. 499.

103   *Sax'schen Instrumenten*: letter from Wagner to King Ludwig II, 16 September 1865. Referred to in Raymond Bryant (rev. Anthony C. Baines and John Webb), article on 'Wagner tuba' from *Grove Music Online* (published 2001). www.oxfordmusiconline.com.

107   *This is Alberich's dream come true*: CWD, Vol. 1 (25 May 1877), p. 965.

110   *Endless melody*: 'Music of the Future', RWPW, Vol. 3, p. 338.

114   *the work's meaning*: SLRW, p. 310.

115   *At present I have no time [. . .] of indestructible power*: Wagner to Liszt, 8 June 1854, *Correspondence of Wagner and Liszt*, ed. Francis Hueffer, Vol. 2: 1854–1861 (Cambridge: Cambridge University Press, 2009, first published 1888), pp. 39–40.

115   *the love of that young woman [. . .] since there never could be*: Wagner to Clara Wolfram, 20 August 1858, SLRW, p. 399.

116   *Ich liebe dich*: quoted in Chris Walton, *Richard Wagner's Zurich: The Muse of Place* (Rochester, NY: Camden House, 2007), p. 202.

116   *how curious these contrasts are*: *Correspondence of Wagner and Liszt*, ed. Francis Hueffer, Vol. 2, p. 41.

118   *become a close-knit unity*: SLRW, p. 310.

120   *one of my younger friends*: 'On the Application of Music to Drama', RWPW, Vol. 6, p. 184.

121   *visiting card [. . .] they never appear*: Claude Debussy, 'Impressions of the Ring in London', *Gil Blas*, 1 June 1903, trans. Richard Langham Smith in *Debussy on Music: The Critical Writings of the Great French Composer* (Ithaca: Cornell University Press, 1977), p. 203.

126   *Wagner changes his mind*: CWD, Vol. 1, p. 909, entry for 30 May 1876.

128   *glorification of Brünnhilde*: quoted in Carolyn Abbate, *Unsung Voices: Opera and Musical Narrative in the Nineteenth Century* (Princeton: Princeton University Press, 1991), p. 206.

129 *I often sat before my pencilled pages*: ML, p. 526.

134 *fearfully majestic music*: letter to Mathilde Maier, 15 January 1865, quoted in Curt von Westernhagen, *The Forging of the 'Ring': Richard Wagner's Composition Sketches for 'Der Ring des Nibelungen'*, trans. Arnold and Mary Whittall (Cambridge: Cambridge University Press, 1976), p. 145.

135 *I have led my young Siegfried*: letter to Liszt, 28 June 1857, *SLRW*, p. 370.

136 *scared away from the older work*: ML, pp. 551, 549.

137 *My soul rejoices*: Wagner to Mathilde Wesendonck, 7 April 1858, *SLRW*, pp. 381–3.

137 *eternal love*: quoted in Chris Walton, *Richard Wagner's Zurich*, p. 206; see chapters 9 and 10 of this book for more information about Wagner's continuing relationship with the Wesendoncks.

140 *belong to each other alone*: ML, p. 729.

145 *art of the most delicate and gradual transition*: Wagner to Mathilde Wesendonck, 29 October 1859, *SLRW*, p. 475.

145 *it must sound like the proclamation of a new religion*: Porges, p. 103.

146 *under the protection of my exalted friend*: ML, p. 739.

146 *introduce recitative [. . .] music, he says, transfigures*: CWD, Vol. 1, p. 73.

147 *the theme which had come to him*: CWD, Vol. 1, p. 330.

148 *there suddenly occurs to me*: letter to Mathilde Wesendonck, 9 July 1859, translated by Anthony Newcomb in Nicholas John (ed.), *Richard Wagner: Siegfried (Opera Guide 28)* (London: John Calder, 1984), p. 40.

151 *R. appears to be sketching out 'Götterdämmerung'*: CWD, Vol. 1, p. 151.

158 *we are expecting bad experiences*: CWD, Vol. 1, p. 381.

161 *This is the book I have been longing for*: CWD, Vol. 1, p. 447.

162 *calls me his priestess of Apollo*: CWD, Vol. 1, p. 445.

164 *It is only through the spirit of music*: Friedrich Nietzsche, *The Birth of Tragedy: Out of the Spirit of Music*, trans. Shaun Whiteside, ed. Michael Tanner (London: Penguin, 1993), p. 79.

Chapter 5

177 *that it would not be impossible*: SLRW, p. 724.

180 *enchanted with the genuine charm*: CWD, Vol. 1, p. 362.

180 *to our delight, we read*: CWD, Vol. 1, p. 196.

182 *Therefore economize [. . .] With this building we are offering*: SLRW, p. 793.

184 *'Society in Support'*: Nicholas Vazsonyi, *Richard Wagner: Self-Promotion and the Making of a Brand* (Cambridge: Cambridge University Press, 2010), p. 179.

189 *Fortunate century*: Ludwig II to Wagner, quoted in Ernest Newman, *The Life of Richard Wagner, Vol. 4: 1866–1883* (reprinted Cambridge: Cambridge University Press, 1976), p. 482.

Chapter 6

191 *in Frau Grün*: CWD, Vol. 1, p. 773.

191 *Frau Grün again comes over*: CWD, Vol. 1, p. 775.

191 *would be inclined to take over*: CWD, Vol. 1, p. 783.

191 *Frau Grün . . . comes to our house*: CWD, Vol. 1, p. 801.

195 *delighted to get*: CWD, Vol. 1 (19 April 1876), p. 902.

196 *beautifully done*: Porges, p. 119.

196 *the intensity of a flash of lightning*: Porges, p. 113.

197 *there was nothing he hated so much*: Porges, p. 65.

197 *fear and feverish haste*: Porges, p. 125.

198 *even in passages of lyrical abandon*: Porges, p. 69.

198 *if she has an instinctive*: Porges, p. 129.

198 *slowly and broadly [. . .] in the throwaway style*: Porges, p. 12.

199 *Last Request to my dear comrades*: original notice reproduced in Árni Björnsson, *Wagner and the Volsungs: Icelandic Sources of Der Ring des Nibelungen* (London: Viking Society for Northern Research, University College London, 2003), p. 59. Translation mine.

201 *No photographs survive of the sets*: see Barry Millington, *Richard*

Wagner: The Sorcerer of Bayreuth (London: Thames and Hudson, 2012), pp. 227–9, and Patrick Carnegy, *Wagner's Theatre: In Search of a Legacy* (Cambridge: Lutterworth Press, 2024), Chapter 3, for interesting accounts of Hoffmann's work and the complex story of its rediscovery in recent years, and for illustrations of the designs he envisioned for *The Ring*.

202 *outstandingly beautiful*: CWD, Vol. 1, p. 913.

203 *references to the costumes of the Germanic peoples*: SLRW, p. 846.

203 *Red Indian chiefs*: CWD, Vol. 1, p. 917.

205 *Splendid sight [. . .] heavenly sound*: CWD, Vol. 1 (23–8 July 1875), p. 857.

207 *his facial expression and characteristically eloquent gestures*: Porges, p. 119.

207 *Oh Richter, I nearly forgot all about you!*: Fifield, p. 90.

208 *you are bound too much*: Fifield, p. 109.

209 *sublime joy*: Porges, p. 114.

209 *absolutely definite instruction*: Porges, p. 98.

209 *taken a shade faster*: Porges, p. 103.

209 *should combine the forward movement*: Porges, p. 86.

210 *of reminiscence or premonition*: Porges, p. 102.

210 *straining her physical and mental faculties to the limit*: Porges, p. 136.

210 *Piano pianissimo – then all will be well*: Frederic Spotts, *Bayreuth: A History of the Wagner Festival* (New Haven and London: Yale University Press, 1994), pp. 68–9.

211 *The curtains part in the middle*: see Patrick Carnegy, *Wagner's Theatre: In Search of a Legacy* (Cambridge: Lutterworth Press, 2024), Chapter 2, for Pringsheim's impressions of the Festspielhaus and the production.

212 *This is where my musicians have to sweat*: Fifield, p. 114.

213 *realistic [. . .] left to the onlookers' imaginations*: Robert Hartford (ed.), *Bayreuth: The Early Years* (London: Victor Gollancz, 1980), p. 68.

213 *a true giant in the history of art*: Spotts, *Bayreuth: A History of the Wagner Festival*, p. 71.

213 *a new epoch in art has arisen*: Joseph Horowitz, *Wagner Nights: An American History* (Berkeley: University of California Press, 1998), p. 139.

213 *the most remarkable*: Horowitz, *Wagner Nights: An American History*, p. 139.

Chapter 7

219 *conscientious, affectionate regard*: Oswald Georg Bauer, *Richard Wagner: The Stage Designs and Productions from the Premières to the Present* (New York: Rizzoli, 1983), p. 237.

225 *nonsense*: Brigitte Hamann, trans. Alan Bance, *Winifred Wagner: A Life at the Heart of Hitler's Bayreuth* (London: Granta Books, 2005), p. 457.

226 *pitted, honeycombed, geological*: Patrick Carnegy, *Wagner and the Art of the Theatre* (New Haven and London: Yale University Press, 2006), p. 293.

226 *the most topical and modern of living dramas*: Wieland Wagner, quoted in Geoffrey Skelton, *Wieland Wagner: The Positive Sceptic* (London: Victor Gollancz, 1971), p. 178.

232 *rougher, deeper voice*: John Culshaw, *Ring Resounding: The Recording in Stereo of 'Der Ring des Nibelungen'* (London: Secker & Warburg, 1967), p. 186.

232 *baking them*: See https://www.soltiring.com for further information on this.

235 *swindle which presides over his existence*: Patrice Chéreau, quoted in Carnegy, *Wagner and the Art of the Theatre*, p. 359.

further reading, viewing and listening

This list of books is not intended as a comprehensive bibliography of the hundreds of sources I have consulted, but as a personal selection of titles in English that might be of interest to readers who would like to explore the themes of the present book in further detail. As those who do will rapidly discover, there is more than enough interesting reading on Wagner to occupy a lifetime: this list is only a partial and selective starting point. For reasons of space, I have included among commentaries and interpretations only books that focus exclusively on *The Ring*: there is, of course, much on *The Ring* also to be found in the many books that deal with Wagner's work as a whole.

Wagner's life, work and ideas

Callow, Simon, *Being Wagner: The Triumph of the Will* (London: William Collins, 2017).

Deathridge, John, *Wagner Beyond Good and Evil* (Berkeley: University of California Press, 2008).

Deathridge, John, and Carl Dahlhaus, *The New Grove Wagner* (London: Palgrave Macmillan, 1984).

Furness, Raymond, *Wagner* (London: Reaktion, 2013).

Geck, Martin, trans. Stewart Spencer, *Richard Wagner: A Life in Music* (Chicago: University of Chicago Press, 2013).

Gregor-Dellin, Martin, trans. J. Maxwell Brownjohn, *Richard Wagner: His Life, His Work, His Century* (London: Collins, 1983).

Köhler, Joachim, trans. Stewart Spencer, *Richard Wagner: The Last of the Titans* (New Haven and London: Yale University Press, 2004).

Magee, Bryan, *Aspects of Wagner*, revised and enlarged edition (Oxford: Oxford University Press, 1988).

Magee, Bryan, *Wagner and Philosophy* (London: Penguin, 2001).

Millington, Barry, *Wagner (The Master Musicians)* (London: Dent, 1984).

Millington, Barry, *Richard Wagner: The Sorcerer of Bayreuth* (London: Thames & Hudson, 2012).

Newman, Ernest, *The Life of Richard Wagner.* Volume 1: 1813–1848, Volume 2: 1848–1860, Volume 3: 1859–1866, Volume 4: 1866–1883. All four volumes reprinted in paperback (Cambridge: Cambridge University Press, 1976).

Newman, Ernest, *Wagner Nights*, paperback edition (London: Pan, 1977).

Tanner, Michael, *Wagner*, paperback edition (London: Flamingo, 1997).

Tanner, Michael, *The Faber Pocket Guide to Wagner* (London: Faber and Faber, 2010).

Trippett, David (ed.), *Wagner in Context* (Cambridge: Cambridge University Press, 2024).

Vazsonyi, Nicholas, *Richard Wagner: Self-Promotion and the Making of a Brand* (Cambridge: Cambridge University Press, 2010).

Walton, Chris, *Richard Wagner's Zurich: The Muse of Place* (Rochester, NY: Camden House, 2007).

Watson, Derek, *Richard Wagner: A Biography* (London: Dent, 1979).

The Ring: sources

Björnsson, Árni, *Wagner and the Volsungs: Icelandic Sources of 'Der Ring des Nibelungen'* (London: Viking Society for Northern Research, University College London, 2003).

Magee, Elizabeth, *Richard Wagner and the Nibelungs* (Oxford: Clarendon Press, 1990).

The Nibelungenlied: The Lay of the Nibelungs, trans. Cyril Edwards (Oxford: Oxford University Press, 2010).

The Poetic Edda, trans. Carolyne Larrington (Oxford: Oxford University Press, revised edition, 2014).

The Saga of the Volsungs, trans. Jesse L. Byock (London: Penguin, 1999).

The Saga of Didrik of Bern: with the Dwarf-King Laurin, trans. Ian Cumpstey (Cumbria: Northern Displayers, Skadi Press, 2017).

Sturluson, Snorri, *The Prose Edda*, trans. Jesse L. Byock (London: Penguin, 2005).

The Ring: translations and commentaries

Sabor, Rudolph, *Richard Wagner: 'Der Ring des Nibelungen': a Companion* (London: Phaidon, 1997).

Sabor, Rudolph, *Richard Wagner: 'Das Rheingold'*, *'Die Walküre'*, *'Siegfried'*, *'Götterdämmerung'*, with translation and commentary. Four separate volumes (all published London: Phaidon, 1997).

Spencer, Stewart and Barry Millington, *Wagner's 'Ring of the Nibelung': A Companion* (London: Thames & Hudson, 1993). Includes complete translation by Stewart Spencer.

Wagner, Richard, *Der Ring des Nibelungen*, trans. Nico Castel, ed. Marcie Stapp (New York: Leyerle Publications, 2003).

Wagner, Richard, *The Ring of the Nibelung*, trans. and ed. with an introduction by John Deathridge (London: Penguin, 2018).

Wagner, Richard, *The Ring of the Nibelung*, trans. Andrew Porter (London: Faber and Faber, 1977).

Andrew Porter's translations, which were intended for singing rather than aiming for strict accuracy, can also be found in the ENO Opera Guides to each music drama (General Editor: Nicholas John), which have been reissued in recent years by Overture Publishing. These Guides also contain essays on each work and an invaluable catalogue of the musical themes of the cycle prepared by Lionel Friend: each theme is numbered and the numbers are also given in the libretti at the points where the themes are heard.

Wagner's writings

Diary of Richard Wagner: The Brown Book, 1865–1882. Presented and annotated by Joachim Bergfeld, trans. George Bird (London: Victor Gollancz, 1980).

My Life, trans. Andrew Gray, ed. Mary Whittall (Cambridge: Cambridge University Press, 1983).

Richard Wagner's 'Beethoven', in a new translation by Roger Allen (Woodbridge: Boydell & Brewer, 2014).

Richard Wagner's Essays on Conducting, in a new translation with critical commentary by Chris Walton (Rochester, NY: University of Rochester Press, 2021).

Richard Wagner's Prose Works, translated by William Ashton Ellis. Eight volumes. Originally published in London by Kegan

Paul, Trench, Trübner & Co. between 1892 and 1899, now reprinted in various editions. Also currently available online at www.imslp.com.

Richard Wagner: Stories and Essays, selected, edited and introduced by Charles Osborne (New York: Library Press, 1973).

Selected Letters of Richard Wagner, trans. and ed. by Stewart Spencer and Barry Millington (London: Dent, 1987).

Three Wagner Essays ['Music of the Future', 'On Conducting', 'On Performing Beethoven's Ninth Symphony'], trans. Robert L. Jacobs (London: Eulenberg, 1979).

Wagner's Ring in 1848: New translations of 'The Nibelung Myth' and 'Siegfried's Death' by Edward R. Haymes (Rochester, NY: Camden House, 2010).

Wagner Writes from Paris . . . : Stories, Essays and Articles by the Young Composer, ed. and trans. Robert L. Jacobs and Geoffrey Skelton (London: George Allen & Unwin, 1973).

The Ring in production

Bauer, Oswald Georg, *Richard Wagner: The Stage Designs and Productions from the Premières to the Present* (New York: Rizzoli, 1983).

Carnegy, Patrick, *Wagner and the Art of the Theatre* (New Haven and London: Yale University Press, 2006).

Carnegy, Patrick, *Wagner's Theatre: In Search of a Legacy* (Cambridge: Lutterworth Press, 2024).

Fifield, Christopher, *True Artist and True Friend: A Biography of Hans Richter* (Oxford: Clarendon Press, 1993).

Fricke, Richard, trans. George R. Fricke, ed. James Deaville with Evan Baker, *Wagner in Rehearsal, 1875–1876: the Diaries of Richard Fricke* (Stuyvesant, NY: Pendragon, 1998).

Hartford, Robert (ed.), *Bayreuth: The Early Years* (London: Victor Gollancz, 1980).

Millington, Barry and Stewart Spencer (eds), *Wagner in Performance* (New Haven and London: Yale University Press, 1992).

Neumann, Angelo, trans. Edith Livermore, *Personal Recollections of Wagner* (London: Archibald Constable & Co., 1909).

Porges, Heinrich, trans. Robert L. Jacobs, *Wagner Rehearsing the 'Ring': an Eye-Witness Account of the Stage Rehearsals of the First Bayreuth Festival* (Cambridge: Cambridge University Press, 1983).

Spotts, Frederic, *Bayreuth: A History of the Wagner Festival* (New Haven and London: Yale University Press, 1994).

Interpretation of *The Ring*

Berry, Mark, *Treacherous Bonds and Laughing Fire: Politics and Religion in Wagner's 'Ring'* (Aldershot: Ashgate, 2006).

Berry, Mark and Nicholas Vazsonyi (eds), *The Cambridge Companion to Wagner's 'Der Ring des Nibelungen'* (Cambridge: Cambridge University Press, 2020).

Cooke, Deryck, *I Saw the World End: A Study of Wagner's 'Ring'* (London: Oxford University Press, 1979).

DiGaetani, John (ed.), *Penetrating Wagner's 'Ring': An Anthology* (New York: Da Capo Press, 1978).

Donington, Robert, *Wagner's 'Ring' and Its Symbols* (London: Faber and Faber, 1963).

Kitcher, Philip and Richard Schacht, *Finding an Ending: Reflections on Wagner's 'Ring'* (Oxford: Oxford University Press, 2004).

Scruton, Roger, *The Ring of Truth: The Wisdom of Wagner's 'Ring of the Nibelung'* (London: Penguin, 2017).

Shaw, George Bernard, *The Perfect Wagnerite: A Commentary on the Niblung's Ring* (New York: Dover Publications, 1967).

After Wagner: family members, performers, influence

Carr, Jonathan, *The Wagner Clan* (London: Faber and Faber, 2007).

Culshaw, John, *Ring Resounding: The Recording in Stereo of 'Der Ring des Nibelungen'* (London: Secker & Warburg, 1967).

Hamann, Brigitte, trans. Alan Bance, *Winifred Wagner: A Life at the Heart of Hitler's Bayreuth* (London: Granta Books, 2005).

Horowitz, Joseph, *Wagner Nights: An American History* (Berkeley: University of California Press, 1998).

Ross, Alex, *Wagnerism: Art and Politics in the Shadow of Music* (London: 4th Estate, 2020).

Skelton, Geoffrey, *Wieland Wagner: The Positive Sceptic* (London: Victor Gollancz, 1971).

Thielemann, Christian, trans. Anthea Bell, *My Life with Wagner* (London: Weidenfeld & Nicolson, 2015).

Wagner, Cosima, trans. Geoffrey Skelton, *Cosima Wagner's Diaries*. Vol. 1: 1869–1877, Vol. 2: 1878–1883 (London: Collins, 1978 (Vol. 1), 1980 (Vol. 2)).

Wagner, Nike, trans. Ewald Osers and Michael Downes, *The Wagners: The Dramas of a Musical Dynasty* (London: Weidenfeld & Nicolson, 2000).

Recordings

Details of the most recent (2022) remastering of the ground-breaking Georg Solti/John Culshaw recording of *The Ring* may be found at www.soltiring.com; several earlier versions also remain available. The set includes an invaluable audio guide on 2 CDs to the leitmotifs of *The Ring*, written and narrated by Deryck Cooke and generously illustrated with musical examples. Both the *Ring* productions discussed in detail in Chapter 7 are available on DVD and Blu-ray. The Patrice Chéreau/Pierre Boulez Bayreuth Festival *Jahrhundertring* is available from Deutsche Grammophon, who recently (2022) produced a remastered high-definition version. The Stefan Herheim/Donald Runnicles *Ring* from the Deutsche Oper Berlin is distributed by Naxos. Hans-Jürgen Syberberg's five-hour documentary *The Confessions of Winifred Wagner*, also discussed in Chapter 7, is currently available to watch on YouTube.

Readers wishing to investigate the music of *The Ring* for the first time may be interested in Naxos's two-CD *Introduction to Wagner: Ring of the Nibelung*, engagingly written and narrated by Stephen Johnson. The set includes excerpts from the Staatsoper Stuttgart's recording under Lothar Zagrosek, and a guide to the leitmotifs that, although less detailed and technical than Deryck Cooke's exegesis in the Solti set, offers a helpful starting point.

In addition to the interpretations discussed in this book, numerous other performances of the complete cycle are of course available both on DVD/Blu-Ray and on CD/audio streaming platforms. Advising on a choice between them is a fraught business: judgements are inevitably subjective, recordings enter and leave catalogues, and space limitations necessarily preclude a full discussion here. Nonetheless, among DVDs, Warner's release of the cycle that played at Bayreuth between 1988 and 1992 may be strongly recommended: it is perceptively directed by Harry Kupfer and magisterially conducted by Daniel Barenboim, and features John Tomlinson as Wotan, Anne Evans as Brünnhilde and Siegfried Jerusalem as Siegfried. The cycles directed by

Pierre Audi for De Nederlandse Opera (1999, Opus Arte, conducted by Hartmut Haenchen), by Kaspar Holten for the Royal Danish Opera (2006, Decca, cond. Michael Schønwandt), and – unusually – by four different directors for Staatsoper Stuttgart (2002, Euroarts, cond. Lothar Zagrosek) all also offer fresh and arresting insights. Also worth investigating are the two Deutsche Grammophon DVD sets conducted by James Levine with New York's Metropolitan Opera, both with productions that are, in different ways, more conventional than most now witnessed in continental Europe: by Otto Schenk (2002); and by Robert Lepage (2012), for which Fabio Luisi took over the conducting for the final two instalments due to Levine's health problems. Lepage's production became notorious for its 'machine' – a huge contraption used as the set for all four dramas, which all too often malfunctioned in performance – but the DVDs reveal a number of outstanding individual performances, notably from Bryn Terfel (Wotan), Jonas Kaufmann (Siegmund) and Eva-Marie Westbroek (Sieglinde).

Where CDs and audio downloads are concerned, the scope for choice is almost overwhelming, with well over thirty recordings from the last seventy-five years – Rudolf Moralt's pioneering radio broadcasts with the Vienna Symphony Orchestra were made in 1949 – still readily available. Only a small fraction can be mentioned here. Among the (pre-Solti) mono recordings, the pair made by Wilhelm Furtwängler – with La Scala Milan (and Kirsten Flagstad as Brünnhilde) in 1950 and with Rome's RAI Orchestra three years later – are pre-eminent, though Wagnerians still debate which is the finest of these two surprisingly different interpretations. Clemens Krauss's recording from 1953 and Hans Knappertsbusch's from 1957 – both taken from Bayreuth performances, both with Hans Hotter in his prime as Wotan – are also particularly impressive, notwithstanding what inevitably seem today like technical inadequacies in the recording process. Of the stereo studio recordings that followed in Solti's wake, Herbert von Karajan's with the Berlin Philharmonic (1966–70) is the most beautifully played, though perhaps marred by his choice of Wotans (Dietrich Fischer-Dieskau and Thomas Stewart). From the same era, the recording taken from Karl Böhm's 1966 and 1967 Bayreuth Festival performances is still frequently cited as a first choice, such is the excellence of its cast (including Birgit Nilsson as Brünnhilde) and the excitement generated by Böhm's pacy conducting.

For those who would like to listen to *The Ring* in English, Reginald Goodall's much-loved 1970s recordings with English National Opera, using Andrew Porter's translations, remain available: though Goodall's tempi are extremely leisurely by the faster standards of today, there are several very fine performances, including Norman Bailey as Wotan and Alberto Remedios as Siegfried. Of the many more recent recordings, the Bayreuth Festival recordings of Daniel Barenboim (1991–92) and Christian Thielemann (2008), perhaps the leading Wagnerian conductors of their respective generations, deserve particular mention; Thielemann also made an excellent live recording with the Wiener Staatsoper three years later. Finally, at the time of writing, Simon Rattle is three-quarters of the way through a beautifully paced and superbly engineered cycle taken from concert performances with the Bavarian Radio Symphony Orchestra, whose chief conductor he became in 2023; in its orchestral playing in particular, Rattle's recording promises to become one of the finest of recent years, once it is completed with *Götterdämmerung*.

Illustrations and credits

PAGE 1 OF THE IMAGE INSERT

Richard Wagner, drawn by Ernst Benedikt Kietz in Paris between 1839 and 1842. *Lebrecht Music & Arts/Alamy Stock Photo*

Gottfried Semper's first opera house in Dresden, built between 1838 and 1841, destroyed by fire in 1869. Drawing from about 1850. *Wikimedia Commons*

PAGE 2 OF THE IMAGE INSERT

Fighting in the Altmarkt during the Dresden uprising, 6 May 1849. *INTERFOTO/Alamy Stock Photo*

Portrait of Mathilde Wesendonck, painted by Karl Ferdinand Sohn in 1850. *Stadt Museum, Bonn/Wikimedia Commons*

Coronation portrait of King Ludwig II of Bavaria, painted by Ferdinand von Piloty in 1865. *King Ludwig II Museum, Bavaria/Wikimedia Commons*

PAGE 3 OF THE IMAGE INSERT

Josef Hoffmann, oil sketch of a design for the ending of *Das Rheingold*. *Nationalarchiv der Richard-Wagner-Stiftung, Bayreuth*

Carl Emil Doepler, costume designs for Wotan and for Waltraute. *DeAgostini/Getty Images*

PAGE 4 OF THE IMAGE INSERT

Exterior of the Bayreuth Festspielhaus, engraving from 1880. *Sunny Celeste/Alamy Stock Photo*

Interior of the Bayreuth Festspielhaus, photograph from the early twentieth century. *Lebrecht Music & Arts/Alamy Stock Photo*

Musicians in the orchestra pit during the 2017 Bayreuth Festival. *B. O'Kane/Alamy Stock Photo*

PAGE 5 OF THE IMAGE INSERT

Richard, Cosima and Siegfried Wagner, pictured in Bayreuth in 1873. *Sueddeutsche Zeitung Photo/Alamy Stock Photo*

Cosima and Siegfried Wagner, pictured in around 1920. *ullstein bild/Getty Images*

The first Metropolitan Opera House on Broadway and 39th Street, New York, photo from 1905. *Library of Congress Prints and Photographs division/Wikimedia Commons*

PAGE 6 OF THE IMAGE INSERT

Winifred Wagner at the 1938 Bayreuth Festival with Adolf Hitler and Josef Goebbels. *Lebrecht Music & Arts/Alamy Stock Photo*

Act III, scene 1 of *Die Walküre* from Wieland Wagner's 1950s *Ring* cycle. Photograph by Siegfried Lauterwasser from the 1953 Festival. *Nationalarchiv der Richard-Wagner-Stiftung, Bayreuth – Zustiftung Wolfgang Wagner*

Act III, scene 1 of *Götterdämmerung* from Wieland Wagner's 1950s *Ring* cycle. Photograph by Adolf Falk from the 1957 Festival. *Nationalarchiv der Richard-Wagner-Stiftung, Bayreuth – Zustiftung Wolfgang Wagner*

PAGE 7 OF THE IMAGE INSERT

Scene 1 of *Das Rheingold* from Patrice Chéreau's 1976 *Ring* cycle. *Nationalarchiv der Richard-Wagner-Stiftung, Bayreuth – Zustiftung Wolfgang Wagner*

Act I, scene 3 of *Siegfried* from Patrice Chéreau's 1976 *Ring* cycle. *Nationalarchiv der Richard-Wagner-Stiftung, Bayreuth – Zustiftung Wolfgang Wagner*

PAGE 8 OF THE IMAGE INSERT

Scene 4 of *Das Rheingold* from Stefan Herheim's Deutsche Oper *Ring* cycle. Photograph by Bernd Uhlig, 11 May 2024. *Deutsche Oper Berlin*

Act III, scene 3 of *Siegfried* from Stefan Herheim's Deutsche Oper *Ring* cycle. Photograph by Bernd Uhlig, 12 November 2021. *Deutsche Oper Berlin*

Acknowledgements

When I first began mentioning to friends that I was considering writing a book on *The Ring*, several expressed well-meaning scepticism about whether such a volume was really needed. I can't blame them: I'd probably have said the same in their position.

I am very fortunate to be part of a stimulating and supportive musical community in St Andrews, and I have enjoyed sharing my developing ideas about the book with friends, colleagues and students there. These conversations have been too numerous for me to mention all my interlocutors individually, but I am indebted to them all. Especial thanks to Garry Taylor and Huw Lloyd Richards, stalwarts of the McPherson Singers' redoubtable bass section, for reading everything from the earliest drafts onwards, and for appreciation that nurtured my faith in the project's value at a crucial stage; to Stephen Read, for his repeated and close readings of each successive chapter and his keen eye for anything that was less than clear; and to Emma Sutton, for making time in a frantic semester to undertake detailed scrutiny of the entire manuscript and for her suggestions for improvement, small in number and scale but highly beneficial in import. I am grateful also to Bettina Bildhauer for her help with the passages on the *Nibelungenlied* and *The Ring*'s other mythological sources, and to Nicholas Davey for a fascinating discussion about the philosophical influences on and implications of Wagner's work.

Among those further afield, my greatest debt is to Lionel Friend: my first conducting teacher and now my mentor once again. This book has benefited enormously from his extraordinary knowledge of *The Ring* and all things Wagnerian, and from his generosity with his time and advice. Thanks, too, to Nicholas Edwards for putting his phenomenal command of acoustic science at the service of helping me understand what is (and isn't) significant about the design of the Festspielhaus; and to Anselm Hagedorn for offering me the perspective of a Wagnerian living in Germany and for his many helpful suggestions on the manuscript. And it has been a delight to discuss the intricacies of the book's development with my daughter Olivia, newly settled in London and embarking on a writing career of her own; I much appreciated her last-minute reading of the final proofs, which eliminated infelicities that were by then too familiar for me to notice.

I am grateful to Martin Randall Travel and ACE Cultural Tours for inviting me to lead tours encompassing places and performances that enhanced my understanding of Wagner, and for the illuminating conversations with my fellow travellers that resulted from those visits. Thanks also to the Wagner Society of Scotland for inviting me to give two presentations of work in progress, and for the helpful feedback from its members.

I would also like to express my gratitude to Tanja Dobrick of the Richard Wagner Museum in Bayreuth for her advice and for locating and supplying images from various Bayreuth *Ring* productions, and to Bernd Uhlig for kindly allowing me to reproduce his photographs of Stefan Herheim's production for the Deutsche Oper.

My most heartfelt acknowledgement is of my family, for their love and belief in me and for sustaining me during an intense period of writing. I thank my parents, Peter and Pamela Downes, for encouraging my musical interests from an early age and for their support ever since. I have enjoyed discussing the book at dinner tables from Houston to West Byfleet to Brussels, and have been touched by the enthusiastic support of my extended family on both sides of the Atlantic. My beloved Madhavi Nevader, though not (yet?) a Wagnerian, from the outset understood what I was aiming to achieve with a clarity that often exceeded my own. I thank her for her selfless encouragement of repeatedly rearranged pandemic-era trips to Germany, for her unerring sense of when it was a good idea to ask me how the book was going and when it wasn't, and for creating within a busy household the physical and psychological space that allowed me to complete it. The book has impinged upon my children's lives, too, to an extent made clear during a recent Cornish holiday, when four-year-old Gabriel spontaneously named a fierce-looking seagull 'Wagner'. As a small token of appreciation for the massive contribution they have made to its realisation, it is dedicated to them all, with much love and with profound gratitude for all they bring to each other's lives and to mine.

Index

Abt, Franz, 41, 42
Albert, Prince Consort, 82
Altenburg, *Ring* production (1943), 224–5
Altmeyer, Jeannine, 238
Anderson, George Frederick, 82
Angerer, Victor, 201
Apel, Theodor, 9
Appia, Adolphe, 225

Bakunin, Mikhail: appearance, 25; arrest
  and imprisonment, 35; Dresden uprising,
  34–5; in Dresden, 25; Liszt's view of, 94;
  love for Beethoven's Ninth, 34; political
  beliefs, 25, 26, 40; relationship with RW,
  25–6, 28, 85–6; suspected of arson, 30;
  used as model for Siegfried, 234; 'Young
  Hegelian', 85–6
Barbarossa, *see* Friedrich Barbarossa
Baudelaire, Charles, 138
Baumgartner, Wilhelm, 39, 41, 45–6
Bayreuth: choice for location of festival
  theatre, 180–1; Dammallee house, 165;
  hotel accommodation, 211; Margravial
  Opera House, 165, 181, 185–6, 191;
  Ninth Symphony concert (1872), 34,
  165; numbers of festival visitors, 211–12;
  rail connections, 181; restaurants, 212;
  RW's first visit, 181; RW's grave, 218–19;
  town council, 181; Wagner Foundation,
  46; Wahnfried villa, 46, 165, 187–8, 191,
  195–6, 197, 227
Bayreuth Festival: control of, 221, 222,
  227, 233; Cosima's management,
  219–20; date of inaugural festival, 182–3,
  185; filming, 237–8; first *Rheingold*
  performance, 199, 210–11; fund, 188–9;
  fundraising scheme, 70, 183–5; Hitler's
  support for, 220–2; *Jahrhundertring*
  (1976), 232–7; Jewish singers, 223; King
  Ludwig's attendance, 211; King Ludwig's
  financial support, 185–9; Nazi support
  for, 220; *Parsifal* production (1951),
  220; *Parsifal* production (1966), 227;

patronage certificates, 70, 183–4, 185,
  187, 188; plans for, 180–1, 182–3; private
  performance of *Rheingold* for King
  Ludwig, 189; rehearsals, 126, 195–9;
  reviews, 213; *Rheingold* production
  (1951), 220; *Ring* premiere (1876), 103,
  112, 120, 210–13, 218; *Ring* production
  (1896), 218, 219; *Ring* production (1933),
  223–4; *Ring* production (1951), 220,
  225–6, 228–9; *Ring* production (1965),
  226–7; Wesendoncks' support for, 137;
  Wieland's role, 222, 224–7, 228, 233,
  236; Winifred's management, 221, 222–
  3; Wolfgang's role, 222, 226, 227, 233
Bayreuth Festspielhaus: acoustics, 188,
  205–6; applause prohibited, 212;
  audiences, xvii–xviii, 200, 210–13;
  auditorium, 200, 205–6, 211, 212;
  costumes, 202–3, 215, 226; curtain
  calls, 212; design team, 182; designs
  and sets, 200–2, 215, 226; fanfares,
  210–11; foundation stone laid, 34, 165,
  182; funds for, 183, 187; King Ludwig's
  financial support, 182, 183, 186, 188;
  lighting, 202, 224, 225, 235; orchestra
  pit, 205–6, 207, 212, 213; performance
  of Beethoven's Ninth Symphony (1951),
  220; plans for, 158; 'princes' gallery', 212;
  rehearsals, 126, 188, 195–9, 205, 206–10;
  royal box, 189, 211, 212; seating layout,
  212; site, 181; stage, 188, 194, 200, 204,
  205, 211, 226; stage machinery, 186, 201,
  204; technical director, 201; technical
  issues, 204, 212–13; technical rehearsal,
  205; temperature in, 210, 212; topping-
  out ceremony, 186
Bayreuther Blätter (journal), 121
Beck, Karl, 52
Beethoven, Ludwig van: Bayreuth
  performance of Ninth Symphony
  (1951), 220; career, 24; *Egmont*, 5; Ninth
  Symphony conducted by RW (1846),
  30–1, 32–3; Ninth Symphony conducted

297

INDEX

INDEX

Wagner, Richard: birth, 9; father's death, 9; mother's remarriage, 9; life in Leipzig, 9, 31, 63, 85; Würzburg chorus master, 7, 185; Magdeburg music directorship, 7–8, 17, 185; first staging of opera (*Das Liebesverbot*), 7, 21; Riga music directorship, 18; in Paris (1839–42), 2, 18–19, 31, 32, 43; *Rienzi* premiere, 17, 19–21; Royal Saxon Kapellmeister in Dresden, 1–6, 11–12, 17, 21–3, 25–7, 29–33, 37, 40, 46–7; in Vienna, 23; Dresden uprising (May 1849), 12, 17, 23–4, 28–30, 36; warrant for arrest and escape to Zurich, 12, 16–17, 35–6, 71–2; in Paris (1849), 35–6; life in Zurich (1849–59), 36, 39–43, 45–6, 56, 61, 65–7, 69–73, 79–83, 86–7, 95–6, 131, 136–8; in Paris (1850), 43–4, 103; in Bordeaux (1850), 44–5; fortieth birthday (1853), 69–70; in La Spezia (1853), 71, 100, 101; in Paris (1853), 71, 100, 102–3, 106; first meeting with Cosima (1853), 71; departure from Zurich (1858), 115; in Venice, 137–8; in Paris (1859–61), 138–9, 175; separation from Minna, 139; first meeting with King Ludwig, 140–1; birth of daughter Isolde, 141; exiled from Bavaria (1865), 142, 170; Minna's death, 142; Tribschen home with Cosima, 142–3, birth of son Siegfried, 143; *Rheingold* premiere, 148; *Walküre* premiere, 149; marriage to Cosima, 157–8; festival theatre plans, 142, 158, 167–9, 170–3, 180–3; plan for German school of musical drama in Munich, 168, 170–1; Bayreuth festival theatre plans, 158, 181–2, *see also* Bayreuth Festspielhaus; Bayreuth festival plans, 182–5, *see also* Bayreuth Festival; move to Bayreuth (1872), 165; sixtieth birthday, 185–6; move to Wahnfried, 187–8; *Ring* casting concerns, 191–5; *Ring* rehearsals, 195–9, 206–10; King Ludwig attends private performance of *Rheingold* in Festspielhaus, 189; first Bayreuth festival, 210–13; responses to first Bayreuth festival, 213–14; death, 137, 216, 218; burial, 218–19
APPEARANCE: portrait, 40; skin infection (erysipelas), 57, 83; uniform, 3
FINANCES: anonymous gift, 53; attitude to money, 6; cash advance from King

Ludwig, 169–70; commission of *Siegfrieds Tod*, 55–6, 57; contract with King Ludwig, 169–70, 174; contracts with Schott, 175; cost of transcribing *Ring* scores, 84; costs of birthday festival in Zurich, 70; costs of first Bayreuth festival, 214; creditors in Dresden, 46; debts, 2, 18, 27, 37, 46, 79–80, 140–1, 169, 175, 187; extravagant lifestyle, 65, 70, 72; fee for writings, 41; fees for conducting, 42, 73, 82; financially disastrous concerts in Paris, 175; fundraising for Bayreuth festival theatre, 168–9; fundraising for festival, 183–5, 206; fundraising ideas, 186–7; German royalties, 81, 138, 188; income in Paris, 18; living beyond his means, 79–80; loan from family, 19; loan from King Ludwig, 187; loans from Liszt, 36, 43, 55, 84; London conducting fee, 82; offer of support from Laussots, 44–6; quarterly allowance to Minna, 139; rent of house in Bayreuth, 165; rent of Zurich apartments, 44, 45–6, 65, 70, 79–80; requests for financial support, 43, 80, 186; *Ring* scores publishing negotiations, 94, 95, 131, 174–5; salary, 3, 8, 37; Starnberg villa, 141, 147, 169; support from Julie Ritter, 44, 46, 57, 65, 79, 84, 94–5, 137; support from King Ludwig, 142, 169–70, 188; support from Otto Wesendonck, 80, 84, 95–6, 137, 174, 175–6; Tribschen villa, 142; Wahnfried villa, 165, 187–8, 195–6
MUSICAL CAREER: conducts across Europe, 140; conducts Beethoven, 30–2, 33, 34, 42, 66, 165; conducts birthday concert, 69; conducts *Don Giovanni*, 7; conducts French and Italian operas, 31–2; conducts *Lohengrin*, 139; conducts *Rienzi*, 20; conducts in Dresden, 27, 30–1, 32, 33, 34; conducts in London, 82, 129; conducts in Riga, 31; conducts in Zurich, 42, 65–6, 69, 73, 81–2; idea of *Gesamtkunstwerk*, 42, 43; Magdeburg musical director, 7–8, 185; organisational skills, 33–4; rehearsal methods, 196–7, 206–10, 214; Riga music director, 18; Royal Saxon Kapellmeister, 1–6, 11–12, 17, 21–3, 25–7, 29–33, 37, 40, 46–7; Wagner tubas, 103–4, 111; Würzburg chorus master, 7, 185
MUSICAL WORKS: *An Webers Grabe*, 33;

'Christ in the nave', 16; *Faust* symphony
overture, 32, 81; *Die Feen* (first opera),
10, 75; 'Friedrich and Freedom' (theme),
9; *Die Hochzeit* (unfinished score), 10;
Kaisermarsch, 180; *The Love Feast of the
Apostles*, 33; operas performed, *see* their
titles; 'political overture', 9; Ride of the
Valkyries arrangement for concerts,
176; system of working, 100; *Siegfried
Idyll*, 147; *Trauersinfonie* (symphony of
mourning), 33; use of leitmotifs (themes),
9, 55, 120–5, 128, 134, 154, 156, 162,
198–9, 210; *Wesendonck Lieder*, 136–7
PERSON: appearance, 3, 40, 57, 83;
character, xviii, 6; health, 20–3, 56–7, 83,
99, 100; library, 16, 46–7, 48, 58, 60–1,
63, 64, 85; organisational skills, 33–4;
pets, 36, 46, 83; readings of his works,
39, 45, 47, 66–7, 69, 87, 136
POLITICAL VIEWS: antisemitism, xviii,
53–4, 133, 173, 183; *Art and Revolution*
essay, 36; articles in *Volksblätter*, 26; belief
in potential of political change, 84–5;
denied pardon without examination in
Saxony, 81, 92; Dresden uprising (May
1849), 23–4, 28–30, 34–5; escape from
Dresden, 34–5; Feuerbach's influence,
86–7; friendship with Bakunin, 25–6, 28,
86; Hegel's influence, 85–6; involvement
in revolutionary politics, 9, 23–30, 85;
Leipzig rioting (1830), 9; loss of belief in
power of political action, 87–8; motivation
in political activities, 23–4; 'Open Letter
to the Soldiers', 25; pardon from King
Johann, 139; partial amnesty from King
Johann, 139; pessimism, 87–8; progressive
faction, 22; revolutionary, 9, 17, 28, 86;
Schopenhauer's influence, 88, 90–1, 129;
speech in support of King Friedrich
August, 22; view of the new Germany,
173–4; warrant for arrest and flight, 35–6;
Vienna visit, 23; views on sexual morality,
85; 'Young Germany' movement, 9, 85
RELATIONSHIPS: Bakunin, 25–6, 28,
85–6; Bülow, 73, 136, 171, 179; children,
141, 143, 220; Cosima, 139–40, 141,
142–3, 177, 180, 193; dog, 36, 46, 83;
female admirers, 139; Hitler, 21, 221;
identification with Wotan, 129; Jessie
Laussot, 45–6; King Friedrich August
of Saxony, 3, 12, 19; King Ludwig of
Bavaria, 140–2, 146, 168–70, 173–4,

178–80, 189, 214; Liszt, 35, 43, 70–2,
186; Lüttichau, 3, 6, 23, 40; Mathilde
Maier, 139, 141; Mathilde Wesendonck,
81–2, 115–16, 119, 137; Meyerbeer, 18,
19, 36; Minna, 8, 36, 71, 42–6, 115, 129,
137, 139; Nietzsche, 161–2, 164, 165;
parrots, 36, 46, 83; Richter, 178, 191,
207–8; Röckel, 24–5, 26, 28–9; Semper,
28, 83, 172, 181
WRITINGS: account of Dresden
uprising, 24; *Achilles* (drama), 15, 16;
Art and Revolution (essay), 36, 41,
161; *The Artwork of the Future*, 41–2,
43; autobiography (*Mein Leben*), xx,
8, 10, 15, 17, 24, 28, 29, 30, 32, 39,
44, 47, 81, 86, 87, 88, 99, 132, 140,
146; *A Communication to My Friends*
(autobiographical essay), 51, 58, 74–5;
correspondence, 1, 12, 24, 28, 44, 56–7,
74, 79, 88, 90, 93, 114, 115, 116, 118,
135, 137, 143, 148; diary for Mathilde,
137; *Friedrich I* (scenario), 12, 16; *German
Art and German Politics*, 180; 'Germany
and its Princes' (article), 26; 'How Do
Republican Aspirations Stand in Relation
to the Monarchy?' (speech), 22; *Jesus of
Nazareth* (project), 15–16, 25; *Jewishness
in Music*, 53–4, 133; *Eine Kapitulation*,
179–80; 'Man and Existing Society'
(article), 26; 'Morning Confession'
(letter to Mathilde), 137; *Music of the
Future* (essay), 110; 'The Nibelung
Myth as Sketch for a Drama' ('Die
Nibelungensaga'), 13–14, 15, 52, 59, 63,
64; 'On the Performing of *Tannhäuser*',
66; *Opera and Drama*, 54–5, 78, 91, 125–
6, 129, 153; 'Plan for the Organisation
of a German National Theatre for the
Kingdom of Saxony', 4–6, 21; poems
for *The Ring*, 51, 63, 64, 66–7, 73–9, 87;
Der Raub des Rheingoldes, 58; 'Report
Concerning the Royal Orchestra', 1–2,
3, 4; 'The Revolution' (article), 26;
Rheingold poem, 66; *Die Sieger* (The
Victors), 92–3, 141; *Siegfrieds Tod* (poem),
39, 47, 51; 'A Theatre in Zurich', 56;
'To the German Army in Paris' (poem),
180; *Walküre* poem, 66; 'The Wibelungs:
World History from Legend', 12–13, 15,
60; 'Zurich writings', 41, 54
Wagner, Rosalie (sister of RW), 10
Wagner, Siegfried (son of RW): baptism,